80-1637

日本の都市化と労仂力

The Urbanization of

Japanese Labor, 1868-1955

BY THOMAS O. WILKINSON

THE UNIVERSITY OF MASSACHUSETTS PRESS
AMHERST, MASSACHUSETTS · 1965

Acknowledgments

This book is the result of an interest in Japan which began to develop during my two-year tenure (1946-47) as a Department of the Army employee in the Occupation. During this period I became one of the thousands who, as representatives of a victorious United States occupying a defeated Japan, were in turn captured by a lasting fascination with the Japanese and their way of life. Such a fascination, however, must be molded and refined before it can become the basis of a productive interest. I have been exceedingly fortunate in the group of teachers and colleagues who have contributed to my attempt to attain this goal.

My debt to Professor Kingsley Davis is far more than can be expressed in any formal acknowledgment. During my three years of graduate work at Columbia University, Professor Davis, with force as a teacher and rigor as a researcher, opened up for me the intellectual excitement of applying sociological and demographic approaches. He also made possible my appointment as Research Sociologist in his project International Urban Research at the University of California, Berkeley in 1957-58, where the initial planning and processing of data for this manuscript took place. His continued interest in the study has been a constant source of encouragement.

Professor Eiichi Isomura of Tokyo Metropolitan University has kindly served as stimulating counselor and critic in my attempt to comprehend the complexities of Japanese population. He has introduced me to Japan's leading urban scholars and made available to me the major sources of urban data. He has also extended friendship and help to a *gaijin* attempting to adjust to Japan. The calligraphy which appears with this book is his. Professor Isomura's ability to work in this essentially artistic medium shows clearly his adherence to the long Japanese tradition which combines practical scholarly activity with a deep esthetic sense.

A book of this sort requires extensive and time-consuming processing of raw demographic data; I have been most fortunate in receiving financial assistance to aid in this task. The University of Massachusetts Research Council granted me three stipends from 1959 to 1962 which enabled me to employ research assistants. A grant from the Population Council in 1959 made it possible to process and incorporate the results of the national census of Japan for 1955. The Four College Non-Western Studies Committee of Amherst, Mount Holyoke and Smith Colleges and the University of Massachusetts subsidized a one-month stay in Tokyo in June, 1963. During this time I was able to explore sources of Japanese urban data not available to me in the United States and also to consult Japanese scholars concerned with urban development. Professor J. Henry Korson, as chairman of my department, has been willing to reduce my departmental duties, providing that most valuable of assists—time. The University of Massachusetts Labor Relations and Research Center has made the publication of this book possible through a generous subsidy.

The editors of *The American Sociological Review* have granted permission to incorporate materials on Japanese metropolitan structure and family system which I originally published in that journal. My articles on agricultural activities in Japanese urban areas which appeared in *Rural Sociology* are also incorporated with the permission of the editors of that journal. I have leaned heavily upon the works of Dr. Irene Taeuber, as will be obvious to those familiar with her outstanding contributions to Japanese population analysis; I wish to mention specifically the permission granted by Princeton University Press to use materials in three tables (Tables 1 and 2 in Chapter IV and Table 13 in Chapter VII) which contain data taken from Dr. Taeuber's *The Population of Japan.*

Leone A. Barron, director of The University of Massachusetts Press, has given freely of her time and advice in the preparation of this book. She has faced with admirable good humor the difficulties of preparation with an author some 10,000 miles away. Dr. Terence Burke, who designed the charts and maps, and Mrs.

Virginia M. Brown, who executed them, have my sincerest thanks.

My wife, Edith Lewis Wilkinson, patiently and efficiently assisted me in the preparation of the manuscript, typing the many drafts and working through the bibliography and index with me. Her eagle-eyed proofreading was indispensable.

I acknowledge with gratitude the cooperation of all those mentioned above, but such acknowledgment in no way lessens my own responsibility for the interpretations, conclusions, and unintentional errors which this book contains.

Thomas O. Wilkinson

Tokyo
May, 1965

Contents

Tables

Figures

Introduction | I

The modern world is an urban world. Even those who live and labor outside the boundaries of cities—and by administrative definition, the majority of the earth's population are nonurban —rarely escape the consequences of the decisions and the material production of those who do reside within these boundaries. From the city, as adminstrative and technological center, constantly flows a stream of influences which sets the tone of contemporary existence. The politico-economic problems associated with this urban-centered control are the major problems of our day. The technological implements created, multiplied and perfected by the Industrial Revolution have made simple the satisfaction of man's basic needs for food, clothing and shelter. That these needs are frequently not satisfied for segments of the world's population is not the result of technological inadequacies but rather of organizational or administrative inadequacies. In other words, the effective administration of the modern urban-industrial social organization stands as our greatest contemporary challenge. As a consequence, an increasing effort is being expended inside and outside the academic community to understand the processes underlying the creation of and the mechanisms contributing to the maintenance of the urban-industrial social system.

This search for understanding has been hampered in several significant respects. First, the emergence of urban-industrialism historically is most closely associated with Western Europe and areas of most intensive Western European settlement. From the fifteenth century onward Europeans created the technological implements which made possible the production of agricultural and industrial surpluses. These surpluses, in turn, made possible the population growth and redistribution which support an emerging urban system. Cities and towns obviously had been possible prior to the appearance of the new technologies, but never in such numbers and with such large permanent populations. For several centuries, then, urban-industrialism was exclusively a Western European phenomenon.

Attempts to analyze the nature and consequences of this transition from agrarian to urban organization unavoidably incorporated major aspects of the Western European cultural context. The major theoretical works relating to this adjustment in the West have had a quality of inevitability with respect to its consequences for the larger social system. Such ecological factors as increased population density in urban areas and the separation of place of residence and place of employment, coupled with rising occupational specialization, bring specific kinds of changes in familial, religious, and all other major areas of social organization. This is to say that the social changes inherent in the development of a capitalistic social organization, which historically paralleled Western urban-industrialization, have tended to be incorporated into theoretical conceptualizations of the agrarian-industrial transition per se. Given the historical context within which these theories were created, and specifically the lack of any non-Western experience with the urban-industrial transition, one might well say that Western social adaptation *had* to be made part of these theories.

Weber's and Tawney's works on the mutual influence of religion and economics in the growth of rational capitalism, Durkheim's mechanical and organic solidarity, Toennies' *Gemeinschaft* and *Gesellschaft*, and the mass society concept developed by MacIver are major examples of analyses concerned with this segment of Western cultural history. Students of the agrarian-industrial transition, and especially those who focus on non-Western societies must face the rather difficult task of distinguishing between the specific adaptation of the West, which has been the primary concern of the writers cited, and the urban-industrialization process as a distinct phenomenon in its own right. The almost unavoidable conclusion to be drawn is that it takes the drive of a Protestant ethic or, at the least, a solid Western European cultural orientation to succeed in the urban-industrial process.

Recent history has made such conclusions untenable. The

startling advances in Soviet Russia are but the most constantly visible evidence that urban-industrialism can thrive in a framework where significant elements of Western European cultural traditions are absent. Japan, as well, provides a case in which urban-industrialism has developed and with an historical background even further removed than Soviet Russia's from the Western European orientation. When used in such cross-cultural comparisons, the term urban-industrialism of necessity must be defined in a narrowed organizational sense. An urban-industrial system is any system in which individual subsistence production is absent or at a minimum. Technological devices are available which expand the productive capacity of individuals far beyond that necessary for their own or their dependents' survival. These devices, plus a high level of specialization, make mass or group production a necessity. Where this production of goods or services has a small space requirement, concentration of population becomes functionally necessary. This approach stresses the interrelationships between the growth of cities and the development of a nonextractive labor force. These interrelationships are further emphasized when it is noted that one of the major indices of level of urban development is specifically the composition of national labor force. In other words, expanding productive capacity plus a high level of specialization are the implementing mechanisms for the growth of urban settlements, both in size and in number.

Urban-industrialism viewed in these terms becomes a conceptual tool with broad applications. When approaching the development of cities and modern technology in non-Western societies, one is not drawn into searching for social or psychological traits associated with urban-industrialism in contemporary or historical Western European systems. The significance of defining urban-industrialism in these terms is that it suggests that there are alternatives to the Western European patterns of over-all social organization within which the implementing mechanisms of urban-industrialism existed in the past or currently exist. A highly efficient urban-industrial system is possible in the absence of a deeply ingrained individualistic profit motive. Or the mass migration of an agrarian labor force to cities can occur without necessarily disrupting the channels for the flow of traditional familial or religious values. It is analytically profitable, therefore, to view urban-industrialism as a distinct process in its own right, stripped of all the necessary *but variable* elements of cultural organization which form its context.

The Japanese experience provides a unique opportunity for just such an analysis of the emergence of an urban-industrial social system. Japan is the only genuinely non-Western nation to have successfully gone through the peasant-agrarian to urban-industrial transition. Modern Japan displays all the major characteristics of an urbanized and industrialized nation. Well over one-half of her total population resides in localities administratively defined as urban; two-thirds of her economically active males are employed in non-agricultural pursuits. Indeed, numerous social, economic, and political indices justify placing her at a level of development comparable to that of leading urban-industrialized nations of the West. Yet the social organization supporting Japan's urban-industrialism reveals focuses markedly different from those found in the West. Traces of feudal-agrarian modes of organization and motivation are still strong in such areas as employer-employee relations, handicraft production, and law enforcement. Japan represents the paradox of a highly industrialized society whose social organization contains viable elements characteristic of the peasant-agrarian social system. Analysis of this paradox in Japan's modernization involves exploration of a specific case in which the alternatives to Western experience in the adjustment of an agrarian society to urban-industrialism are clearly visible.

It would be presumptuous to claim that the present study is an analysis which explores all the dimensions of a cross-cultural study of Japanese urban growth and industrial labor force development. The focus here is a relatively narrow one: the specification, largely in quantitative terms, of the demographic history of city growth in Japan, measured essentially by the movement of employment from an agrarian to an industrial focus. The task is to explore three basic areas:

1) How urban has Japan been throughout her modern period? What variations have occurred in rates of change during this period, and why?

2) What are the demographic and ecological traits of Japan's

urbanizing population, and specifically her employed population? How can these be related to the level and impetus
of her urban-industrialization?

3) What are the significant parallels and contrasts between
Japanese urbanization and that of the West?

Chapter I sets down the historical background for a consideration of Japanese urbanization as a whole. Chapters II through V
are focused principally upon the questions noted in 1) above.
Chapters VI through X deal with the topics covered in 2). Chapter
XI is a summary of the major dimensions of Japan's urbanization
and a series of comparisons with Western urban experience. The
comparative materials are not, however, confined exclusively to
Chapter XI.

One of the principal difficulties in approaching Japanese city
growth is the specification of her urban population from one
period to another. As an ideal type, an urban population is an
occupationally heterogeneous, functionally interdependent and
permanently settled population occupying a limited spatial area.
The crucial distinction between rural and urban populations is
essentially the labor force concentration in agricultural or other
extractive pursuits for the rural population as against a concentration in nonextractive activities for the urban.

In applying such a distinction certain arbitrary choices as to
population size and density must be made. The city incorporation
policies and census reports of all nations include such decisions.
The consistency with which these decisions are applied is frequently open to question, but the demographer must in most
cases accept these basic data as given. Until roughly 1930 in Japan,
for instance, incorporation as a city carried highly regarded elements of administrative prestige. Most incorporated cities (*shi*)
were 20,000 or more in population, but many units of this size
were not administratively defined as cities because of the political
commitments and status relationships of prefectural leaders. The
official urban population of Japan, therefore, under-reports the
urban level in early estimates and census returns. Taeuber and
Beal, in discussing Japanese city growth prior to 1935, disregard
urban data as reported and rely upon enumerations of persons

in all places of 10,000 or more.[1] This method has the disadvantage, however, of including as urban those genuinely rural places where the area is sufficiently large to meet the population size level chosen to designate cities, but which functionally lack the distinctive urban traits. Using size and density alone as criteria for classification as urban creates difficulties, especially for Japan, where cultivatable areas are extremely limited and where, consequently, rural densities reach levels largely unknown in the West.[2]

The present study utilizes official estimates and census enumerations of city populations since the characteristics necessary for analysis are frequently reported only for officially recognized urban places. This is to say that the areas administratively designated as urban by Japanese census officials are here treated as urban in specifying broad trends of urban growth. However, agricultural and extractive activities of urban populations are highlighted, as well as the nonextractive pursuits of populations outside official city boundaries. In this way the actual urban-oriented or industrial segment of the Japanese labor force becomes more clearly delineated. Further, the functional classification of cities presented in Chapter VIII designates clearly those cities whose levels of agricultural employment call into question their official recognition as urban. In attempting to delineate metropolitan areas (Chapter X), on the other hand, administrative units officially classed as rural where employment in nonextractive pursuits is high are incorporated into functional urban agglomerations. In summary, though the difficulties of dealing with the rural-urban continuum in Japan are here far from solved, the analyses related to distinctions between rural and urban populations are so presented as to indicate significant areas of overlap or interpenetration by the two categories.

---

[1] Irene B. Taeuber and Edwin G. Beal, "The Dynamics of Population in Japan," *Demographic Studies of Selected Areas of Rapid Growth* (New York: The Milbank Memorial Fund, 1944), pp. 11-15.

[2] The Japanese national census of 1960 used for the first time the Densely Inhabited District as an enumeration category. These units are defined essentially in terms of minimum density and are independent of official boundaries. Preliminary analysis using these units indicates that they encompass a more functionally meaningful urban population for Japan. Studies of changes over time in this urban population will be hampered, however, since the area covered by the Densely Inhabited Districts will change as densities change from one census year to the next.

BIBLIOGRAPHICAL NOTE

The demographic data upon which this volume is based fall roughly into two categories, those official enumerations and estimates made prior to 1920 and those compiled on the basis of official national censuses following 1920. Beginning in 1872, the Japanese government required the registration of all nationals by households; these figures became the base for yearly estimates of total population through addition of births and subtraction of deaths from registers. With minor variations, this system prevailed for the computation of population and vital statistics until the first national census of 1920. Even after the institution of official enumerations in 1920, vital statistics continued to be computed from household registers. Not until 1947 was the collection of vital statistics separated from domicile registration. The inadequacies of this system make the interpretation of pre-1920 population statistics difficult and the conclusions drawn must be accepted with reservations.[3]

Japanese population statistics following 1920 are fairly accurate and moderately extensive. The censuses of 1920, 1930, 1950, and 1955 include not only data on number, location, and demographic characteristics of the population but details of occupational-industrial structure and place of birth. Only a small part of the data collected for the 1940 census was published; scattered materials are available for this census from yearbooks and post-World War II publications. The quinquennial censuses of 1925 and 1935 were made using shortened schedules which yield results only for population, age, sex, residence, and marital status. Specialized census surveys were conducted in 1945, 1946, 1947, and 1948, but the first complete post-World War II census was that of 1950. The adequacy and reliability of specific data will be evaluated in detail as they are utilized. In summary, however, it can be said that Japanese statistical materials from the Imperial Restoration until 1920 are questionable and most frequently lacking in sufficient detail for the purposes of this study; from 1920 Japanese population statistics are greatly improved in reliability and de-

---

[3] For discussions of specific problems related to Japanese statistics prior to 1920, see Ryoichi Ishii, *Population Pressure and Economic Life in Japan* (London: P. S. King and Son, Ltd., 1937), pp. 48-56, and Irene B. Taeuber and Edwin G. Beal, *op. cit.*, pp. 4-11.

tail. The result is that any detailed analysis of Japanese urban structure is confined largely to the period from 1920 to the present.

In addition to official census publications, a number of works in both Japanese and English have provided valuable data and interpretations of Japanese population development and urbanization. In Japanese, the following works of Professor Eijiro Honjo have been most helpful: *Jinkō oyobi jinkō mondai* (Population and Population Problems), *Nihon jinkōshi* (History of Japan's Population), and *Hyakushō chōnin no rekishi* (History of Farmers and Townsmen). The historical background of the emergence of Japanese cities is presented in Akitsugu Ono's *Toshi no hattatsu* (Development of Cities) and Takeshi Toyoda's *Nihon no hōken-toshi* (The Feudal Cities of Japan). In addition, the following Japanese works contain significant discussions of aspects of Japanese urbanization: Ayanori Okazaki, *Nihon jinkō no jisshoteki kenkyū* (A Factual Study of the Population of Japan); Naotaro Sekiyama, *Kinsei nihon jinkō no kenkyū* (Study of the Population of Modern Japan); and Kunio Yanagida, *Toshi to nōson* (City and Village).

Of the works in English, Irene Taeuber's *The Population of Japan* has been a continuous reference point for the interpretation of Japanese population structure and change. In addition, these works have provided demographically relevant materials: George C. Allen, *A Short Economic History of Modern Japan, 1867-1937*; Ryoichi Ishii, *Population Pressure and Economic Life in Japan*; Edwin O. Reischauer, *The United States and Japan*; E. B. Schumpeter, *The Industrialization of Japan and Manchukuo, 1930-40*; Glenn T. Trewartha, *Japan: A Physical, Cultural and Regional Geography*.

The broader trends of Japanese social and economic history, both pre-Restoration and modern, are taken principally from these major secondary sources available in English: Hugh Borton, *Japan's Modern Century*; Eijiro Honjo. *The Social and Economic History of Japan*; William W. Lockwood, *The Economic Development of Japan*; the three volumes of James Murdoch's *A History of Japan*; E. Herbert Norman, *Japan's Emergence as a Modern State*; George Sansom, *Japan: A Short Cultural History*, *The Western World and Japan*, and his most recent three-volume work, *A History of Japan*; and Chitoshi Yanaga, *Japan Since Perry*.

This has been by no means an attempt to cite the complete bibliography for this volume; rather, the purpose has been to highlight those works of major relevance to the analysis of Japanese urban growth. A complete bibliography of sources is provided at the end of this volume.

Preindustrial Urbanization in Japan | II

The fall of the Tokugawa regime and the restoration of the Emperor in 1868 mark for most students of Japanese history the beginning of Japan's modern era. The convenience of using a single date or event for marking the onset of a period of dynamic change in Japan does not, however, weaken the recognition that much that was new in modern Japan developed prior to 1868, and that, conversely, much of the old continued under the new Emperor. The fact remains that the greater portion of the official restrictions upon intercourse with Western nations was lifted with the Imperial Restoration, and Western influences upon Japan were intensified.

These Western influences, bound up as they were with concerns for industrial technology and international commerce, were essentially urban oriented. They fell upon a fertile urban tradition in Japan. Under the Tokugawa Japanese administrators had had to deal with the effects of the seductiveness of city life upon an agrarian peasantry, the growth of urban based radical movements, and the appearance of an independent-minded commercial middle class. A city way of life as such, therefore, was not one of the many borrowed elements present in modern Japanese social structure. Her modernization has entailed an extensive expansion of urban population, but this expansion has carried with it significant aspects of the preindustrial modes of urban life.

As a background for exploring the nature of modern Japanese urbanization, it is necessary to highlight those pre-1868 elements which are relevant to contemporary urban processes. Specifically, the number and characteristics of urban dwellers will be directly related to three major causes of city growth from one historical period to another. The first major problem in this historical summary will be to characterize the periods of Japanese history prior to the mid-nineteenth century in terms of their dominant locus of social influence, especially as this influence fostered or retarded the growth and multiplication of cities and the movement of labor force into employment geared for city life. Essentially this constitutes an attempt to answer the question of how much urbanization there was in pre-modern Japan, and why.

The second relevant historical problem is an extension of the first, but applied to specific cities. Where significant shifts in the impetus for urban expansion can be shown, how did they influence the standing of particular cities? What was the hierarchy of cities in terms of size and influence during each era? Were new cities brought into being with the appearance of new urbanization forces, or were the older centers able to absorb these new functions and thus maintain dominance?

The answers to these questions will of necessity incorporate a survey of the geography of Japanese preindustrial total population as well as urban settlement. The traditional patterns of Japanese settlement, both rural and urban, are in large measure the product of the distribution of cultivatable plains throughout a series of volcanic islands. Historically, villages and towns sprang up on locations dominating these plains. Within this over-all pattern, however, shifts in governmental form, the variation in intensity of sea-oriented trade, and the appearance of specialized production areas are but a selection of the factors which influenced the relative distribution of population among the habitable areas.

A glance at a topographic map of the nation reveals the paucity of agriculturally useful land. After generations of effort to make even marginal areas productive, today, in spite of modern techniques, less than one-fifth of the total national area of 142 thousand square miles is under cultivation.

The four main islands which make up the Japanese nations are dominated by great mountainous spines. The limited lowland areas are typically small isolated patches of river- and wave-worked sediments developed in a coastal indentation or in a mountain basin. The largest of these plains, which contains the city of Tokyo, has an area of only some 5,000 square miles. Being predominantly peripheral, most of the plains have sea frontage. They are seldom continuous along the coast, being frequently interrupted by spurs and larger masses of hardrock hill land that extend to the sea.[1] The picture which emerges is that of a nation composed of a series of relatively small, sea-border plains, largely of riverine origin, separated by mountainous barriers. Numerous rivers run from the mountains through these plains.

The earliest historical records indicate settlements in northern Kyushu and along the borders of the protected sea area between Shikoku and southern Honshu. The development of Japan as a nation has been a penetration of her peoples to the east and north, establishing concentrations of population in each of the alluvial plains.

EARLY JAPANESE URBANIZATION

Given the influences of the geographical background, the cities, towns, and villages which appeared in the course of the early development of the Japanese nation came in response to one or a combination of three major forces: politico-military administration, religious administration, and commerce. In this respect the history of Japan's early cities differs little from that of other nations. Contrasts are evident, however, in the relative strength of any one of the three forces favoring city growth in the history of a given nation.

The dominant characteristic of the premodern Japanese city was its politico-military administrative focus. This is not to say that trade and commerce were insignificant in the development of towns and villages, but one is struck with the overriding influence of political and military, and to a lesser degree religous, functions as bases for city growth. Early Japan, as Murphey says of early China, most frequently presents a picture of the city "based upon administration from a central location, where trade flows in largely in response to the existing structure of officials, troops, court, hangers-on, and the host of people necessary to support them."[2] As a consequence, the trade process ap-

---

[1] Glenn T. Trewartha, *Japan: A Physical, Cultural and Regional Geography* (Madison, Wisconsin: The University of Wisconsin Press, 1945), pp. 17-19.

[2] Rhoads Murphey, "The City as Center of Change: Western Europe and China," *Annals of the Association of American Geographers*, XLIV, 4 (December, 1954), pp. 353-354.

pears to have lacked the dynamic quality familiar to students of Western European city growth.

The history of Western European cities is not, however, lacking in periods of non-commercial foci for town life. The period following the Islamic invasions, for example, saw the cities of Western Europe exist almost exclusively as centers of ecclesiastical and manorial administration, with only minor activities in local trade.[3] From the seventh century onward, however, the continuous expansion of both domestic and foreign commerce in Western Europe fostered a parallel revival and expansion of commercially based city growth. Never again were trade and commerce to lose their dominant roles as urbanization factors in Western Europe. On the other hand, though the evolution of Japan as a nation prompted the growth of trade and commercial activities, the merchant classes and the urban centers in which they functioned were never able to throw off the controls of government as effectively as their Western European counterparts.

The political administrative focus of urban growth is evident at the very inception of the Japanese nation. As early as the first century A.D. the leaders of Japan's numerous clan states extending over the southwestern area of the home islands ruled their areas from village capitals. By the fourth century the Yamato clan, centered in the Yamato Basin east of present-day Osaka, had unified the clans under a single leader. Each succeeding Yamato emperor founded a new capital city within the Basin until the construction of a permanent capital at Nara in the eighth century, soon to be followed by Heian (Kyoto).[4]

These cities were more than mere expanded agrarian villages prospering from the location of an Imperial residence. They were cities laid out as capital cities by Japanese students following Chinese models of city planning. Extensive production and com-

---

3 Henri Pirenne, *Economic and Social History of Medieval Europe* (New York: Harcourt, Brace and Co., 1956), pp. 40-41. The whole of this work as well as his *Medieval Cities* (Garden City, N. Y.: Doubleday and Co., Inc., 1956) traces the increasing commercial activities throughout the Middle Ages and their consequences for city growth. See also Melvin M. Knight's *Economic History of Europe to the End of the Middle Ages* (New York: Houghton Mifflin Co., 1926), especially the last three chapters.

4 For details of the development of the Yamato Basin see Robert B. Hall, "The Yamato Basin, Japan," *Annals of the Association of American Geographers,* XXII, No. 4 (December, 1932), pp. 243-290.

mercial activities developed to service the large aristocracy which the Imperial Court fostered. Estimates of 500,000 inhabitants for Kyoto during the ninth century seem exaggerated, but there is no doubt that the city reached unprecedented size and that it was possibly one of the world's largest cities during that period.

From Nara, and later from Kyoto, representatives of the court bureaucracy traveled to the domains of vassal clans. These representatives, with the local provincial administrators, formed cores about which numerous secondary towns developed. The spread of Buddhism and the building of its temples further added to the population concentrations; Sansom cites the fact that some forty-six Buddhist temples had been erected in Japan by 640 A.D.[5]

Japanese cities during the early phases of the nation's history can be characterized as stemming largely from the concentration of populations about the administrative centers of a unified aristocratic rule. The capital city and secondary centers of political control were dominant functional urban types. Geographically, the cities and towns were concentrated on the periphery of the Inland Sea. Nara and later Kyoto topped the hierarchy of cities, and significantly these were overwhelmingly political and religious centers. Important handicraft production and commercial activities developed in these capitals, especially Kyoto, but the abiding dominance of these cities rested upon their politico-religious functions.

This characterization of Japanese urban structure holds until the disintegration of Imperial rule in the mid-twelfth century. The economic strain of maintaining elaborate capitals, the military expenses of a continued subjugation of Ainu aborigines in eastern and northern areas, and finally debilitating court intrigues combined to produce a decline in aristocratic control of the nation. The growth of large tax immune estates (*shoen*) in the hands of strong military and religious factions undercut Imperial authority and led to the emergence of a decentralized feudalism. With the appearance of a series of military dictators (*shogun*), beginning with Minamoto Yoritomo in 1185, effective aristocratic rule came to an end. The Hojo regents ruled in the name of the shogunate from 1205 to 1333, and the Ashikaga shogunate was in

5 G. B. Sansom, *Japan: A Short Cultural History* (New York: D. Appleton-Century Co., 1938), p. 143.

national control from 1338 to 1477. The disintegration of Ashikaga control marked the beginning of a period of civil wars which
lasted until the mid-sixteenth century. The cities which developed
during the period from the decline of the aristocracy to the end of
the civil wars (the twelfth to sixteenth centuries) reflected the
changes in politico-military leadership, the evolution of strong
religious factions, and the economic demands of a decentralized
feudal order.

The most important urban development during these four
centuries, however, was the rise of the commercial city. Unstable
national leadership and the turmoil of civil war provided an at-
mosphere conducive to the spread of social mobility and a freer
commercial activity. Growing trade with China, the extension of
this trade to the Philippines and Indo-China, and the arrival of
European traders and missionaries in the sixteenth century contributed to this process.

An excellent illustration of city growth during this period is
the rise of Sakai, an important city in the Greater Osaka area of
today. Beginning as a salt production center, Sakai rose to become
the "Venice of Japan," according to descriptions by early Jesuit
missionaries.[6] As a departure point for overseas trade and a supply
center for Kyoto and nearby provinces, the city produced a
thriving merchant class. Her inhabitants exercised a degree of
self-government and judicial autonomy previously unknown to
townsmen in Japan; this power extended even to the maintenance
of their own military forces.

Yamaguchi, Onomichi, Hyogo, and Hakata followed much the
same pattern, though on a smaller scale. Even the towns which developed around the seat of feudal power, the castle, did not escape
the so-called *chonin sabaki* (townsmen's jurisdiction). The merchants of Matsuyama in Shikoku during the Tensho period
(1573-91), for example, were sufficiently powerful to prohibit the
entry of the lord's military forces into the commercial quarters
of the town.[7]

In addition to these trade cities, the new centers of politico-

---

[6] James Murdoch, *A History of Japan* (London: Kegan Paul, Trench, Trubner
and Co., Ltd., 1925-26), Vol. II, pp. 146-154.

[7] Takeshi Toyoda, *Nihon no hōken toshi* (Feudal Cities of Japan), (Tokyo:
Iwanami, 1956), p. 69.

military control flourished. Seeking to avoid pressures from the older Imperial and aristocratic factions, the first *shogun*, Yoritomo, made Kamakura his capital. In so doing, Yoritomo pushed the effective boundaries of the Japanese nation to the north and east into the Kanto region. This action also created an urbanizing focus removed from the traditional area of city life dominated by Kyoto and Nara. Except for the period under the Ashikaga shogunate (1338-1477) when the political bureaucracy again returned to the Kyoto area (Muromachi), the Kanto region has been the seat of political administration in Japan since the twelfth century. Present-day Japan's national capital and largest city, Tokyo, commands the Kanto region; the city owes its dominance in large measure to this early northeasterly shift of national control.

Influential religious centers, e.g., Ujiyamada, Ishiyama, also developed during this period. The administration of large rice-producing fiefs in the hands of religious factions led to the growth of towns which, in addition to their more sacred functions, served as centers of secular commercial activities. Trade and commerce also aided the recovery of Kyoto and Nara, which had suffered declines with the passing of aristocratic rule.

In summary, during the four centuries between the failure of Imperial control and the rise of the Tokugawa in the seventeenth century, urbanization reflected the major changes which took place in Japan: 1) an expansion of domestic and foreign trade leading to the rise of the genuinely commercial city, e.g., Sakai, 2) the shift of politico-military control to the northeast away from Imperial and aristocratic rule, e.g., Kamakura, 3) the growth of important religious communities wielding significant economic power in the form of feudal fiefs, e.g., Ujiyamada.

The apex of the hierarchy of cities during this period was no longer exclusively the domain of the political administrative center. The dynamic stimulus of foreign trade coupled with a highly organized domestic trade made the commercial city a strong rival for urban dominance. As noted above, the merchant classes exercised levels of political and economic autonomy historically absent in Japanese town life. Wholesale and retail monopoly systems, guilds, and a whole battery of other economic devices were established to generate and maintain effective control by the merchant groups. If the nation had not passed into a period of nearly complete isolation from contact with the outside world in the early seventeenth century, no doubt the characteristics of her economic structure and urbanization would resemble more closely those of the urban-industrial nations of Western Europe.

The two and one-half centuries of Japanese exclusion preceding Perry's visit in 1853 effectively destroyed foreign commerce or even an unrestricted domestic commerce as a force for city growth. Foreign commerce was one of the major sources of wealth and power for the commercial classes of Western Europe on the eve of the Industrial Revolution. This source of power was not rigidly bound to the political structure of any given nation. The dynamic nature of Western European commerce in the centuries preceding the Industrial Revolution was directly related to this element of independence among the commercial classes. Japanese commerce, on the other hand, in the crucial centuries before her industrial revolution was limited to the boundaries of her homeland. The politico-military structure of the nation, therefore, looms large in the development of a merchant class and the economic structure out of which her modern industrialization and urbanization sprang.

Though the commercial centers of sixteenth-century Japan resemble in important respects the free cities of preindustrial Europe, the extent and depth of their "freedom" were not sufficient to withstand the pressures of a reunified national political authority. Once this authority turned upon the cities as potential centers of independent power, the cities either fell rapidly into decay or were absorbed into the new administrative structure. The military leader Hideyoshi's wholesale movement of the merchants of Sakai to his Osaka castle area in 1583 and his subsequent destruction of the principal canal of Sakai in 1586 illustrate the basic weakness of the merchant class.[8] It is true that the autonomous cities of Western Europe also fell before emerging nation states, but the extended period of resistance by the European cities before their downfall implies a much stronger economic and political base than that which underlay these Japanese commercial centers.

8 Murdoch, *op. cit.,* Vol. III, pp. 1-61.

The period of civil wars in Japan was brought to a conclusion in the latter part of the sixteenth century, and the reunification of the nation took place under the successive leadership of Nobunaga, Hideyoshi, and Tokugawa Ieyasu. During the late fifteenth and early sixteenth centuries the feudal lords had consolidated and stabilized their holdings. The multiple feudal rivalries of the civil war period evolved into relatively stable alliances under the more powerful of the feudal lords. The culmination of this process was the re-establishment of effective national unity under Tokugawa Ieyasu in the early seventeenth century. The Imperial court, the powerful Buddhist hierarchy, and the embryonic merchant class of the cities all came under the authority of the powerful Tokugawa *shogun*.

URBANIZATION UNDER THE TOKUGAWA

Tokugawa rule had dynamic consequences for subsequent Japanese history and particularly for the character of Japanese city growth and structure. The two and one-half centuries of Tokugawa rule were a period of relative peace, during which the shogunate made strenuous efforts to maintain the society as an isolated feudal nation. From the mid-seventeenth century all forms of international contact were prohibited except for regularized, limited trade at Nagasaki with the Dutch and Chinese.[9] Every effort was made to maintain Japan as a society in which an hereditary military hierarchy administered, an agricultural peasantry produced, and a heavily circumscribed class of merchants and artisans was accepted as necessary but not to be encouraged.

The economic base of Tokugawa society rested firmly upon peasant agricultural productivity. Feudal lords were allocated their fiefs on the basis of the amount of rice produced by the area. By choosing Edo (Tokyo) as his administrative capital, Tokugawa Ieyasu controlled access to the most productive of Japan's alluvial plains, the Kanto, and hence controlled a dominant source of economic strength. In order to maintain the elaborate political machinery and standard of living of the ruling hierarchy, the

---

[9] Donald Keene, *The Japanese Discovery of Europe* (New York: Grove Press, 1954), pp. 5-20, and C. R. Boxer, *Jan Compagnie in Japan, 1600-1850* (The Hague: Martinus Nijhoff, 1950). The broader aspects of Western contact with premodern Japan are presented in G. B. Sansom, *The Western World and Japan* (New York: Alfred A. Knopf, 1951).

Tokugawa and their vassal lords assessed as taxes and tribute approximately one-half of the harvest of the peasant. Frequently during periods of poor harvest and natural catastrophe, the peasant found his share of the harvest below that necessary for subsistence. Rice assessment policies thus brought about a widespread practice of abortion and infanticide among the agricultural population. The relative stability of Japan's total population, ranging between an estimated 28,000,000 and 30,000,000 during the Tokugawa period, speaks for some attempt at reproductive control. Thus, for nearly three hundred years Japanese society existed as one in which an extensive peasantry was maintained at near-subsistence levels while a relatively small political hierarchy administered the whole of any resources produced above peasant subsistence needs.

The economic and political importance of agricultural produce in feudal Japan is reflected in the concentrations of population which developed during the Tokugawa period. The largest of the alluvial plains are sea-border plains, and all the great cities, with the sole exception of Kyoto, developed within these areas. As already noted, the Kanto Plain, containing Edo (Tokyo), is by far the largest and most productive. The Tokai, the belt of lowlands extending from the Kanto to the Nagoya Plain, saw the growth of Nagoya as its dominant city. To the southwest is the Kinai district which contains Osaka. The Inland Sea region developed its marine as well as agricultural resources as a base for numerous population concentrations, among them the city of Okayama. The fifth area of important agricultural resources is western Kyushu, and here the cities of Kagoshima and Fukuoka flourished. The population centers of the major alluvial plains, given impetus for growth under the Tokugawa, remain today the areas of highest population concentration within Japan.

All cities of any importance at the inception of the Tokugawa shogunate were incorporated into the administrative system. Kyoto and Nagasaki, for example, became parts of the personal holdings of the *shogun*. Cities located at points of stategic importance were developed with the building of castles; others were placed under the direct control of the *shogun*. More important for future Japanese city growth, however, were the new population concentrations created during the Tokugawa period.

The numerous castles built at strategic points during the civil wars and the period of unification, and on orders from Tokugawa in the early seventeenth century, became nuclei about which cities and towns sprang up. As a means of tightening administrative control, the Tokugawa in 1615 decreed the destruction of all but one castle in each fief. The impetus for urban growth inherent in Tokugawa political structure was thereupon focused largely upon a limited number of locations. The consequent growth of these castle centers meant the decline of previously existing towns, except where they could be incorporated into the new defense or communication system. The castle town, then, can be termed the dominant urban form throughout the Tokugawa era.

The outstanding illustration of Tokugawa urbanization is the capital city of Edo (Tokyo). The Edo site had been used by an Ashikaga warrior, Ota Dokan, for the contruction of a castle as early as 1456, but when Tokugawa Ieyasu selected it for the location of his own castle in 1590 it was merely a swampy fishing village. The city flourished under the Tokugawa, reaching an estimated 1.3 million in the latter half of the Tokugawa period.[10]

Of major significance is the fact that the geographical distribution of the castle towns to a large degree set the pattern of urban settlement in modern Japan. Of the thirty-nine cities incorporated under Japan's first urban legislation in 1889, some thirty-three were former castle towns. It is estimated that in 1952, 124 of Japan's 268 incorporated cities were either former castle towns or were cities which formed and developed on the castle town pattern.[11] In large measure the castle town constitutes the urban base on which modern Japanese urbanization was founded.

The growth of Edo illustrates well the basic form which the castle settlement took during this period. The *shogun* occupied a huge castle which served as residence and military stronghold, as well as political-administrative center. The feudal lords through-

10 See Appendix II for a survey of Tokugawa population. The largest city in Europe, London, had in 1801 an estimated 865,000 population. On the basis of this estimate, Edo appears to have been the largest city of the world in the eighteenth century. Takao Tsuchiya, "An Economic History of Japan," *Transactions of the Asiatic Society of Japan*, 2nd series, XV (December, 1937), p. 193.

11 For a detailed analysis of the influence of castle towns upon modern urban structure see Robert B. Hall, "The Cities of Japan: Notes on Distribution and Inherited Forms," *Annals of the Association of American Geographers*, XXIV, No. 4 (December, 1934), pp. 175-200.

out Japan were allocated large tracts directly surrounding the *shogun's* castle upon which they were required to construct residences. The practice of *sankin kotai* or alternate residence instituted by the *shogun* required that the lord spend a specified period of each year in residence in Edo. The location of the residence tract in relation to the castle was assigned according to the rank of the lord.

The area surrounding the residences of the lords was given over to those engaged in commercial and handicraft activities necessary to supply the extensive bureaucracy. The outer areas of the city were the assigned quarters of the lower warrior ranks and other feudal retainers. These areas were often densely settled and poorly laid out. Skirting the outer boundaries of the city were numerous religious settlements centered upon shrines and monasteries. From the central castle outward, succeeding areas represent strategic lines of defense; even the outlying religious settlements served as military observation points from which initial warnings of attack could originate.

Modern Tokyo remains essentially a castle town in its spatial pattern. With the Imperial Restoration in 1868, the *shogun's* castle became the residence of the Emperor. The lands of the former feudal lords within the city were used for public buildings. The street pattern, the distribution of public buildings and parks, and the zoning of utilities are still dictated largely by the castle town pattern. The large estates maintained by the lords during the Tokugawa period now form foci from which secondary street systems flow. The complex street pattern of Tokyo becomes somewhat more comprehensible when the influence of the earlier city form is emphasized.[12]

The concentration of the population in Edo under the Tokugawa directly reflects the concentration of political and economic functions about the seat of the *shogun's* control. Beginning in the early eighteenth century, the non-*samurai* or townsmen population of Edo was enumerated and published on order of the *shogun*. These figures indicate that the nonmilitary population of the city ranged between 450,000 and 550,000 from 1721 through 1855. The proportion which townsmen constituted of that total popu-

---

12 Hall, *loc. cit.*

lation is estimated to have been approximately 40 per cent; this estimate, yielding an estimated total population range of 1.1 to 1.4 million, is reasonable when it is noted that Edo was the center of the political administration of the country and as such contained the heaviest concentration of military administrators. A high ratio of *samurai* to townsmen was not only characteristic of Edo, but of the seats of strong feudal lords as well, e.g., Sendai and Kagoshima.[13]

The factors underlying the growth of Edo were also influential in drawing population to the lesser castle towns. Unification of numerous small feudal centers of power throughout the territories into a smaller number of powerful centers meant that the individual domains came more and more under the absolute control of one dominant feudal lord. This fact, combined with the new military and tactical requirements, made it necessary for the lord to draw his retainers more and more into permanent residence within the castle area. The pattern of enforced residence practiced by the *shogun* in Edo was also present in the larger feudal domains as a further means of assuring loyalty. The warrier class had originally been landholding agriculturalists who in time of military necessity became military personnel. With the creation of the castle town as a permanent military garrison, the warriors became a distinct town-dwelling group whose ties to the land had been severed.

In addition to the castle towns, a number of secondary population centers developed during the Tokugawa era. The extensive travel which the Tokugawa required of the lords and their retainers made necessary the maintenance of a nationwide network of travel routes along which numerous service towns appeared. By Tokugawa fiat, local communities through whose boundaries the routes passed were responsible for repairs and general maintenance of the roads, as well as provisioning official travelers and their retinues. The most famous of these routes were the East Sea Road or *Tokaido* and the *Nakasendo,* an alternate route between Edo and Kyoto. The posting and market towns along these routes grew to appreciable size, especially when they were also castle towns. Shinagawa, Kanagawa, Ejiri, Shimada and Yokkaichi all

13 Toyoda, *op. cit.,* p. 152.

had populations of over 5,000, while the ferry stations of Otsu and Atsuta were more than 10,000 in population. Such castle towns as Odawara, Numazu, Okazaki, and Kuwana, which served also as posting stations, were even larger. Significantly, the modern railroads in this region follow closely the path of the *Tokaido*. The many towns which grew up to service the earlier Tokugawa travelers are today thriving industrial and commercial settlements.[14]

In addition to the post towns serving the major travel routes, there were a few towns specializing in textile handicrafts. The most important of these were Hachioji, Kiryu, and Ashikaga, none of which had more than 10,000 population in Tokugawa times.[15] The post stations and handicraft centers constitute the limited urbanization which took place outside the castle towns in Tokugawa Japan.

This survey of Tokugawa urbanization makes possible a comparison of Japanese and Western European patterns of urban settlement on the eve of their respective industrial revolutions. With respect to the distribution of cities, the impetus for city growth was relatively more diffuse in Japan than in Western Europe in the period just prior to the Industrial Revolution. Through their feudal lords, the Tokugawa had to control the whole country, and therefore administrative centers existed in areas which otherwise would not have encouraged urban settlements. The concentration of city population about only one castle in each fief made for a widely dispersed system of relatively large urban centers. This dispersal did not imply isolation, however, for the requirement of alternate residence in Edo by the local lord meant an almost constant interchange of personnel and ideas between the castle town and the capital. Though the geographical distribution of cities was such that no region was without an urban population, the urban population as such was not equally distributed throughout the nation. The areas extending to the south and west of Edo, covering Nagoya and Kyoto and the regions bordering the Inland Sea, were the most heavily urbanized. Edo was the nation's

---

14 Naotaro Sekiyama, *Nihon jinkō-shi* (History of Japanese Population), (Tokyo: Shikaiminzo, 1942), pp. 186-187; Robert B. Hall, "Tokaido: Road and Region," *Geographical Review*, XXVII, No. 3 (July, 1937), pp. 353-377.
15 Sekiyama, *op. cit.*, p. 188.

largest city, with Osaka and Kyoto never very far behind in total population. Following these three were a number of relatively large urban centers. Nagoya, Nagasaki, Kanazawa, Okayama, Wakayama, Hiroshima, Kagoshima, and Sendai were all estimated to have surpassed the 50,000 population level. A host of lesser cities contained an estimated 20,000 or more population; among these were Matsue, Tokushima, Kochi, Fukuoka, Akita, Himeji, and Takada.

To attempt to state with assurance the proportion of Japan's total population which was urban during the Tokugawa period is hazardous, to say the least. It is useful, however, to employ existing data to arrive at a rough estimate. Honjo's estimate of 30 million total population for Japan in the latter Tokugawa period has been cited previously. Some two million of this total were of the warrior class, which means that they were predominantly town dwellers. Assuming that at a minimum there were as many non-*samurai* as *samurai* residents in towns,[16] we arrive at an estimated four million town or urban population. These figures result in an estimate of between 13 per cent and 14 per cent urban for Japan in the latter Tokugawa era.

A diffuse pattern of settlement of Tokugawa Japan's estimated 13-14 per cent urban population offers a significant contrast with Western Europe in the eighteenth century. Western European urbanization appears more narrowly focused than that of Tokugawa Japan. The growth of large European cities was fostered by two major factors: the rise of powerful monarchs with a tendency to settle in permanent capital cities and the development of foreign commerce about deep-sea ports. Cities favored with one or both of these factors had a tendency to outstrip other urban centers in the nation. London in 1700, for example, was almost eleven times larger than England's next three largest cities combined, while Paris at the same time was six times larger than Marseilles,

16 The assumption is based upon Toyoda's estimates that as a general rule approximately 40 per cent of the castle town population was made up of *samurai* (Toyoda, *op. cit.*, p. 152). In some special cases, notably Edo, Sendai, and Kagoshima, the proportion was even higher. The higher proportion of *samurai* in these cities is to some extent counterbalanced in estimating the total urban population by the fact that some towns, e.g., the post and market towns, contained an insignificant number of warriors. An estimate of a one-to-one relationship between *samurai* and other townsmen would seem, therefore, to be a conservative one.

France's second city.[17] The urban settlement pattern which emerges is one in which there is a great gap between the first city, with its overwhelming concentration of population and functions, and the nation's other urban areas.

There is no denying the dominance of Edo in Tokugawa urbanization, but the degree of its dominance was lower than that revealed in the illustrations from Western Europe cited above. Edo at its peak of over one million had not much more than twice the population of either Osaka or Kyoto. Osaka with its great merchant houses and Kyoto as Imperial capital and handicraft center were never completely overshadowed by Edo in either size or functions.

The lack of any extensive foreign trade capable of concentrating commercial activities in a favored deep-water port contributed to this urbanization pattern in Tokugawa Japan. Further, the very nature of Tokugawa administrative policies fostered concentrations of large bureaucratic staffs in *all* centers of political control, not in the capital city only. This second factor helps to explain the relatively high level of urban residence in nonindustrialized Japan vis-à-vis Western Europe in the century preceding the Industrial Revolution. Compared to Japan's 13-14 per cent urban in the late eighteenth century, it is estimated that Europe's population living in places of 5,000 or more never climbed above 10 per cent prior to 1800. As late as 1819, only 14 per cent of France's population was in places of this size. England and Wales, which by the late seventeenth century was the most highly developed area of Europe, is estimated to have had only 20 per cent of her population in places of 5,000 or more in 1750. These contrasts become even more striking when it is noted that England and Wales and France had experienced considerable industrialization at the time of these estimates.[18]

THE ECONOMIC BASES OF TOKUGAWA URBANIZATION

Inherent in Tokugawa rule, which sought to maintain Japan as a rigidly stratified, feudal society, were the seeds of downfall for the very system it sought to preserve. First, the administrative machinery directed by the shogunate fostered the city growth

---

[17] Kingsley Davis, *Patterns of World Urbanization* (in preparation).
[18] *Ibid.*

(discussed above) which in itself served to weaken agriculturalism as a national way of life. Second, the whole system, heavily dependent upon a rice economy, placed those who manipulated this basic commodity in a strategic position. The collection, transportation and marketing of rice were in the hands of the *chōnin* (merchant townsmen) and of an expanding number of *samurai* who turned from military to commercial pursuits. These men, supported by the dynamic young *samurai* who rose to political power in groups opposing the continuation of Tokugawa policies, formed the core of the politico-economic leadership of the emerging modern Japan.

The Imperial Restoration brought the removal of many, but not all, of the Tokugawa restrictions upon commerce and trade. The merchant classes, as the center of a dynamic commercial expansion, unavoidably depended heavily upon traditional principles of economic practice. The result was that the early phases of Japan's modernization maintained a distinct feudal tone. The significance of this fact for Japanese urban history is that the pattern of city growth following the Imperial Restoration was conditioned by this "feudal" economic system. Japan's post-Restoration urbanization was a correlate of her industrialization. The nature of the background of this industrialization as observed in the history of the merchant class which took part in its administration becomes crucial to the understanding of the nature of Japan's modern urbanization.

The pattern of urbanization in Tokugawa Japan reflected a consolidation of political and military power in the castle town. This consolidation also brought changes in the economic structure of the nation and created opportunities for the evolution of an influential merchant class. The castle towns rapidly assumed importance as commercial and consumption centers when population was concentrated about the permanent residences of the lords and their retainers. The initial impetus for castle town growth was the assemblage of manpower and material required for the construction of the castle itself. Once the castle construction was completed, however, these centers continued to be the focus of commercial activities. The lord and his retainers, as permanent town dwellers, created an expanding urban market.

The lowly merchant served as the commercial link between the city and its hinterland. Larger and larger numbers of merchants were attracted to the castle town in preference to continued location in older trade settlements. Thus as it developed, the castle town brought forth factors basically antagonistic to the land-centered feudal regime conceived by the Tokugawa. These factors are well illustrated in the evolution of the merchants from dependent commercial middlemen for the lords to an important power group during the eighteenth and nineteenth centuries.

The establishment of the castle town had concentrated large numbers of the merchant and artisan classes under the protection of the lord. The merchants served as warehousemen for the lord's rice income allocated by the *shogun*. They also handled the production and transportation of the wealth of handicraft goods necessary to maintain the lavish level of living by the lord both in his local castle and in Edo. In return for their services the townsmen received the protection of the local lord. The merchants, however, still suffered the lowly prestige assigned their class and increasing restrictions were applied to them as feudal authorities perfected their administrative techniques. The evolution of a money economy, however, placed the merchant group in a position to amass extensive power in Tokugawa society.[19] The initial steps in the appearance of a money economy are visible prior to the Tokugawa shogunate, but Tokugawa policies speeded the process and aided the rapid outmoding of rice as a means of exchange.

An essential weakness in the Tokugawa economic system was the possibility of fluctuations in rice production or in the exchange value of the crop. The constant outlay necessary to maintain extensive bureaucratic staffs and to meet the frequent levies of the Edo shogunate made a consistent income level for the lords a necessity. In times of crop failure or low exchange value, the lords mortgaged future rice income to the merchants. This practice became so widespread that in the late Tokugawa period the

[19] For detailed analyses of the evolution of a money economy see Matsuyo Takizawa's *The Penetration of Money Economy in Japan* (New York: Columbia University Press, 1927), and Delmer M. Brown's *Money Economy in Medieval Japan* (New Haven: Far Eastern Association, 1951).

shogunate itself was under the financial domination of merchant-townsmen. This development gradually made the merchants bankers and only secondarily warehousemen and merchandisers.

The merchants were joined in many of their commercial activities by the lower ranks of the warrior class (*samurai*), who found it increasingly difficult to maintain themselves on fixed rice allocations. The peace and prosperity of the Tokugawa period made the military services of the warrior class superfluous. The *shogun* and the local lords attempted to hold their large military staffs together by overstaffing their administrative bureaucracies, but they succeeded only in increasing their economic obligations. The traditional way of life of the military aristocracy was thus undermined further as large numbers of the *samurai* took up commercial activities. The local lord often unintentionally contributed to this alienation of his military followers by granting monopolies in the handicraft specialities of the domain to his economically depressed *samurai*. These products in turn were traded through the commercial monopolies of the merchants in Edo and Osaka. The lines separating the warrior and the merchant classes were thus blurred. The willingness of hard-pressed *samurai* to be adopted into merchant families or the outright sale of *samurai* rank to the prestige-hungry townsmen further obscured the distinctions.

The relevance of these developments for Japanese urbanization lies in their creation of a social structure within which urban-oriented commercialism took precedence over feudal agriculturalism, but was not independent of it. The emergence of Japan's merchant class into a position of economic significance represented the foundation of an urban way of life for Japan, but one firmly rooted in the feudal social order. Unlike the great merchant bourgeoisie of France and England on the eve of the Industrial Revolution, the merchant class of late Tokugawa Japan was closely tied to the existing political order. The power of the French and English merchants, though certainly not independent of their national political systems, was based firmly upon international commerce and thus gained strength from sources outside any one nation's boundaries. Japanese merchants in contrast grew economically strong wholly through the manipulation of an internal economic structure. Among their principal sources of income was interest upon loans made to the feudal aristocracy. Since international trade, or even an unrestricted internal trade, was denied the commercial class by Tokugawa seclusion policies, merchants lacked an economic power independent of the existing feudal system. Hence the merchants' participation in anti-Tokugawa activities which culminated in the fall of the shogunate did not represent a frontal attack upon the feudal system but were attempts at political realignment within the existing social order.[20]

The blending of the older feudal order with the newer commercialism is further illustrated by the fact that some of the feudal lords themselves turned to industrial and commercial activities as an escape from the financial hardships of a decaying clan system. By means of manufacturing and marketing monopolies, these lords engaged in limited commercial activities at a more advanced level than the traditional handicraft system. The porcelain industry of Owari, the paper manufacture of Tosa, and the silk weaving of Kozuke and Shimotsuke are illustrations of clan monopolies sponsored by the local lords.

In the late Tokugawa period some of the stronger lords ignored the *shogun's* restrictions upon foreign contact and sponsored Westernized industrial developments in their fiefs. The lords of Satsuma, a fief at the southwestern tip of Kyushu, early in the nineteenth century had established a sugar monopoly in the northern Ryukyu Islands. Working through the Dutch at Nagasaki, by the early 1850's the Satsuma leaders had obtained the technological knowledge necessary to construct smelting works and blast furnaces for cannon manufacture. The fief of Hizen, which contained the port of Nagasaki, also profited from the acquisition through the Dutch of Western technology pertaining to shipbuilding and smelting. The more progressive of the lords took advantage of the *shogun's* policy of local autonomy to sponsor these industrial developments within their fiefs.[21] The extent of these developments, however, was never great, and they were carried out with the constant threat of reprisal by a hostile national government.

20 Thomas C. Smith, "Old Values and New Techniques in the Modernization of Japan," *Far Eastern Quarterly*, XIV, No. 3 (May, 1955), pp. 355-363.
21 Hugh Borton, *Japan's Modern Century* (New York: The Ronald Press Co., 1955), pp. 22-25.

THE IMPERIAL RESTORATION

During the early nineteenth century international pressures for the opening of Japan combined with expanding internal urbanism and commercialization to weaken further Tokugawa control. The visit of Perry in 1853 led to international commercial treaties in 1858. The period from 1858 to the restoration of Imperial rule in 1868 found the Tokugawa leadership distracted from attempts to revive its domestic administration by an increasing volume of foreign intercourse. The shogunate fell in 1868, and the Emperor Meiji became the nominal ruler of Japan.

The factors underlying the Imperial Restoration in Japan reveal a significant contrast in the role of cities in the modernization of Japan and of Western Europe. The three centuries preceding the Industrial Revolution, roughly from 1500 to 1800, saw dramatic changes in the organization and functions of the cities of Western Europe. The autonomous, guild-dominated city of the medieval period was possible only where a philosophy of isolation and self-sufficiency of separate communities held. Even before the impact of discoveries of new lands was deeply felt, the free city had shown signs of decline. The development of woolen manufacture in England in the fifteenth century illustrates the initial stages in the breaking of town-based guild control of industry. A group of embryonic capitalists, the clothiers, who realized the advantages of a wider production and distribution base, initiated the "putting out" system. The importance of this domestic system of production in contrast to the guild system was that it was centered in the homes of the predominantly rural working force. Industry was expanding beyond old town boundaries and hence beyond the restrictions of urban guilds.[22]

Of even more importance for English urbanization was the nascent factory system which can be seen underlying the creation of new industrial villages. Seeking locations nearer raw materials and power sources as well as a more obvious escape from the restrictions of the towns, many manufacturers moved into new areas and established villages whose populations were employed exclusively in the factories established at their centers. This movement

---

[22] H. deB. Gibbins, *The Industrial History of England* (London: Methuen and Co., Ltd., 1926), pp. 68-70.

is clearly reflected in the rapid growth of the northern English counties beginning in the sixteenth century.[23]

English town autonomy was dealt an even heavier blow by the economic expansion inherent in the commercial exploitation of newly discovered lands. The demands of these wider commercial horizons were for an orientation toward trade per se in contrast to self-sufficiency of the local community. The political correlate of this economic development was the creation of the unified, centrally administered nation state. For the society which could marshal its resources behind a strong centralized government, the economic and political rewards of exploiting the new world as well as nearby markets were limitless. Spain under Ferdinand and Isabella and later England under Elizabeth I showed the strength inherent in this new political order.

The role of the merchant-capitalist was a crucial one in the development of the European nation-state. Through the formation of giant mercantile companies and the perfection of commercial techniques, the deep-sea commerce centered in such cities as London, Lisbon, and Amsterdam put unheard-of financial resources at the disposal of the merchant class. The monarchy was constantly in need of capital to defend and strengthen the evolving nation-state and to maintain a royal way of life. The merchant-capitalist desired a stronger voice in national policy. Throughout the Tudor period in England, for example, the alliance between the monarchy and the rising bourgeoisie was a growing one. Tudor sovereigns were quick to see the advantages of hastening the decay of the power of the feudal aristocracy by supporting and being supported by the urban-based middle class.[24] Ultimately, however, political control moved into the hands of the merchant middle class itself. This victory was more clear-cut in France than in England, but even in England, the middle-class, commerce-oriented policies carried the day. The rising merchant classes of Western Europe were ever ready to ally themselves with an absolute monarchy during the formative periods of capitalism; once the system was sufficiently mature, the alliances were discarded in favor of self-determination through more democratic governmental forms.

[23] Gibbins, *op. cit.*, pp. 77-78.
[24] *Ibid.*, pp. 71-72.

The emergence of a merchant class in Japan during the three centuries prior to industrialization was of a different order. The alliance between the merchants and the authoritarian political system was too strong to be easily changed. The lines dividing the ruling hierarchy, especially the lower military ranks, and the developing merchant class had been obscured earlier in the Tokugawa period (see above). Further, the capital accumulation potential in foreign trade and colonial exploitation was denied Tokugawa merchants by the seclusion policies of the shogunate. Tokugawa merchants were unable to utilize their financial resources to establish their independence from the existing feudal social order. The antagonisms between money-hungry Osaka creditors and the Tokugawa shogunate and their feudal lords were frequently intense, but they were all bound closely within a land-based feudalistic economy. The essential wealth of the society was its land, and the shogunate had effectively severed the tie between the warrior class and the land by making them permanent castle town residents. This is not to say that large portions of the income from land were not in the hands of individuals, but rather that the concept of private ownership of resources to be exploited for personal gain was weak. Even the most powerful of the merchant houses were without a tradition of legal protection from debt cancellation, forced levies, or even outright confiscation by political authorities. It is true that a limited amount of private capital was accumulated through trade and usury by a few great merchant families and by the more progressive lords through monopolistic industrial activities in their fiefs, but this accumulation lagged far behind the financial resources of the merchant-capitalists of Western Europe.

The Industrial Revolution came to Western Europe at the culmination of a long period of revolutionary pressure from below, from an urban-based merchant class clamoring for destruction of the old social order and creation of a new one in which new institutions generated in an urban, commercial context could flourish. In contrast, the Industrial Revolution in Japan was carried out by leaders who had gained their opportunity to exercise power by the manipulation of an essentially feudalistic social order. The pressures to modernize the nation came largely from above, from those who were desirous of effecting revisions in the old order but not its drastic overthrow.

The differences in sources of economic power and in political philosophy between the preindustrial merchant classes of Japan and those of England and France were reflected in the tenor of urbanism in the respective countries. From at least the fifteenth century the urban merchant classes of these Western European countries made the cities centers of rebellion against their feudalistic rulers. The growth of modern Europe was in many respects the growth of this dimension of her cities. Preindustrial European cities were largely creatures of trade and commerce where developments antithetical to a feudal social order were bred.[25]

The cities of Tokugawa Japan were essentially administrative centers about which commercial activities clustered. The developing urban commercialism of Tokugawa Japan evolved in a context of dictation from and compromise with the authoritarian, feudalistic shogunate. Anti-Tokugawa pressures were inherent in the expanding urban population, but these pressures were far from being revolutionary in the sense of being anti-feudal. It is to be emphasized again that those who realized the advantages of expanding the opportunities of urban life were willing to attempt change in political leadership to gain these advantages, but not any basic revolution in the existing social structure.

SUMMARY

This brief survey of Japan prior to her industrial revolution has been focused primarily upon major parallels and divergencies in the pre-modern histories of urbanization in the West and in Japan. The major parallel is the growth of cities in response to the integration of larger and larger populations. This integration may arise from the creation of larger political units and/or from the development of trade relations between regions or nations. The evolution of effective political units in the form of European nation-states or of the Tokugawa shogunate in Japan expanded the bases for urban life in their respective areas by creating a need for administrative activities concentrated in strategic locations.

25 Pirenne, *Medieval Cities*, pp. 153 ff. and E. Herbert Norman, *Japan's Emergence as a Modern State* (New York: Institute of Pacific Relations, 1940), pp. 50-52.

The European urban growth which appeared with the revival of interregional trade in the late Middle Ages and the development of Japanese cities associated with expanded domestic and foreign trade in the thirteenth and fourteenth centuries also illustrate similar patterns of urbanization in response to commercial integration.

Divergencies in the patterns of preindustrial urbanization in Japan and the West are associated with the unique aspects of historical backgrounds. This is especially true of the political and economic factors which influence a nation's ability to support a segment of its population in occupations other than those concerned with basic subsistence. The contrasts between Japan and the group of Western nations which are today characterized as urban-industrial must be drawn in broad strokes since the Western nations among themselves have dissimilarities in historical elements influencing urban development. Valid contrasts can, however, be made between Japan and, for instance, England concerning the nature of the context of their respective industrial revolutions. In contrast to Japan, England as well as France and Holland maintained extensive political and commercial relations with areas outside their boundaries on the eve of the Western European Industrial Revolution. The structure and extent of urbanization within these European nations were influenced by these relations. The circumstances under which commerce and industry developed in these European areas were drastically different from those surrounding the later developments in Japan.

In summary, Japan began her modernization possessing the following major characteristics which were largely absent from the nations of the urban-industrial West:

1) A densely settled population living in an area containing few natural resources and lacking any channels for extensive emigration.

2) A strong tradition of authoritarian political administration, essentially feudalistic in character.

3) No extensive diplomatic or commercial relations beyond her own boundaries.

4) Limited accumulated capital in the hands of a merchant class with little entrepreneurial experience.

5) A keen awareness on the part of her leadership of the failure of other Asiatic nations (e.g., China) to cope with foreign and especially Western influence.

The consequences of the interplay of these factors form the background for the analysis of Japan's modern urban growth which is to follow.

Japanese Urban Growth since 1868 | III

How Japan was able to telescope a process encompassing several centuries for Western European nations into the relatively short span of fifty-odd years (assuming we are justified in characterizing Japan as urban-industrial at the close of World War I) has absorbed the efforts of numerous students of the nation's history. The manner in which the growth and structure of Japanese cities influenced and were influenced by the process of modernization is the framework within which we here view Japan's modern century.

RATE OF URBAN GROWTH

We begin by examining the changes in the magnitude of Japanese urbanization from the Imperial Restoration onward. What has been the over-all trend in modern Japanese city growth and what were the major factors moulding this growth? Further, within this over-all trend of urban expansion, what have been the variations in rate of expansion from one period to another? The basic assumption in answering these questions is that the transition from agriculturalism to industrialism implemented by the opening of Japan to the West is causally linked to the growth of her cities. The over-all rate of urbanization as well as variations of this rate are related not only to the fact of Japan's industrialization per se, but to the specific traits of her developing industrial organization. Hence, an increased level of industrial productivity at a given time is significant for urban growth, but whether the labor force involved was predominantly male or female, old or young, and employed in home workshops or outside the home in large factories also become crucial factors. The nature of the industrial activity itself was also influential in this respect. For example, export-oriented textile production and industries geared to domestic consumption had different consequences in terms of their impetus as urbanizing factors.

The striking trait of Japanese urban growth was the relative speed with which it was accomplished. From 1889 to 1940, the percentage of Japan's total population in cities of 20,000 or more increased from 9.7 per cent to 37.5 per cent. In approximately fifty years Japan had moved from less than 10 per cent urban to over one-third urban. England and Wales at the time reliable figures became available (1801) already had 16.9 per cent of her population in cities of this size. Assuming that it took at a minimum two decades to move from approximately 10 per cent in cities of 20,000 and over to the level she had reached by 1801, England and Wales required roughly eighty years (1780-1860) to match the Japanese level of urbanization. In moving between the same points, the United States took approximately seventy-five years (1850-1925). The urbanization of Germany, however, is roughly comparable in rate to that of Japan; in some fifty-five years (1860-1915) Germany's proportion of total population in cities of 20,000 or more increased from 10 per cent to 38 per cent (Figure III-1). The same relative rates of increase are evident for the growth of large cities (100,000 and over).

The post-World War II figures show Japan to have outdistanced the United States and to compare favorably with England and Wales in degree of urbanization as measured both in the 20,000 and the 100,000 and over categories:

Country	Per Cent of Total Population	
	In cities 20,000 and over	In cities 100,000 and over
United States (1950)	49.0	29.4
Japan (1955)	56.3	34.9
England and Wales (1951)	69.3	38.4

The comparative rates of urban growth summarized above suggest that the more recently a nation goes through an industrial revolution, the more rapid tends to be the expansion of its urban population. The causes underlying the rapidity of city growth in such recently modernized nations as Germany and Japan are complex and contain factors unique to the specific nation's history. No casual analysis can be expected to explain completely and

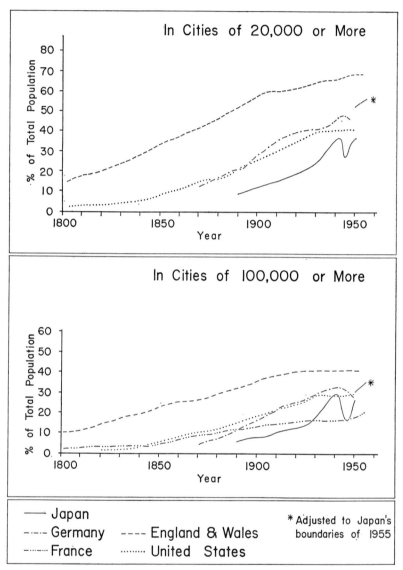

FIGURE III-1: Growth in City Populations for Selected Countries, 1800-1955 (Sources: National Censuses and Yearbooks)

definitively the great social changes which these transitions represent, but the influence of dominant elements upon the success or failure of a nation's modernization can be elaborated. It is within this framework that four major factors in Japan's rapid urbanization will be discussed.

First, a rapid population increase following the Restoration among an already densely settled agricultural population created a reservoir of labor force from which an expanding industrialization could draw. Second, industrial and commercial techniques which facilitate the capacity to support large urban concentrations were available to Japan from the West. Third, Japan's post-Restoration leaders were determined to secure for Japan these Western techniques as means of assuring Japan's independent economic and political development. Finally, a series of fortuitous military and diplomatic events secured for post-Restoration Japan not only an enhanced international prestige but expanded raw material sources and demands for the products of a developing industrial system. These factors, though phrased largely in terms of pressures toward industrialization rather than urbanization as such, emphasize a potential weakening of peasant-agriculturalism as the Japanese way of life. Hence, the factors making for a rapid industrialization of Japan in turn increased her urban orientation.

As cited previously, the total population of Japan during the last half of the Tokugawa period was relatively stable. Abortion and *mabiki* ("thinning" or infanticide), which were widespread among the hard pressed agriculturalists, had held the nation's population at approximately 30,000,000 for roughly a century prior to the Restoration. Governmental and private groups devoted to curtailing abortion and infanticide became active soon after the Restoration and contributed to the steadily increasing total population. Modest expansion of economic opportunity offered by the abolition of feudal restrictions upon occupation and migration removed some of the pressures producing these crude methods of population control.

Emigration played a relatively minor role in the relocation of Japan's increased population. In 1936, the number of Japanese residents abroad was less than 1,000,000 and over one-third of these were in Japanese-held Manchuria. Outside Asia, only the United States, Hawaii, and Brazil had more than 100,000 Japanese at this time. The only significant immigration to Japan has been by Koreans, who numbered nearly a million in 1939.[1]

Increases in population following the Restoration provided a reservoir of population which could be drawn relatively easily into cities. The mere existence of the reservoir did not cause urban growth, but given this population with its tenuous economic ties to agriculture, an urban-oriented industrialization could draw freely from it for its labor supply.

As for the second factor underlying Japan's rapid urbanization, the availability of Western technology, a brief illustrative summary is sufficient. Japan could avoid going through decades of trial and error in the invention and perfection of industrial and commercial techniques necessary for the support of an urban labor force. Her use of transport technologies well illustrates this point. Within four years of the Imperial Restoration Japan had her first railroad, an eighteen-mile line from Tokyo to Yokohama. Within the next decade more short lines were constructed under government auspices; private interests showed little interest in railways until the mid-1880's when the government guaranteed an eight per cent income in investments over the next twenty years. The next fifteen years brought a rapid increase in railroad mileage. The total mileage in 1900 was 3,885 miles (953 miles were in government hands, 2,902 miles were privately owned); by 1920 the total had increased to 8,475 miles.[2]

The pattern of development in shipbuilding shows much the same trend of rapid expansion. The Tokugawa shogunate had limited Japanese ships to tonnages capable of interisland transport only as a means of enforcing its policies of seclusion. This meant that Japan was opened to the West totally dependent upon foreign shipping in the early phases of her foreign trade. By offering attractive government subsidies and importing Western technical personnel and equipment, Japan made rapid strides toward providing for her own needs in shipping. In 1893, less than ten per cent of both exports and imports were carried in Japanese bot-

1 E. B. Schumpeter, et al., The Industrialization of Japan and Manchukuo (New York: The Macmillan Co., 1940), p. 70.
2 Nobutaka Ike, "The Pattern of Railway Development in Japan," Far Eastern Quarterly, XIV, No. 2 (February, 1955), pp. 222-228.

toms; by 1913, over half of all foreign trade was moved in national ships.[3]

Engineering, mining and chemical production, as well as railroads and shipping, progressed rapidly. The utilization of Western experts both as administrators and instructors of Japanese nationals was sponsored by the government and private industry.

The role of the national government in Japan's adoption of Western technology was a vital one.[4] Modernization became an active policy, with national preservation as its goal. Governmental policies encouraging the development of Westernized industry in Japan had appeared even prior to the Imperial Restoration. Following Perry's visit of 1853, Tokugawa leaders had ordered strengthening of coastal defenses through the manufacture of cannon utilizing Western methods. The Dutch were asked to supply a warship to the shogunate, and in 1855 Japan received her first steamship. The Dutch also supplied the Tokugawa with the necesary personnel and technical equipment for the construction of the first iron foundry. Further, a school for instruction in foreign languages was established in Edo with the support of the Tokugawa government.

This zeal for the acquisition of Western learning was even more obvious among the leaders of the post-Restoration period. The Imperial Charter Oath proclaimed in 1868 contains the following injunction for the pursuit of foreign technology:

> Knowledge shall be sought for all over the world and thus shall be strengthened the foundation of Imperial polity.

Early Meiji leaders saw in rapid modernization and industrialization the means to secure Japan's position as an independent nation.[5] They were keenly aware of the details of England's defeat of China in the Opium War of 1840.[6] A rapid buildup of

3 Hugh Borton, *Japan's Modern Century* (New York: The Ronald Co., 1955), pp. 271-272.

4 An excellent summary of governmental participation in Japan's industrialization is given in William W. Lockwood, "The State and Economic Enterprise in Modern Japan," in Simon Kuznets, *et al.*, eds., *Economic Growth: Brazil, India and Japan* (Durham, North Carolina: Duke University Press, 1955), pp. 537-602.

5 See the statements of Marquis Hirobumi Ito in Alfred Stead, ed., *Japan by the Japanese* (New York: Dodd, Mead, and Co., 1904), pp. 64-72.

6 For an analysis of the differences in Japanese and Chinese responses to Western influences see Marion J. Levy, Jr., "Contrasting Factors in the Modernization of China and Japan," Kuznets, *op. cit.*, pp. 496-536.

Japan's military strength was the only hope for avoiding the fate of China in dealing with the West. For this reason the application of modern techniques was almost exclusively confined to areas directly affecting national security, e.g., the so-called strategic industries of shipbuilding, railroads, iron and steel production, chemicals, and mining. Government subsidies and direct ownership by the government were focused predominantly upon these areas. These industries which were useful in advancing Japan's national standing developed at the expense of agriculture and consumer production. For instance, in 1885-89, 69.4 per cent of the government's revenue still came from land taxes, while favored industrial areas escaped the burden of taxation almost completely. During the same period, business taxes accounted for only 3.8 per cent of the government's revenue. Problems related to expanding the domestic market for the absorption of domestic production were largely ignored, as government and industry cooperated to strengthen Japan's international standing. That is, the national standard of living was of little concern to political and industrial leaders who were absorbed in closing the military and economic gaps between Japan and the industrial West.

A lasting consequence of Meiji policies of industrialization was the concentration of financial control of Japanese industry in the hands of a few favored merchant groups. The Tokugawa background of interdependence between merchants and feudal political leaders lent the weight of tradition to Meiji economic policies. Both the scarcity of venture capital and the lack of capitalistic experience among private businessmen in post-Restoration Japan caused a certain hesitancy on their part to initiate industrial ventures. The government, therefore, undertook entrepreneurial functions. The extent of government ownership of industry is revealed in this listing of the holdings of the Imperial Japanese Government in 1882.[7]

3 shipbuilding yards	10 mines
51 merchant ships	75 miles of railway
5 munition works	1 telegraph system
52 factories	

Once established, some of these concerns were offered for sale

[7] Borton, *op. cit.*, p. 155.

by the government to private interests. Through shrewd purchases, a limited number of private industrialists were able to gain effective control of Japanese economic development.

The point to be emphasized is that Meiji leaders, utilizing a tradition of authoritarianism inherited from the Tokugawa, were able to unify national efforts toward the kind of industrialization conceived as necessary to preserve the nation. This early "unified" industrialization contrasts vividly with the modernization of Western Europe, where industrialization came through the efforts of numerous and often conflicting private enterprise groups.[8] By intensifying even her narrowed industrialization, Japan intensified as well the impetus for urban expansion.

Japan's efforts toward modernization were not confined to domestic policies alone. Her leaders pursued diplomatic and military policies in the international sphere which served to implement advancement. Beginning with a treaty with Britain taking effect in 1899, Meiji representatives were successful in ridding international treaties of extraterritoriality clauses. The Sino-Japanese War (1894-95) gave Japan Formosa and the Pescadores and helped prepare the way for annexation of Korea in 1910. The Anglo-Japanese alliance of 1902 greatly increased Japan's international prestige. The conclusion of the Russo-Japanese War (1904-05) found Japan with the southern half of Sakhalien and other important concessions in China and Manchuria. Though one of the Allies in World War I, Japan suffered little or no losses by her participation, while gaining control of Germany's Chinese and northern Pacific holdings. In addition, Japan's industries prospered by supplying her allies as well as the customers of her allies with goods no longer available from a war-torn Europe. By the end of the war Japan's leadership throughout East Asia had been greatly strengthened with only limited costs.[9]

During the 1930's and early 1940's the leaders of Japan sought to make of their nation a new British Empire: a home island

---

[8] Detailed analyses of Japanese economic development are found in William W. Lockwood, *The Economic Development of Japan* (Princeton, N. J.: Princeton University Press, 1954) and in G. C. Allen, *A Short Economic History of Japan* (London: George Allen and Unwin, Ltd., 1950).

[9] Hugh Borton, "War and the Rise of Industrialization in Japan," in Jesse D. Clarkson and Thomas C. Cochran, eds., *War as a Social Institution* (New York: Columbia University Press, 1941), pp. 224-234.

group functioning as the financial, processing, and administrative center of vast colonial holdings. Aggression in China during the 1930's was an attempt to implement this policy, and it gave Japan greater sources of raw materials and natural resources for her industrial plant. World War II, however, brought the failure of attempts to extend still further Japanese control.

Japan's rapid urbanization since the Restoration is, therefore, linked closely with the speed of her shift away from agriculture and towards industry as her dominant economic activity. This shift was facilitated by the availability of Western technology and the determination of an authoritarian government to see this technology utilized as a means of gaining national strength and independence. In addition, developments in the international sphere placed Japan in a position whereby her domestic advance could be aided through military and diplomatic activities.

VARIATIONS IN RATE OF URBAN GROWTH

Though urban growth in Japan has shown a trend of constant increase, there have been significant variations in the rates of increase since the Restoration. Table III-1 shows the average yearly rates of change in urban population since 1891. (For purposes of analysis, growth rates have been divided into five periods as indicated in the last column.) It is noteworthy that from the earliest date to 1908, the rates of change are relatively high (6.8 per cent average yearly increase for the whole seventeen-year period). The twelve-year span from 1908 to 1920 shows the lowest rate of increase for any period since 1891. For the twenty years following 1920, the rates again are high (8.7 per cent average annual increase). The effect of World War II on city growth is clearly seen in the lower rate of increase during 1940-44, and the loss of approximately one-third of the city population by 1945. Post-World War II figures again show high rates of increase.[10]

The Japanese economy during the first period, extending roughly into the first decade of the twentieth century, displayed three dominant traits: 1) rapid development of international trade, 2) heavy dependence upon the textile industry for export

[10] These comparisons are based upon the growth of population in incorporated cities (*shi*) (see Chapter I, above).

production, and 3) exploitation of mineral resources within the home islands. This complex of factors was the context for Japan's first rapid increase in urban population, but there were inherent limitations upon the degree of urbanization that such an economic structure could support. For one thing, overseas trade was restricted by treaty to a limited number of ports during this early period; hence the impact of international contact was focused upon these centers. Osaka and Nagasaki, commercial centers un-

TABLE III-1. Growth of Japanese Urban Population, 1891-1955

Year	Population in Incorporated Cities (Shi) (000's)	Percentage Increase from Last Date	Average Annual Increase from Last Date		Average Annual Increase for Period
1891	3,812	—	—		
1898	5,518	44.8	7.4	I	6.8
1903	6,748	22.3	4.5		
1908	8,227	21.9	4.4		
1913	8,920	8.4	1.7	II	1.8
1920	10,020	12.3	1.8		
1925	12,823	28.0	5.6		
1930	15,363	19.8	4.0	III	8.7
1935	22,582	47.0	9.4		
1940	27,494	21.8	4.4		
1944	29,650	7.8	1.9	IV	—5.4
1945	20,022	—32.5	—32.5		
1950a	46,660	133.0	26.6	V	15.1
1955	50,288	7.8	1.6		

a Population adjusted to boundaries of 1955 census.

Sources: 1891-1913 figures from *Résumé Statistique de L'Empire du Japon*, Vols. 8-31. 1920-1955 figures from *Population Census of Japan, 1955*, Vol. I, p. 27.

der the Tokugawa, experienced rapid growth. In addition, relatively new ports, e.g., Yokohama and Kobe, attracted large population concentrations. In essence, urban expansion during this first period was the response of Japan to its initial contact with the world, the congregation of population about the points which served as gateways to international contact. No other cities approached the rates of growth experienced by the major port cities until well into the twentieth century.

The maintenance of extensive trade centered in these ports rested upon Japan's ability to supply exportable commodities. It is in this period that one of Japan's traditional handicrafts, silk processing, played a vital role in her modern history. Lacking either extensive mineral resources or the facilities for producing manufactured goods desired by the rest of the world, Japan could easily have developed into the weak, commercially dependent nation common in Asia during this period. The blight which had hit the silk-producing areas of Eastern Europe in the 1850's largely saved Japan from this fate and provided her with the opportunity to establish herself in the silk-export field.

The export structure of Japan from 1870 until the early 1930's reveals how dependent she was upon textiles. In 1870, 49.9% of total exports was made up of textiles; by 1920-30, 59% of total exports was in this area. The percentage of exports in textiles, however, showed a steady decline from this peak because of world depression and Japan's industrial diversification.[11] A further indication of the dominance of textiles in the Japanese economy is the fact that 33.2 per cent of the total Japanese export trade in 1870-74 was made up of raw silk alone; in 1900-04 and 1910-14, raw silk accounted for 27.1 per cent and 28.6 per cent respectively of her exports. Even as late as 1929, over 2,000,000 (approximately 40 per cent) of Japan's farming households were engaged in cocoon raising.[12]

Not only silk but cotton, and to a lesser extent wool, became important sources of Japanese textile exports. Cotton has been grown in Japan for centuries, but only on a limited scale. The importation of machine-woven cottons directly after the signing of the first commercial treaties quickly destroyed the Japanese cotton handicraft industry. The establishment of cotton textiles in the nation came with the importation of power looms and raw cotton. India and the United States provided Japan with the major portion of her raw cotton, which, after processing, was offered for export as finished goods. The Japanese cotton industry has been centered largely in factories utilizing modern technology to process an imported raw material. In contrast to silk, the cotton industry is almost exclusively a processing activity rather than a joint production and processing activity. Historically, then, the

[11] Tanzan Ishibashi, ed., *Foreign Trade of Japan: A Statistical Survey* (Tokyo: Oriental Economist, 1935), pp. 4-151.

[12] Mitsubishi Economic Research Bureau, *Japanese Trade and Industry, Present and Future* (London: Macmillan and Co., Ltd., 1936), pp. 253-255.

Japanese cotton industry has lacked the rural-oriented handicraft character of silk.

In large measure the production and processing of textiles was the major area of industrial activity in Japan until well after World War I. The national income from the textile exports provided the largest part of government and private investment capital during the first half century after the Restoration. The relative ease of Japan's development of the textile industry was brought about by three factors. 1) The previously cited world-wide shortage of silk fibers coincided with the opening of Japan to international contact. There existed, then, just that need which one of Japan's traditional handicraft industries was able to satisfy. 2) The technological and financial investment necessary for the establishment of a textile industry is relatively small compared to that of other types of industry. Japan's investors placed their limited industrial capital precisely where returns would be the highest and fastest. 3) The essentially rural nature of the Japanese silk industry provided a means whereby masses of the rural population became "industrialized" without the disruptions associated with large scale rural-to-urban movements of population. The production and processing of Japan's most important export became largely supplementary employment for a great segment of Japan's agriculturalists.

The second phase of Japanese urbanization, roughly from 1908 to 1920, was a period of relatively low rates of increase. Industrialization based largely upon a narrow export production, i.e., textiles, and the exploitation of limited mineral resources had almost reached a plateau. The international trade ports had reached sufficiently high population levels to perform their function. Throughout the twelve-year period these ports grew little: Nagoya, 13.7 per cent; Yokoyama, 7.3 per cent; Osaka, 2.1 per cent; and Nagasaki, less than 0.1 per cent. Among the major ports, only Kobe, with an increase of 60.9 per cent, showed a growth greater than the 21.8 per cent in the total urban population during the period 1908-1920. The cities which led in urban growth during this phase were those associated with the continued exploitation of mineral resources: Sapporo and Hakodate in Hokkaido and Niigata, the oil center on the Sea of Japan. Their increases were not sufficient, however, to bring the national urban increases up to previous levels.

The key to later diversification of Japan's economy and hence to increased urban orientation lies in Japan's relationship to the Allies during World War I. Japan's limited chemical, munitions, and heavy industries were given impetus for expansion by the orders placed with her by the Allies as European production was curtailed (see above). Japan's participation in the world's economy as a genuine industrialized nation dates from this period. It is true that in the period following World War I she lost many of her gains as European production rose, but her foothold in international markets and her domestic industrial base were never completely destroyed. The consequences of this expansion of the Japanese industrial structure can be read in the shift in the rate and character of her urbanization in the third phase of her urban growth (1920-1940). From 1920 to 1930, the average annual rate of increase in total urban population was 5.3 per cent; the rate jumped to 7.9 per cent from 1930 to 1940. Japan had eighty-one incorporated cities in 1920; by 1930 the total had increased to 107. By 1940, there were 164 incorporated cities. The urban population was expanding vertically in total proportion of the population residing in cities, and horizontally in the number of urban centers.

Paralleling this urban expansion, the proportion of total males which were in nonextractive employment increased steadily: 51.8 per cent in 1920, 57.0 per cent in 1930, and 64.3 per cent in 1940. Significantly, the textile industry was gradually declining in importance.[13]

Per Cent of Total Factory Workers in Textile Industries

1923	1929	1933	1936
53.2	50.4	43.4	37.9

Per Cent of Total Value of Factory Output in Textiles

44.6	40.0	35.7	28.5

One of the dominant causes underlying the change in Japanese post-World War I industrial structure was the heightened imperialistic policies of Japan beginning with the Manchurian Incident of 1931, continuing through the opening of the Sino-

---

[13] Schumpeter, *op. cit.,* p. 484.

Japanese War in 1937, and on into World War II. The element of national survival in the world's commercial and political spheres which dominated much of Japanese political and economic policy prior to the 1920's was replaced by an aggressive policy of national self-sufficiency and colonialism. During the decade preceding World War II large government expenditures were made for armaments; the chemical, oil, shipbuilding, and munitions industries were encouraged through subsidies. With the collapse of the silk market following the world-wide depression of the early 1930's, large groups of displaced agricultural workers poured into the urban areas, providing abundant labor for the expanding strategic industries.

This pattern of growth was halted by the bombing of Japanese cities in 1944-45. Japan lost approximately one-third (32.5 per cent) of her urban population through casualties and evacuation from roughly June of 1944 to August of 1945. The larger cities, as centers of administration and industrial production, suffered the greatest share of the total urban loss:

City Size	Per Cent Change 1944-45
1,000,000 +	—56.7
500-1,000,000	—33.9
100-500,000	—29.8
Under 100,000	— 6.2

The final period of Japanese urbanization, that following World War II, has been one largely devoted to recouping war losses in population. In addition, some attempt has been made by administrators to redefine urban boundaries to reflect the urban expansion which has taken place since the close of the war. During the five-year period 1945-50, cities regained some 11,000,000 of their populations to give a total of 37.5 per cent urban. This figure was still some four percentage points below the urban peak of 41.4 per cent urban in 1944. None of the four cities which had over 1,000,000 inhabitants in 1944 had reached their 1944 population level by the time of the national census of 1950. Administrative boundary expansion plus continued population growth in urban areas between 1950 and 1955 combined to wipe out Japan's war losses in urban population. In spite of this, Osaka and Nagoya (among the major cities) and Kure, Sasebo, and Yokosuka (in the 200-400,000 size group) were still below their 1944 populations in the national census of 1955. The major portion of the urban expansion indicated in the increase from 37.5 per cent urban in 1950 and 56.3 per cent in 1955 was accomplished by the incorporation of 243 new cities. When the proportion of total urban population is figured for 1950 using these revised urban boundaries, the total urban population is increased by some 15.4 million, to a proportion of 53.5 per cent urban in 1950.

As a consequence of post-World War II urban growth and redefinition, urbanization of a relatively high level is characteristic of the whole of Japan. Whereas in 1940 four of Japan's forty-six prefectures had less than 10 per cent urban, by 1955 the lowest proportion of urban (Tokushima Prefecture in eastern Shikoku) was 28.5 per cent. An outstanding illustration of this spread of urban residence is Shimane Prefecture in southern Honshu. In 1940 this prefecture was the least urbanized in Japan (7.2 per cent); in 1955, 43.0 per cent of its population was defined in the census as urban.

SUMMARY

The differential rates of urban growth in Japan are shown to have been closely linked with the character and speed of her economic development. Soon after the Restoration her ports expanded rapidly to accommodate foreign trade, supported largely by Japan's capacity to produce textiles for export. As this impetus for development reached its limits, World War I spurred the creation of a more diversified and genuine industrialized economy. Japan's most rapid urbanization took place during the decade preceding World War II as the nation strove for self-sufficiency within her empire. Rapid urbanization is characteristic of the post-World War II period as urban losses were regained and industry was revived.

Japanese urbanization has been rapid, compared to the nations which first experienced an industrial revolution. She is at present among the most urbanized nations. The correlation of urban expansion with industrialization found in the history of the West is also found in modern Japanese history.

The Sources of Japanese Urban Growth | IV

The economic transition of Japan from an agrarian to an industrial society entailed a dynamic population redistribution within the nation. This redistribution was essentially the movement of agrarian labor force into those areas where the need for industrial labor was expanding. The rapid increase in the proportion of total population residing in urban areas is the clearest evidence of such redistribution. The problem of specifying the magnitude and direction of this internal migration, however, remains.

The essential difficulty of this task is one not peculiar to Japanese population data. Few nations compile precise data on internal migration, e.g., points of departure and arrival, age, sex, or economic activity of migrants. Any assessment of population redistribution must, therefore, of necessity be based upon indirect measures. These measures for Japan are largely derived from the place-of-birth data collected in the censuses of 1920, 1930 and 1950. In addition, rural to urban migration can be gauged, again indirectly, from correlations of level of urbanization and magnitude of nonagricultural employment with rate of total population growth by prefecture. The positive association of prefectural urban-industrialism with high levels of population increase and the converse association of little urban residence and industry with low rates of growth imply a movement of population at least equal to the natural increase in agrarian areas to urbanized areas.

From 1872 to 1955, the total population of Japan increased from 34.8 million to 89.3 million, an increase of 156.6 per cent. This increase in total population is of vital importance since it took place in a nation which had only approximately one-third acre of cultivated land per capita as early as 1880. Post-Restoration population increases placed an increasing burden of support upon an already crowded agricultural base. During this same period the urban population increased from an estimated two million to 50.3 million, an increase of over nineteenfold. The total population increased in absolute numbers 54.5 million, while the increase in urban population was approximately 48 million. The absence of any significant international migration means that almost 90 per cent of the Japanese increase from 1872 to 1955 was absorbed by urban areas. Japan's modern urban growth represents in essence the natural increase in her population since the Restoration.

While the proportion of population outside incorporated cities has declined steadily since the Restoration, the absolute number of persons in these areas showed a steady increase until 1930: the population outside incorporated cities in 1872 is estimated to have been some 34.2 million (93.1% of total population); in 1930, this population was 75.9% of the total, or some 48.5 million. The war years, with the dispersal of urban populations, saw a jump to an all-time high of 52.2 million in rural areas in 1947, but the census of 1955 shows a return to a decreasing noncity population (39.0 million, 43% of the total population). These data imply a constant flow of excess population from rural areas into the cities throughout the whole of Japan's modern history.

The threefold increase in total population since the Restoration has given to each Japanese prefecture an increase in absolute population. However, only fourteen of the forty-six prefectures have held or increased the proportion of the total population which they contained in 1891 (Figure IV-1).[1] The largest gains in the proportions of total population are shown in the prefectures containing the cities of Tokyo, Osaka, and Fukuoka. These areas are closely followed by the chain of prefectures running southwest from Tokyo along the Pacific Ocean and Inland Sea, including the northern Kyushu area. The agrarian prefectures facing the Japan Sea and those of the northern half of Honshu experienced the greatest proportionate losses. The post-Restora-

---

[1] The greatest proportionate increase took place in Hokkaido where the total population has increased some sixfold. The absolute increase, however, is a relatively small part of Japan's total population: 340,374 in 1892 as against 4,773,087 in 1955. The proportion of Japan's total population in Hokkaido has increased from less than one per cent in 1892 to 5.3 per cent in 1955.

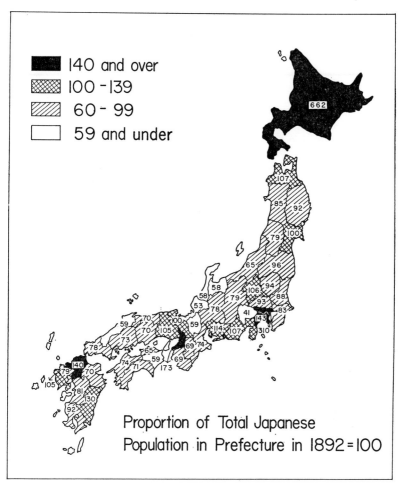

FIGURE IV-1: Population Changes by Prefecture, 1892-1955 (Sources: *Résumé Statistique de L'Empire du Japon*, Vol. 8 [1894], pp. 8-9; *1955 Population Census of Japan*, Vol. 1, pp. 28-31)

tion development of Hokkaido led to an increasing proportion of the Japanese population in this area as well as a smaller increase for Aomori Prefecture, which serves as the gateway to Hokkaido from the central island of Honshu.

The pattern noted for total population distribution within Japan can in large measure be accounted for in terms of the growth and distribution of cities following the Restoration. The prefectures showing the greatest total population increases are

TABLE IV.1. Japan: Level of Urbanization and Net Migration for Selected Prefectures, 1920-1950

	1920		1930		1950	
	% Urban[a]	Net migrants per 100 residents[b]	% Urban[a]	Net migrants per 100 residents[b]	% Urban[a]	Net migrants per 100 residents[b]
Prefectures with greatest net gain through migration (1930)						
Tokyo	59.8	38.6	39.2	41.8	89.1	14.4
Osaka	51.7	32.1	73.7	34.6	78.4	8.8
Hokkaido	21.7	44.0	24.9	30.1	35.5	12.8
Kanagawa	38.8	16.5	51.6	16.2	75.0	16.5
Kyoto	45.9	10.9	51.3	14.6	69.4	7.9
Fukuoka	21.0	15.8	34.9	12.6	45.1	9.1
Hyogo	31.5	7.4	37.0	6.5	51.2	4.2
Aichi	25.5	0.6	44.8	5.3	49.0	3.6
Prefectures with greatest net loss through migration (1930)						
Toyama	13.6	−32.2	16.3	−29.8	29.4	−13.8
Fukui	9.5	−23.6	10.4	−25.4	22.9	−10.7
Kagawa	10.5	−25.0	14.8	−25.0	21.5	−11.1
Ishikawa	17.3	−23.0	20.8	−24.6	37.1	− 8.8
Tokushima	10.2	−22.9	12.6	−23.0	18.7	−12.7
Niigata	9.1	−22.2	11.1	−22.6	18.1	−13.8
Shiga	4.8	−22.9	5.0	−22.6	21.0	− 6.9
Nara	7.1	−19.2	8.9	−22.1	14.3	− 4.5

[a] *1955 Population Census of Japan*, Vol. I, Table 8.

[b] Irene B. Taeuber, *The Population of Japan* (Princeton: Princeton University Press, 1958), Table 43, p. 125. The net migration shown in this table is calculated from place-of-birth enumeration in the censuses for these years. The computations for 1920 and 1930 are only for population born within Japan, while those for 1950 are based upon total population in Japan. The ratios are, therefore, not precisely comparable, but the direction of the differences is valid.

those containing the highest proportion of urban population. The administrative district containing the city of Tokyo, for instance, increased 588.7 per cent in total population from 1891 to 1955; the Osaka area showed an increase of 276.8 per cent. These two urban prefectures stood at 93.7 per cent and 97.4 per cent urban, respectively, in the 1955 census.

The magnitude of this movement is indicated even more clearly in Table IV-1, which shows level of urbanization and net migration by prefecture for 1920, 1930, and 1950. The leading urban prefectures throughout the thirty-year period consistently gained through internal migration, while the reverse is true for the prefectures with lower levels of urban residence. It is significant, however, that although the agrarian prefectures were the major sources for out-migrants, their own levels of urbanization show a steady though relatively small pattern of increase. A significant portion of the rural-urban migration indicated in these data was from rural areas to cities within the same prefecture.

The internal migration viewed here was a movement essentially from an agrarian context to an industrial one, not necessarily a movement from rural areas to those administratively defined as cities. This fact accounts for the higher level of in-migrants to the urban-industrial prefectures as a whole as well as to their cities. The more urban-industrial the prefectures, the higher the proportion of population in the *gun* (that outside incorporated cities) which was born outside the prefecture of residence (Table IV-2).

The same broad patterns of population redistribution reflected in place-of-birth data are also evident in an analysis of interpre-

TABLE IV-2. Japan: Prefectural Level of Urbanization and Place-of-Birth for Population Outside Incorporated Cities, 1930

Prefectures by per cent of population in cities	Per cent of population born within prefecture of residence	Per cent of population born in other prefectures	Total
Less than 10%	93.5	6.5	100.0
10-19%	94.8	5.2	100.0
20-29%	77.5	22.5	100.0
More than 30%	78.6	21.4	100.0
All Japan	89.4	10.6	100.0

Source: Irene B. Taeuber, *The Population of Japan* (Princeton: Princeton University Press, 1958), p. 126.

fectural vital rates. The birth and death statistics for Japan were computed from household registrations and were consequently subject to a whole range of errors resulting from imprecise recording as to place and time of occurrence. The patterns of internal migration observed in the manipulation of these statistics will therefore reflect the inadequacies of the source data. The usefulness of such manipulations is largely in terms of indicating the direction of prefectural variations, not in indicating their

TABLE IV-3. Japan: Natural Increase and Migration by Prefectures, 1920-1952

Prefectures	Date	Total increase (000's) (1)	Natural increase[b] (000's) (2)	Estimated net migration (000's) (1) — (2)[c]
Seven most	1920-30	4,384	1,952	2,432
urban	1930-40	5,687	2,487	3,200
prefectures[a]	1950-52	1,950	722	1,228
Remaining	1920-30	4,097	6,049	—1,952
thirty-nine	1930-40	2,980	6,143	—3,163
prefectures	1950-52	714	1,919	—1,205

[a] Tokyo, Kanagawa, Aichi, Kyoto, Osaka, Hyogo, and Fukuoka.

[b] Total births minus total deaths.

[c] In each time period the positive gain in migration for the seven most urban prefectures is greater than the loss in the remaining prefectures. It can be assumed that the absence of a separate category for migration to and from areas outside the Japanese home islands as well as the inaccuracies inherent in the Japanese system of collecting data upon which natural increase figures are based account for these imbalances.

Sources: Shinichi Mihara, "Internal Migration in Japan," *Proceedings of the World Population Conference, 1954* (New York: United Nations, 1954), Vol. II, p. 603.

magnitude. With these qualifications, Table IV-3 contrasts prefectural natural increases with actual increases for the 1920-1952 period. Once again, the implied source of population gains in urban-industrial prefectures is largely the migration of population increases from the rest of the nation.

Taeuber, in her more detailed analysis of natural increase and internal migration, notes the same general trends. However, she notes further that the rural to urban movement was not sufficient to cause population decreases even in the agrarian prefectures.

Migration removed substantial proportions of the natural increase from the peripheral agricultural prefectures. . . . In the modal agricutural prefectures, net out-migration was equal to little more than one-third of the natural increase during the 1920's and only two-fifths in the years from 1930 to 1935. In the years that followed the outbreak of the China War, out-migration was probably greater than natural increase. . . . It seems evident that migration even of the magnitude of that occurring in Japan in the decades from 1920 to 1940 was not a solution to the problems of an increasing agricultural population.[2]

THE ROLE OF AGRICULTURE IN JAPAN'S MODERNIZATION

The continued stability of this agricultural population in spite of great strides in urban-industrialization lends to Japanese modernization a unique coloring. Unlike the rural to urban population movement which contributed to urban expansion in such nations as the United States and England and Wales, Japanese internal migration has not yet been able to affect significantly the absolute population in rural areas. Agricultural households since the Restoration have shown relatively little variation in total number, and there is no indication that the number of persons per agricultural household has decreased significantly. The number of Japanese agricultural households was 5.6 million in 1872; this figure varied only between 5.4 and 5.7 million until 1946. In 1949 and 1951, the number of households in this category actually rose to over six million.[3] The census of 1960, however, indicates that there has been a drop away from these peaks.

The background and characteristics of Japan's agricultural population are important considerations, for many of the traits of her urban population are understandable only in terms of the rural context from which the great bulk migrated. Many of the feudal remnants that are so much a part of Japan's present-day existence can be traced directly to the tenacity of peasant-agricultural patterns, preserved in the urban social structure by rural migrants.

The agrarian reform directly following the Meiji Restoration was necessitated by the government's need for a constant income

2 Irene B. Taeuber, *The Population of Japan* (Princeton, N. J.: Princeton University Press, 1958), p. 146.
3 T. Honda, "Historical Analysis of Population Problems in Japan," *Jinko Mondai Kenkyu* (Studies in Population Problems), Vol. 6, No. 2 (June, 1950), p. 11, and The Bank of Japan, *Economic Statistics of Japan*, 1951, p. 294.

from taxation. Feudal restrictions upon the right to sell land were removed. The basis of agricultural taxation was shifted from harvest-sharing to a direct taxation of the total value of the land, irrespective of seasonal variation in harvests. As a consequence, the small, isolated cultivator was hard pressed to meet the new tax demands. Larger and larger portions of the agricultural land came into the hands of landlords who retained the former owners as tenants. Landlords were little concerned with agricultural productivity; their primary interest was in the high rents which agricultural holdings yielded. The atomization of holdings went on apace as larger and larger numbers of agricultural population attempted to secure subsistence from the soil.

This pattern represents a significant contrast to the agrarian changes which took place in eighteenth-century England, where the land enclosure policies placed larger and larger tracts in the hands of landlords whose purposes were essentially capitalistic: to increase agricultural productivity, and hence profits, by using improved techniques. In a sense, this was an attempt to "industrialize" agriculture. It is not to be denied, however, that Japanese agricultural productivity did increase following the Restoration, but more as a matter of self-preservation than of the modernization of agriculture. For instance, yields of rice per *cho* increased from 11.6 *koku* in 1880-84 to 18.8 *koku* in 1930-31, but the per capita consumption of rice during the same period increased from 0.8 *koku* to 1.1 *koku*. The fact remains, however, that Japanese agriculture was under the Tokugawa and remains today essentially a gardening activity, utilizing intense hand cultivation. Compared to other industrialized nations, Japanese agriculture is wasteful of manpower. For instance, per square mile of cultivated land Japan has over 400 males employed in agriculture; in contrast, the United States and Canada have only ten male agriculturalists per square mile of cultivated land.[4]

The heavy ratio of men to land throughout the modern period has had profound effects upon Japanese society. The excess population from her dense agricultural areas has moved into cities, where industrialization has been able to absorb only part of it.

[4] Kingsley Davis, "Population and the Further Spread of Industrial Society," *Proceedings of the American Philosophical Society*, Vol. 95, No. 1 (February, 1951), pp. 8-19.

The presence of a large "floating" labor supply has retarded Japan's development of highly capitalized industry. This has been the case until quite recently, when falling fertility has reduced the source of new labor force. Manpower has traditionally been her only relatively unlimited natural resource, and industry has developed accordingly. Major readjustments are currently being made to meet the needs of an industrial structure in which labor is becoming less abundant and in which capital resources have expanded. However, it is still true that the Japanese home market is relatively narrow and dependent upon an over-all low wage scale.

A statistical analysis of Japanese internal migration gives little indication of the dynamic nature of Japan's rural to urban movements. The close ties between rural and urban populations cause constant movements between cities and their hinterlands. Traditional practices of choosing marriage partners from the home area, of returning to the family homestead for childbirth, and the like, are still strong. The younger sons and daughters of rural families frequently migrate temporarily to urban areas, returning later to marry and establish residences in the rural areas. A study of migration to Tokyo during the 1930-39 period, for example, showed that 43 per cent of the population migrating into the city stayed less than five years. This same study revealed that the 900,000 gain in Tokyo's population for the five-year period 1930-35 involved the movement of some 4,000,000 persons into and out of the city.[5]

The major source of Japan's expanding urban population, as in the West, has been her agrarian population. Unlike Western nations, however, the rural to urban movement has carried with it much more of the traditional rural social context. Migration of agrarians toward cities and their industrial activities is characteristic of the industrialization process. In Western nations this movement has been the base upon which a permanent, urban industrial worker class has developed. Urban residence implied a weakening and ultimate severing of rural ties. In contrast, the population making up Japan's rural to urban flow contains significant proportions of persons whose ties to the agrarian village

[5] Toyoura Asakichi, "Quality and Quantity of Population Renewal in Tokyo," *Shakai Seisaku Jihō* (April, May, June, 1939).

are sufficiently strong to bring them back periodically to the point of origin, frequently to re-establish permanent residence.

The nature of this "circulatory migration" is well illustrated during the early periods of Japanese industrialization. Heavy emphasis was placed upon textile production which utilized a predominantly female labor force. These women were usually the young, unmarried daughters of agrarian families who went into industrial plants under contract for specified periods of time. When the employment contract was fulfilled, the daughters returned once again to their rural homes to marry. Thus a segment of early Japanese industrial structure was developed with a minimal disruption of traditional social behavior. Indeed, this textile employment pattern served to implement the attainment of peasant cultural goals through the increased economic contribution of children to family maintenance as well as through the establishment of a new source for dowries in preparation for traditional marriage.

The same pattern of preservation of traditional peasant values is observed in the migration of younger sons from the agrarian household into urban industrial activities. The practice of primogeniture with respect to family agricultural holdings deprived the younger sons in rural families of strong economic ties to the land, but the deeply rooted ethic of familial responsibility did not permit a complete break with their family's village life. The movement of these younger sons into non-agricultural pursuits was encouraged by the family itself. The new migrant continued to contribute economically to his family and frequently returned to his home area to marry a local resident. Further, in times of unemployment in the urban area, he returned to his family and rural village life. The paternalistic structure of the traditional Japanese family, therefore, contributes to what has been termed here "circulatory migration."

The consequences of these and similar elements for Japanese urban-industrialism are far-reaching. The following chapters which deal with the industrial and demographic structure of Japan's urbanization will frequently make use of detailed aspects of these elements as explanatory factors. In summary, it is sufficient at this point to emphasize the dynamic relationship of Japan's rural and urban populations. There is no clear break be-

tween the agrarian and the industrial populations either economically or demographically. Though urban areas have historically increased their populations at the expense of natural increase
in rural areas, the redistribution of population has not been a
one-way flow. The exchange of population between agrarian and
industrial areas has resulted in a penetration of peasant values
and modes of existence into Japan's modern industrialization,
rather than the creation of a wholly new urban value system
capable of destroying the traditional system.

The Regional Pattern of Japanese City Growth | V

The urbanization of a population is a selective process. Internal migration contributes differentially to urban growth from one region to another. The expansion of older industrial complexes tends to attract rural migrants to existing cities, while the creation of new nonagrarian enterprises aids in the establishment of new cities. At the same time, existing cities with their established urban orientation and trained nonagrarian labor force are attractive locales for the introduction of new industrial activities. The result may be some variation of the process of size begetting size. All this is simply to say that from period to period and from region to region there are variations in the quality and quantity of a nation's urban growth.

We document this principle of urbanization by focusing upon two major variables of Japanese urban structure: functional types of cities and city size. Analysis of the first of these variables, functional type of city, makes it possible to plot the pattern of urban growth over time as it is related to the kinds of cities involved, e.g., port cities, inland administrative centers, and heavy industry cities. Shifts in national economic focus as it fosters city growth can, in this way, be read in the kinds of cities experiencing most rapid growth. For example, intensified export of products requiring little industrial processing, e.g., raw silk, encouraged the rapid growth of deep-water port cities. As Japanese industrial technology expanded, manufacturing centers experienced growth of a comparatively high level. The history of urban growth by functional type of city, therefore, provides an insight into the causal relationship between Japanese industrial development and the pattern of her city growth.

Analysis of Japanese urbanization using the city size variable further clarifies this relationship. The historical summary of Japanese city growth contained in Chapter II reveals the extent to which Japan was an urban nation prior to industrialization. This is to say that there were existing urban agglomerations within Japan from which an industrially created urbanization could proceed. The crucial question is to what extent Japan's modern city growth did take place in and around existing cities. Was there a positive association between the large, older cities and rate of growth? Is any such association consistent throughout Japan's modern history? Or, as the industrial impetus for urbanization shifted from period to period, did the influence of size upon patterns of city expansion change as well?

CITY GROWTH BY FUNCTIONAL TYPE

The urban bridge between the pre-industrial Tokugawa period and the Meiji era was the Tokugawa administration center, the castle town. The prosperity of these settlements suffered following the Imperial Restoration as the feudal lords were made nobility and their fief holdings were converted into interest-bearing government bonds. As nobility, the lords tended to become permanent residents of the new national capital of Tokyo. Consequently, many of the smaller cities which had thrived under the Tokugawa are today historical relics of Japan's feudal period. Others were made the seats of new local governments and thus maintained growing populations. Still others, favored by location or natural resources, acquired new importance with the expansion of Japan's domestic and foreign trade. As a group, however, the cities and towns with less than 50,000 population at the time of the Imperial Restoration tended to decline in population. Out of thirty-four cities which had between 20,000 and 50,000 population in 1879, fully one-half had shown decreases in population by 1886, with some decreases as high as 60 per cent.[1]

It was only the very large cities and the commercial seaports which showed positive population growth immediately following the Imperial Restoration. Kobe, opened to foreign trade in 1867, leaped from 13,295 in 1879, to 80,446 in 1886. Osaka during the same period grew from 287,984 to 316,694. Tokyo, as the largest

[1] *Nihon Toshi Nenkan* (Japan City Yearbook) (Tokyo: Zenkoku Shicho-kai, 1956), p. 5.

Tokugawa castle settlement, suffered an initial population decrease with the fall of the shogunate, but as the new imperial capital it quickly recovered, showing a growth from 799,237 (1879) to 1,121,883 (1886).[2]

The first Japanese city incorporation law was promulgated in 1889. This law officially recognized thirty-nine cities, all above 20,000 in population. At the time of incorporation these cities contained 3.8 million persons, approximately 10 per cent of the total population of Japan. By 1955, these original thirty-nine cities still contained 23.8% of Japan's total population. The major portion of this growth, however, was experienced by those cities which were capable of serving functions supporting either the commerce or administration of a new internationally oriented Japan. Tokyo, as the capital, responded to all the factors associated with Japan's modernization. Already a city of over one million at the time of the first incorporation law, the city has maintained its position as the nation's largest city down to the present. In contrast, the existence of many of the smaller cities incorporated in 1889 was based principally upon lingering elements of pre-Restoration society. They still remain today as cities, but they have been far outstripped in size and importance by newer cities created in the context of modern Japan.

The first major urbanizing factor in post-Restoration Japan was the development of her export-oriented textile industry. This factor was most effective in fostering the growth of deep-water ports serving as outlets for international trade. Yokohama, for instance, was little more than a fishing village when it was designated as an open port in 1859. The channeling of raw silk exports from the extensive silk producing areas of central Honshu through the new port underlay its growth to a city of over 100,000 by 1889.

The five cities showing the highest increase in the decade 1888-98 were all port centers (Nagasaki, Osaka, Kobe, Yokohama, and Nagoya), and they maintained this lead for roughly the following two decades. Total urban increase for the 1888-98 period was 5.3%, while for these five cities the increase was 8.1%. For the period 1903-08, Osaka, Kobe, and Nagoya still had increases higher than the 4.4% for the total urban population. Outside the port

---

[2] Yeijiro Ono, *The Industrial Transition in Japan* (Baltimore: American Economic Association, 1890), pp. 27-32.

areas, the impetus for city expansion inherent in Japanese textile production was relatively weak. The taking on of sericulture as a "by-occupation" by agriculturalists and the locating of small processing plants in a widely dispersed pattern in order to take advantage of power available from the many short, rapid streams of the Japanese countryside, tended to retard the growth of large urban concentrations about this industry. It is true, however, that inland urban centers specializing in the collection and processing of silk, cotton, and wool fibers appeared, but their rates of growth were usually less than the over-all urban increases for the country. Again citing total urban rate of increase (5.3%) for 1888-98 as contrast, Yamagata, Kofu, and Fukui increased 3.1%, 2.0%, and 1.0%, respectively, for the period. In addition, the newly incorporated cities of this type, e.g., Maebashi, Nagano, and Matsumoto, had increases ranging from 4.2% to 1.4% in 1898-1903, in contrast to a national urban rate of increase of 6.2%.

Cities which combined textile processing with a coastal site experienced growth rates generally higher than those of inland textile centers. A coastal location was of importance in growth, for during this early period adequate land transportation was largely confined to rail lines between the major cities of central Honshu. Domestic trade, as well as the movement of textile export products, favored those cities located so as to serve both as textile processing and shipment centers. Himeji, Tsu, and Wakayama are representative cities of this type. Their rates of growth for this early period were, however, below that of the total urban population.

Exploitation of mineral resources brought emphasis primarily upon Hokkaido, northern Kyushu, and the northwestern coastal area of Honshu. These areas contained the major deposits of Japan's coal and oil. The impetus given to urbanization by the exploitation of these areas was somewhat later in coming than that given by the textile and port developments discussed above. Hokkaido officially had no cities until 1899, when Sapporo, Hakodate, and Otaru were incorporated. Asahigawa was recognized in 1914, Muroran in 1918, and Kushiro not until 1920. Sapporo and Otaru, both towns of less than 15,000 population in 1880, had reached the 100,000 level by 1920. Hakodate, as the major port for contact with Honshu and an international trade port, had 52,000 population in 1888 and had passed the 100,000 level around 1915. Muroran reached the 100,000 level in 1940; Asahigawa and Kushiro were not to achieve this size until after World War II. Fukuoka, as administrative and commercial center for northern Kyushu, showed consistent increases until 1920, but rapid urbanization came to the area after 1920 when extensive industrial developments appeared. Niigata and Akita, cities in northwestern Honshu, showed continued expansion as the oil resources in their hinterlands were developed.

The diversification of industry, especially after 1930, gave rise to the genuine industrial city in Japan. The development of such cities as Yahata in northern Kyushu, Kawasaki located between Tokyo and Yokohama, and Amagasaki on the western boundary of Osaka marked the appearance of urban growth of a new character. These were cities firmly based upon the development of heavy industries: iron and steel, chemicals, and engineering. These industries were present in Japan previously, but their limited development generally made possible their absorption into existing urban centers. The population concentrations which did grow up around heavy industry outside major cities prior to the 1920's were usually not sufficiently large to qualify the areas for incorporation as cities. The increased urbanization from 1920 to the early 1940's saw, then, not only the expansion of older cities but the appearance of new cities at an increased rate:

The Incorporation of New Cities

Date	Number
1920-29	26
1930-39	57
1940-43	41
Total 1920-43	124

The geographical location of these new cities is significant. The demands of the kind of industrial expansion which took place in the 1930's placed a premium upon a grouping together of integrated industrial complexes, e.g., the clustering of coal mining, iron and steel processing, and shipping facilities of the Yahata, Osaka and Tokyo-Yokohama areas. This trend of urban concentration can be seen from the fact that of the 124 cities incorporated from 1920 to 1943, the Tokyo-Yokohama area and the contiguous prefectures of Chiba and Saitama contained twenty. Osaka and the contiguous prefectures of Hyogo, Kyoto, and Wakayama contained nineteen of the new cities. Fukuoka Prefecture, the center of the industrial area of northern Kyushu, added four new cities; its bordering prefecture, Oita, and Yamaguchi Prefecture, at the southern tip of Honshu, added thirteen new cities. The prefecture containing Nagoya and the bordering prefectures of Shizuoka, Gifu, and Mie saw the appearance of sixteen new cities during this period. In summary, the fifteen prefectures which make up the four major industrial regions accounted for seventy-five (60.5 per cent) of the new urban centers appearing between 1920 and 1943. The 69.5 per cent of the total Japanese urban population which was in those four areas in 1920 had increased to 75.1 per cent by 1940. The greatest share of the average yearly increases in total urban population was contributed by the growth of older cities and of the new industrial centers located on or near their boundaries (Table V-1).

The early years of World War II brought an intensification of industrial activities and hence an increased emphasis upon the industrial city. The evacuations and dislocations of urban populations during the latter half of the war, however, reversed the total urbanization process, especially that focused upon the industrial areas. In the postwar period city growth has been essentially a recouping of wartime losses. The diversified industrial activities upon which Japan's urbanization during the 1930's and early 1940's was based, again appear to be the dominant impetus for city growth. The industrial city has regained its previous lead in Japan's postwar urban recovery and growth.

CITY GROWTH BY SIZE CATEGORY

The functional emphases of Japanese urban areas have been shown to be related to patterns of growth, but this factor is not alone in influencing population increase. The very size of a city itself, irrespective of its functional base, plays no small part in its growth history. The fact that Edo (the new Tokyo) contained approximately one million inhabitants at the time of the Restoration, or that Osaka had some one-half million, was no doubt of significance in attracting migrant population as well as newly established industrial activities. An analysis of Japanese city growth by size categories can answer two questions: first, which sizes of cities have contributed most heavily to total urbanization? And secondly, how has the distribution of Japan's urban population been affected by size class growth differentials?

TABLE V-1. Growth of Selected Japanese Cities, 1920-1940

City	AVERAGE ANNUAL PERCENTAGE CHANGE			
	1920-25	1925-30	1930-35	1935-40
TOKYO	— 1.6[a]	0.7	37.2[b]	3.1
YOKOHAMA	— 4.0[a]	10.6	2.7	7.5
Yokosuka	1.4	2.9	13.2	1.1
Kawasaki	—	18.2	9.7	18.9
Chiba	—	3.5	3.4	12.1
Kawaguchi	—	—	—	16.2
Urawa	—	—	—	6.5
OSAKA	13.8	3.2	4.4	1.8
KOBE	1.2	4.5	3.2	1.2
Sakai	4.7	2.9	3.5	5.8
Nishinomiya	4.2	2.9	25.7	3.1
Amagasaki	3.0	2.6	8.4	30.9
FUKUOKA	10.6	11.3	5.5	1.1
Kokura	10.4	14.1	5.1	11.5
Moji	6.4	2.7	2.5	2.9
Shimonoseki	5.5	1.3	6.9	9.5
Yahata	3.6	8.4	4.8	5.1
Wakamatsu	0.2	3.0	5.6	4.2
NAGOYA	15.7	3.6	3.9	4.5
Yokkaichi	3.0	5.7	2.6	1.8
Ichinomiya	—	4.3	5.3	6.5
TOTAL URBAN	5.6	5.6	9.4	4.4

[a] Earthquake in 1923 destroyed large sections of Tokyo, Yokohama, and surrounding areas.
[b] Extensive boundary changes October 1, 1932.

Source: *1955 Population Census of Japan*, Vol. I, Table 1.

There are two techniques for specifying the role of city size in further urbanization. The first of these, the continuous method, presents growth rates of cities classified by their size at one specified date. For example, if the cities designated in Japan's first urban incorporation law are analyzed in these terms (Table V-2), it is evident that the six largest of the thirty-nine contributed the greatest absolute increases to Japan's post-Restoration urban expansion. Further, the rate of increase for these largest cities was slightly higher than that of the smaller categories. This method has the disadvantage of excluding from consideration any new cities which appear following the base year. Table V-2 does, however, highlight the contributions of the older cities, especially the larger ones, to Japanese urbanization.

TABLE V-2. Growth of Japan's Original Incorporated Cities by Size Category (Continuous Method), 1891-1955

| Size Group in 1891 | Number of Cities | Absolute Increase | PERCENTAGE CHANGE | |
			1891-1955	Average Annual
20-50,000	23	3,238,414	439.4	6.9
50-100,000	10	2,376,119	364.9	5.7
100,000+	6	11,782,574	491.4	7.7
TOTAL	39	17,397,107	456.2	7.1

Sources: *Résumé Statistique de L'Empire du Japon*, Vols. 8, 17, 23, and 28. *Population Census of 1950*, Vol. I. *1955 Population Census of Japan*, Vol. I.

The continuous method of size class analysis applied to the eighty-one cities incorporated by 1920 reveals the effects of a broadening of Japan's urbanization (Table V-3). The number of cities in each size class has roughly doubled since the categorization of 1891, but the ranking of percentage change by size has

TABLE V-3. Growth of Japanese Cities Incorporated in 1920 by Size Category (Continuous Method), 1920-1955

| Size Group in 1920 | Number of Cities | Absolute Increase | PERCENTAGE CHANGE | |
			1920-55	Average Annual
20-50,000	41	3,902,239	256.3	7.3
50-100,000	24	3,797,636	221.9	6.3
100,000+	16	10,358,351	153.3	4.4
TOTAL	81	18,058,326	180.8	5.2

Sources: *Population Census of 1950*, Vol. I. *1955 Population Census of Japan*, Vol. I.

reversed that of Table V-2. The differences in average annual percentage change by size class are small both for the cities incorporated by 1891 (Table V-2) and by 1920 (Table V-3). The important fact to note is the relative similarity of increases by size category.

If growth by size class is analyzed by means of the instantaneous method, i.e., comparison of population in city size classes at each census date irrespective of the specific cities which make up the classes, the over-all similarity of rates of growth by size is again

TABLE V-4. Japanese Urban Growth by Size Category (Instantaneous Method), 1891-1955

Size Group at Census Date	AVERAGE ANNUAL PERCENTAGE CHANGE							
	1891-98	1898-1908	1908-20	1920-30	1930-40	1940-50	1950-55	1891-1955
20-50,000	3.9	3.8	1.4	-1.7	9.5	5.3	30.5	18.4
50-100,000	0.9	9.5	2.2	7.8	2.1	6.4	11.2	21.0
100,000+	6.6	5.8	1.8	6.3	9.3	0.0	9.2	18.7
TOTAL	5.0	6.0	1.8	5.3	7.9	1.4	12.2	19.0

Sources: *Résumé Statistique de L'Empire du Japon*, Vols. 8, 17, 23, and 28. *Population Census of 1950*, Vol. I. *1955 Population Census of Japan*, Vol. I.

TABLE V-5. Japanese Urban Population by Size Category, 1891-1955

Size Group at Census Date	1891		1920		1930		1940		1955		Absolute Increase 1891-1955	
	Population (000's)	Number of Cities	Population (000's)	Number of Cities	Population (000's)	Number of Cities	Population (000's)	Number of Cities	Population (000's)	Number of Cities	Pop.	No.
20-50,000	764	23	1,555	41	1,296	34	2,529	68	9,741	253	8,977	230
50-100,000	651	10	1,711	24	3,037	45	3,673	53	9,403	140	8,752	180
100,000+	2,398	6	6,754	16	11,031	28	21,292	45	31,144	98	28,746	92
TOTAL	3,813	39	10,020	81	15,364	107	27,494	166	50,288	491	46,475	452

Sources: *Résumé Statistique de L'Empire du Japon*, Vols. 8, 17, 23, and 28. *Population Census of 1950*, Vol. I. *1955 Population Census of Japan*, Vol. I.

evident. Table V-4 shows the average annual rates of growth by the three major size classes for the period 1891-1955. Though the appearance of new cities in the smallest size class and the movement of cities from smaller to larger classes create wide variations in the rates for any specific decade, the average annual rates by size class for the sixty-four year period are within three percentage points of each other. As with the specific large cities which made up the 100,000 population and over class in the continuous method analysis, the simultaneous technique shows the greatest absolute urban increases to be those of the largest size class (Table V-5).

Approaching Japanese urban growth through size class analysis shows two significant facts. First, the distribution of urban population among the sizes of cities has remained relatively stable in spite of a significant increase in total urban population. Table

TABLE V-6. Japan: Percentage Distribution of Urban Population, 1891-1955

Size Class	PER CENT OF TOTAL POPULATION IN INCORPORATED CITIES							
	1891	1908	1920	1930	1940	1945	1950	1955
20-50,000	20.0	16.3	15.5	8.4	9.2	18.7	12.3	19.4
50-100,000	17.1	16.4	17.1	19.8	13.4	26.3	19.3	18.7
100,000+	62.9	67.3	67.4	71.8	77.4	55.0	68.4	61.9
TOTAL	100.0	100.0	100.0	100.0	100.0	100.0	100.0	100.0

Sources: *Résumé Statistique de L'Empire du Japon*, Vols. 8, 17, 23, 28. *Population Census of 1950*, Vol. I. *1955 Population Census of Japan*, Vol. I.

V-6 shows the percentage distribution of urban population by size-class for the period 1891-1955. The distribution in 1955 is essentially the same as that of 1891. The domination of the urban structure by a few large cities, which was characteristic of the pre-Restoration Tokugawa era, continued into the modern period of Japanese urbanization. This pattern tended to be emphasized up to the beginning of World War II, by which time over three-fourths of the urban population were residents of cities of over 100,000 population. The urban destruction of World War II broke this trend, but even in late 1945 there were still over 50% of the urban population in the larger cities. The postwar trend has been toward a reassertion of large city dominance, but not to the level of pre-war periods.

The second point to be made with respect to city size relationships is that the *same* cities have constituted the dominance of ur-

TABLE V-7. Rank of Japan's Ten Largest Cities, 1891-1955

Size Rank	1891	1898	1908	1920	1930	1940	1950	1955
1	Tokyo	Tokyo	Tokyo	Tokyo	Osaka	Tokyo	Tokyo	Tokyo
2	Osaka	Osaka	Osaka	Osaka	Tokyo	Osaka	Osaka	Osaka
3	Kyoto	Kyoto	Kyoto	Kobe	Nagoya	Nagoya	Kyoto	Nagoya
4	Nagoya	Nagoya	Yokohama	Kyoto	Kobe	Kyoto	Nagoya	Kyoto
5	Kobe	Kobe	Nagoya	Nagoya	Kyoto	Yokohama	Yokohama	Yokohama
6	Yokohama	Yokohama	Kobe	Yokohama	Yokohama	Kobe	Kobe	Kobe
7	Kanazawa	Hiroshima	Nagasaki	Nagasaki	Hiroshima	Hiroshima	Fukuoka	Fukuoka
8	Hiroshima	Nagasaki	Hiroshima	Hiroshima	Fukuoka	Fukuoka	Sendai	Sendai
9	Sendai	Kanazawa	Kanazawa	Kanazawa	Nagasaki	Nagasaki	Hiroshima	Hiroshima
10	Nagasaki	Sendai	Sendai	Sendai	Sendai	Sendai	Nagasaki	Nagasaki

Sources: *Résumé Statistique de L'Empire du Japon*, Vols. 8, 17, 23, and 28. *Population Census of 1950*, Vol. I. *1955 Population Census of Japan*, Vol. I.

ban structure by large urban areas. Table V-7 ranks Japan's ten largest cities by size for roughly six decades. Tokyo, except for 1930, has held the first rank throughout the period, with Osaka ranking second. The next four ranks, three through six, have been held by the same four cities. The same pattern of stability is noted for the remainder of the list, with the exception of the replacement of Kanazawa by Fukuoka. It is significant that of these ten cities only two, Yokohama and Kobe, are cities which are essentially the creations of post-Restoration Japan. The other eight, led by Tokyo, were thriving centers under the Tokugawa, and these cities have continued their dominance during the period of Japan's modernization.

THE GEOGRAPHICAL DISTRIBUTION OF JAPAN'S CITIES

The rapid urbanization of the post-Restoration period analyzed thus far has obviously not been evenly distributed throughout the nation, nor was this the case during the Tokugawa period. Under the shogunate, political and military strategy largely accounted for regional differences in urbanization; with the expansion of foreign trade and industry following the Restoration such factors as deep-water harbor sites and power and mineral resources assumed importance. New urbanization, however, built out from the settlement pattern established under the Tokugawa. The role of Tokugawa urban centers in post-Restoration city growth has already been cited. Modern urban expansion affected many of the older cities, but added to them cities created in response to the locational demands of Japan's development as an industrial nation.

In the main, Japan's total population and, in turn, her urban population have tended toward concentration in the prefectures running southwestward from Tokyo to northern Kyushu. Reischauer has emphasized the extent of urban concentration in these areas during the pre-World War II period by noting that if a line is drawn from Tokyo 540 miles to northern Kyushu, one finds the great bulk of Japan's urban population within forty miles of either side of this line.[3] Census data of 1955 show that this strip contains all of Japan's cities of one million or more, fifty-eight of the ninety-eight cities of 100,000 or more, and forty-

3 Edwin O. Reischauer, *The United States and Japan* (Cambridge: Harvard University Press, 1950), pp. 82-83.

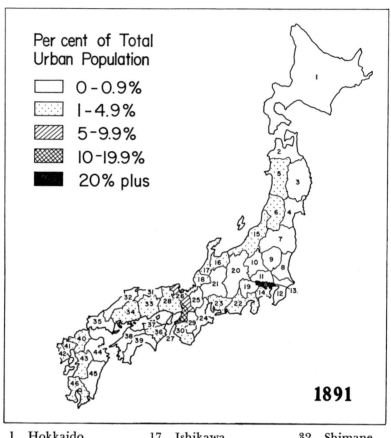

Per cent of Total
Urban Population

☐ 0-0.9%
▢ 1-4.9%
▨ 5-9.9%
▧ 10-19.9%
■ 20% plus

1891

1	Hokkaido	17	Ishikawa	32	Shimane
2	Aomori	18	Fukui	33	Okayama
3	Iwate	19	Yamanashi	34	Hiroshima
4	Miyagi	20	Nagano	35	Yamaguchi
5	Akita	21	Gifu	36	Tokushima
6	Yamagata	22	Shizuoka	37	Kagawa
7	Fukushima	23	Aichi	38	Ehime
8	Ibaraki	24	Mie	39	Kochi
9	Tochigi	25	Shiga	40	Fukuoka
10	Gumma	26	Kyoto-fu	41	Saga
11	Saitama	27	Osaka-fu	42	Nagasaki
12	Chiba	28	Hyogo	43	Kumamoto
13	Tokyo-to	29	Nara	44	Oita
14	Kanagawa	30	Wakayama	45	Miyazaki
15	Niigata	31	Tottori	46	Kagoshima
16	Toyama				

FIGURE V-1: Prefectural Distribution of Urban Population (Source: *Résumé Statistique de L'Empire du Japon*, Vol. 8)

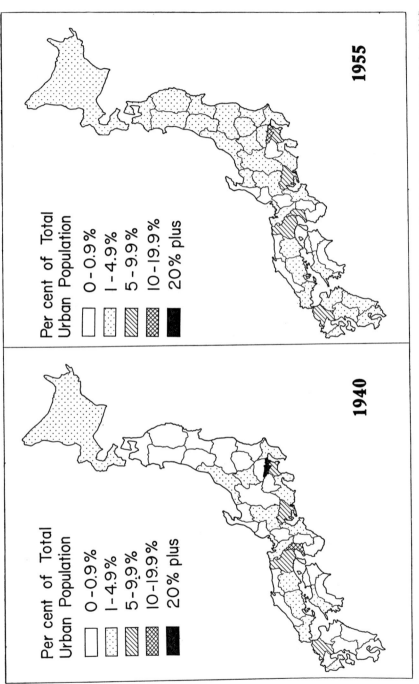

FIGURES V-2 and V-3: Prefectural Distribution of Urban Population (Sources: *Population Census of 1950*, Vol. I; *1955 Population Census of Japan*, Vol. I, Table 12)

seven of the 140 cities between 50,000 and 100,000. Further, the fifteen prefectures which constitute such a strip contained 75.4% of the population in incorporated cities in 1891, a proportion which was increased to 76.7% by 1940. In 1955, with the incorporation of more than 200 new cities, the percentage of urban population in these fifteen prefectures dropped to 60.0%. The fact remains, however, that slightly less than one-third of Japan's 46 prefectures have contained two-thirds or more of her urban population throughout the modern period.

In more detailed and graphic form, the geographical distribution of Japan's urban population can be noted in Figures V-1, 2, 3. The prefectural distributions of the total urban population for 1891 and 1940 show a proportional loss of urban dwellers by the northern Honshu prefectures bordering the Japan Sea and consequent gains by those on the eastern and southern shores of Honshu. The 1955 distribution shows a continued but weakened lead in these prefectures. Again, the almost doubling of incorporated cities between the censuses of 1950 and 1955 accounts for the apparent reversal of the trend toward urban concentration to the south and west.[4]

Historically, the areas to the south and west of Tokyo have been the population centers of the nation, containing the leading Tokugawa centers of Edo (Tokyo), Osaka, Kyoto, and Nagasaki, among others. The most trafficked overland route under the shogunate, the *Tokaido*, falls within this narrow area. Following the Restoration, the plentiful labor of this area made it naturally attractive for industrial developments. Other factors contributing to the population concentration along this strip were the availability of inexpensive sea transport routes and the nearness of natural resources, especially the coal deposits of northern Kyushu. Further, the many short, rapid streams flowing from the mountains of central Honshu to the Pacific provide almost unlimited hydroelectric power sources for the industrial region between Osaka and Tokyo.

Essentially, however, the location of Japanese population concentration, and thus of her cities, has been determined by the agricultural plains and accessibility to the sea. The plains which

---

[4] The validity of the incorporation of these 243 new areas as cities is discussed in Chapters I and III, above.

have served for centuries as the hinterlands of Tokyo, Osaka, and Nagoya, for instance, are the natural locations for population in a mountainous island country. The scarcity of extensive mineral resources makes unnecessary any major shifts away from traditional settlement areas in the period of industrialization. Industrialization has not radically disturbed the traditional population distribution. Northern Kyushu and Hokkaido, the areas containing major portions of Japan's limited mineral resources, have been the areas most affected by population shifts in response to modernization. Urban expansion based upon industrial development in Japan has meant, by and large, the growth of older urban centers and their contiguous regions.

The Economic Bases of Japanese Urbanization | VI

The basic principle underlying the evolution of cities is the capacity of a nation to support a segment of its population in activities other than those concerned with the production of the basic subsistence needs of food, clothing, and shelter. A nation possessing an economic structure within which an increasing number of persons can specialize in nonsubsistence activities is potentially a nation of growing cities. The spatial requirements, for instance, of industrial, administrative, or trade activities in contrast to agriculture, make possible the concentration of persons so engaged within relatively small geographical areas. Such concentration is further necessary for the effective performance of these activities. Industrialization, broadly conceived as the growth of nonagricultural functions, therefore underlies urbanization as a process.[1] An industrial revolution vastly increases a nation's capacity to support nonagricultural specialization. Hence, the introduction of modern industrial and commercial technology is associated with rapid urbanization.

The close association of urbanization with industrialization can be approached from two points of view, the contemporary and the historical. With respect to the contemporary approach, correlation between percentage of total population in cities of 100,000 and over and the percentage of economically active males in nonagricultural employment shows a high level of association. A linear correlation of these two figures for all the countries and territories of the world of over one million population (circa 1945) has an index of correlation (r) of +0.885.[2] This correlation supports the

---

[1] Eric E. Lampard, *Urbanization and Economic Growth: The Creative Force of Cities* (New York: The Social Science Research Council, May, 1954). (Processed.)

[2] Kingsley Davis, "World Regions and the Correlates of Urbanism," paper read at the annual meeting of the American Sociological Society, September, 1952.

contention that currently there exists a close connection between level of economic development and urbanization.

Any attempt to show this relationship in an historical analysis is hampered by the fact that comparable occupational statistics for any considerable period of time are available for relatively few countries. These limited data do, however, imply that the association between urbanization and industrialization holds *within* the history of specific nations in much the same manner as *between* contemporary nations. The results of correlations between percentage of total population in cities of 100,000 and over and percentage of males in nonagricultural employment for selected nations for which data are available are as follows:[3]

Country	Dates	Coefficient of Correlation (r)
England & Wales	1841-1931	+0.9852
United States	1820-1940	+0.9967
France	1866-1946	+0.9701
Sweden	1870-1940	+0.9667

The pattern of Japanese city growth and economic development follows the experience of the West as indicated in the above correlations. Among contemporary nations Japan ranks sixth in percentage of total population in cities of 100,000 and over (1955: 34.9 per cent) and seventeenth in percentage of economically active males in nonagricultural employment (1955: 66.2 per cent). Historically, the expansion of Japan's urban population has been closely associated with her industrialization. The coefficient of correlation (r) for the two items shown in Table VI-1 is +0.9854.

The similarity between Japan and the West with respect to statistical indices of the relationship of industrialization and urbanization is heavily qualified, however, by the unique features of Japan's premodern socioeconomic structure which have been influential upon the character of her industrialization. Japanese modernization was accomplished without seriously disturbing many of the feudal-agrarian elements of her social organization. For instance, Japanese industrial management was able to integrate traditional feudal values, e.g., personal loyalty and subservience of subordinate to superior, into the organization of modern

[3] Davis, *loc. cit.*

industrial activities.[4] The individualism characteristic of industrialization in the West has been largely absent in Japan. Japanese society remains essentially a familial hierarchy which binds the individual to the nation through a series of traditionally defined social relationships. It is within this framework that modernization was conceived as a national mission rather than as an opportunity for self-aggrandizement. Significant inroads in this traditional

TABLE VI-1. Japan: Indices of Urbanization and Industrial Development, 1920-55

Date	Percentage Economically Active Males in Nonagricultural Employment	Percentage Total Population in Cities of 100,000 or More
1920	51.8	12.2
1930	57.0	18.0
1940	64.3	29.4
1950	59.8	25.7
1955	66.2	34.9

Sources: *Population Census of 1950*, Vol. I, Table 6 and Vol. VII pt. 13, Table 14.
1955 Population Census of Japan, Vol. I, Table 9, and Vol. II, pt. 2. Table 7.

pattern have been made by the host of Western, and specifically American, elements introduced widely in Japan during and after the Occupation, but the "old" Japan is still strong and viable in this regard, and contrasts with the Western prototype remain valid.

Interesting contrasts to this aspect of Japanese industrialization are found in Reinhard Bendix's analysis of the justifications for managerial authority in Western capitalism and Russian communism.[5] Bendix sees managerial authority in capitalism justified in terms of managers having earned their power rights by a superior manipulation of means available to all in the society. In contrast, under Russian communism managerial authority rests with those who can most effectively carry out the political purposes of national leaders. These national leaders are, in turn, directing the creation of a society wherein the higher interests of all mankind

---

[4] The consequences of this pattern for Japanese industrial administration are discussed in detail by James C. Abegglen in *The Japanese Factory* (Glencoe, Ill.: The Free Press, 1958).

[5] Reinhard Bendix, *Work and Authority in Industry* (New York: John Wiley and Sons, Inc., 1956).

are served. The contrast is between an *individualistic* and an *altruistic* basis for managerial control. Japan would seem to form yet another category of justification which might be termed *nationalistic*. The goal of industrialization in Japan was conceived as national aggrandizement, rather than either the improvement of the lot of the individual or mankind as a whole. Any sacrifices required to attain the goal were justified in terms of the glorification of Japan vis-à-vis other nations.

The conception of industrialization as essentially a political policy by Japan's leaders in the post-Restoration period meant that those industries most useful for political purposes would receive the greatest impetus for development. Modern technologies and methods were introduced with the creation of the so-called strategic industries of shipbuilding, iron and steel, chemicals, and the like. The cotton textile industry as a vital export producer was also encouraged to utilize Western methods.[6] The result is that large segments of Japanese industry which fall outside the "strategic" category have retained many of the traditional elements of production and organization. This is especially true of the industries which produce Japanese style items for domestic consumption. The small household production unit has been integrated into a contract or "putting out" system which underlies Japan's frequently cited dispersed industrial pattern. A jobber buys raw materials and arranges for the wholesale disposal of the finished goods; actual production is carried on by numerous household units which may be specialized for only one step in production.[7]

Throughout Japan today less than 400 factories employ more than 1000 persons, while over 400,000 have fewer than thirty employees. The existence of relatively few large-scale industrial plants side by side with the household handicraft unit characterizes Japanese industrial activity. The post-World War II period shows evidences of the continuation of this pattern.[8] Table VI-2 shows the distribution by size and number of workers for Japan's industrial and commercial establishments in 1954. The high pro-

6 John E. Orchard, *Japan's Economic Position* (New York: McGraw-Hill Book Co., 1930), pp. 185-91.

7 *Ibid.*, pp. 192-208.

8 Solomon B. Levine, "Labor Patterns and Trends," *Annals of the Academy of Political and Social Sciences*, Vol. 308 (November, 1956), pp. 102-103.

TABLE VI-2. Japan: Percentage Distribution of Establishments by Size and Persons Employed, 1954

Size by Number of Employees	Total Establishments	PERCENTAGE DISTRIBUTION				
		Industrial Establishments			Trade Establishments	
		Light Industry Establishments	Heavy Industry Establishments	Total Persons Employed	Total Establishments	Total Persons Employed
1	14.9	14.6	13.4	1.3	32.1	10.5
2-4	44.2	47.1	33.1	10.5	55.1	44.4
5-9	20.4	20.5	20.8	11.4	8.8	18.2
10-19	11.3	10.5	15.7	13.0	2.9	12.4
20-29	3.8	3.2	6.3	7.7	0.6	4.5
30-99	4.2	3.3	8.0	17.6	0.4	6.0
100-499	1.0	0.7	2.2	17.1	0.1	2.7
500+	0.2	0.1	0.5	21.4	0.0	1.3
TOTAL	100.0	100.0	100.0	100.0	100.0	100.0

Source: *Japan Statistical Yearbook, 1957*, Table 37.

portion of establishments of relatively small size even in the heavy industry category reveals the prevalence of the household production unit.

A discussion of the consequences of this type of economic organization for Japanese industrial efficiency and productive quality and quantity is beyond the scope of the present study. The concern here is with the demographic consequences for that segment of Japan's population engaged in nonagricultural activities. A widespread household industry pattern, paternalistic employer-employee relationships, and a history of a great labor force reservoir in rural areas are all elements which underlie the demographic traits of those who enter the Japanese nonagricultural labor force and the locations in which their employment activities will take place.

THE LOCATION OF NONAGRICULTURAL EMPLOYMENT

Urbanization in Japan has been shown to be centered primarily in the prefectures to the south and west of the Tokyo area. These prefectures therefore lead in those activities capable of supporting large urban populations. Table VI-3 shows by prefecture the ratio of the percentage of total employed to the total employed in the major areas of urban-oriented employment from 1920 to 1950. It is to be noted that the areas historically associated with high levels of urbanization are also those which have consistently had large proportions of their employed populations in nonagricultural pursuits.

If employment in the manufacturing category alone is analyzed in terms of areal distribution, its relation to urbanization reveals two distinct patterns. Textile processing is not so closely identified with highly urban prefectures as are other forms of manufacturing. Table VI-4 shows the ratios of percentage total employed to percentage employed in textiles and in other categories of manufacturing by prefecture for 1950. The twenty prefectures which have a higher proportion of employed in textiles than the proportion of the nation's total employed (those with ratios of 100 or over in Column 9 of Table VI-4) account for 73.9 per cent of those employed in textiles in the whole of Japan, but these twenty prefectures contain only 43.3 per cent of the nation's population in

TABLE VI-3. Japan: Percentage Distribution of Total Employed and of Employed in Nonagricultural Activities by Prefecture, 1920-50

PERCENTAGE OF EMPLOYED IN TOTAL JAPAN

	1920a			1930a			1950b		
Prefecture	Total Employed Activities[c]	In Nonagricultural Activities[c]	(2)/(1)	Total Employed Activities[c]	In Nonagricultural Activities[c]	(5)/(4)	Total Employed Activities[d]	In Nonagricultural Activities[d]	(8)/(7)
	(1)	(2)	(3)	(4)	(5)	(6)	(7)	(8)	(9)
Hokkaido	4.0	3.4	85.0	4.1	3.4	82.9	4.8	3.3	68.8
Aomori	1.4	0.9	64.3	1.4	0.9	64.3	1.6	1.1	68.8
Iwate	1.5	0.8	53.5	1.6	0.8	50.0	1.8	1.0	55.6
Miyagi	1.6	1.2	75.0	1.7	1.2	70.6	1.9	1.6	84.2
Akita	1.6	1.0	62.5	1.4	0.9	64.3	1.6	1.0	62.5
Yamagata	1.9	1.4	73.7	1.7	1.2	70.6	1.7	1.2	70.6
Fukushima	2.6	1.8	69.2	2.5	1.6	64.0	2.5	1.7	68.0
Ibaraki	2.8	1.6	57.1	2.6	1.5	57.7	2.7	1.5	78.9
Tochigi	1.9	1.6	84.2	1.8	1.4	77.8	1.9	1.5	78.9
Gumma	2.0	1.9	95.0	1.9	1.7	89.5	2.0	1.6	80.0
Saitama	2.6	2.0	76.9	2.4	1.9	79.2	2.6	2.3	88.5
Chiba	2.7	1.7	63.0	2.7	1.6	59.3	2.7	2.0	74.1
Tokyo	5.8	12.0	206.8	7.8	14.4	184.6	6.7	12.8	191.0
Kanagawa	2.2	3.3	150.0	2.2	3.1	140.9	2.6	4.2	161.5

a Total Employed.
b Employed Population fourteen years of age and over.
c Manufacturing (including construction), commerce, transportation-communication, official-professional, services.
d Manufacturing (excluding construction), commerce, transportation-communication, government, services.

Sources: *Reports of 1920 Census*, Vol. IV, pt. A-2, pp. 108-09. *Reports of 1930 Census*, Vol. IV, pt. 4, Table 18 in prefectural volumes. *Population Census of 1950*, Vol. VII, Table 11 in prefectural volumes.

TABLE VI-3. (Continued)

PERCENTAGE OF EMPLOYED IN TOTAL JAPAN

Prefecture	1920a			1930a			1950b		
	Total Employed	In Non-agricultural Activitiese		Total Employed	In Non-agricultural Activitiese		Total Employed	In Non-agricultural Activitiesd	
	(1)	(2)	(2)/(1) (3)	(4)	(5)	(5)/(4) (6)	(7)	(8)	(8)/(7) (9)
Niigata	3.4	2.5	73.5	3.0	2.2	73.3	3.2	2.4	75.0
Toyama	1.2	1.0	83.3	1.2	1.1	91.7	1.3	1.2	92.3
Ishikawa	1.4	1.3	92.9	1.2	1.2	100.0	1.3	1.2	92.3
Fukui	1.2	1.1	91.7	1.1	1.0	90.9	1.1	1.0	90.9
Yamanashi	1.2	1.0	83.3	1.0	0.9	90.0	1.0	0.8	80.0
Nagano	3.2	2.8	87.5	3.1	2.6	83.9	2.7	2.0	74.1
Gifu	2.0	1.8	90.0	1.9	1.7	89.5	2.0	2.0	100.0
Shizuoka	2.7	2.4	88.9	2.7	2.6	96.3	2.9	2.9	100.0
Aichi	3.7	4.6	124.3	4.1	5.0	122.0	4.1	5.5	134.1
Mie	2.0	1.8	90.0	1.8	1.7	94.4	1.8	1.7	94.4
Shiga	1.3	1.0	76.9	1.2	1.0	83.3	1.2	1.0	83.3
Kyoto	2.3	3.5	152.2	2.4	3.5	145.8	2.1	3.0	142.9
Osaka	4.3	8.5	197.7	5.3	9.5	179.2	4.1	7.6	185.4
Hyogo	3.9	5.3	135.9	4.0	5.0	125.0	3.8	5.0	131.6
Nara	0.8	0.9	112.5	0.8	0.9	112.5	0.9	0.9	100.0
Wakayama	1.1	1.2	109.1	1.2	1.3	108.3	1.2	1.2	100.0
Tottori	0.9	0.7	77.8	0.8	0.6	75.0	0.8	0.6	75.0
Shimane	1.4	0.9	64.3	1.3	0.8	61.5	1.2	0.8	66.7
Okayama	2.4	2.1	87.5	2.1	1.8	85.7	2.1	1.8	85.7

TABLE VI-3. (Continued)

PERCENTAGE OF EMPLOYED IN TOTAL JAPAN

Prefecture	1920[a]			1930[a]			1950[b]		
	Total Employed	In Non-agricultural Activities[c]	$\frac{(2)}{(1)}$	Total Employed	In Non-agricultural Activities[c]	$\frac{(5)}{(4)}$	Total Employed	In Non-agricultural Activities[d]	$\frac{(8)}{(7)}$
	(1)	(2)	(3)	(4)	(5)	(6)	(7)	(8)	(9)
Hiroshima	2.7	2.8	103.7	2.6	2.7	103.8	2.1	2.8	133.3
Yamaguchi	1.8	1.6	88.9	1.8	1.6	88.9	1.9	1.8	94.7
Tokushima	1.3	1.0	76.9	1.2	0.9	75.0	1.1	0.8	72.7
Kagawa	1.2	1.0	83.3	1.2	1.0	83.3	1.2	1.1	91.7
Ehime	1.8	1.6	88.9	1.7	1.5	88.2	1.8	1.6	88.9
Kochi	1.3	1.0	76.9	1.2	0.9	75.0	1.2	0.7	58.3
Fukuoka	3.8	4.2	110.5	3.7	4.0	108.1	3.9	4.4	112.8
Saga	1.2	0.9	75.0	1.1	0.8	72.7	1.2	0.9	75.2
Nagasaki	2.1	1.8	85.7	1.9	1.6	84.2	1.9	1.6	84.2
Kumamoto	2.3	1.7	73.9	2.2	1.6	72.7	2.3	1.6	69.6
Oita	1.7	1.1	64.7	1.6	1.1	66.7	1.6	1.2	75.0
Miyagi	1.2	0.8	66.7	1.2	0.8	66.7	1.4	0.9	64.3
Kagoshima	2.6	1.5	57.7	2.6	1.4	53.8	2.5	1.2	48.0

TABLE VI-4 Japan: Percentage Distribution of Total Employed and of Employed in Manufacturing by Prefecture, 1950

| | | | | PERCENTAGE OF EMPLOYED IN TOTAL JAPAN | | | | | |
| Prefecture | Total Employed | In Manufacturing^a | (2)/(1) | In Heavy Indus.^b | (4)/(1) | In Light Indus.^c | (6)/(1) | In Textiles | (8)/(1) |
	(1)	(2)	(3)	(4)	(5)	(6)	(7)	(8)	(9)
Hokkaido	4.8	3.4	70.8	2.8	58.3	1.4	29.2	0.9	18.8
Aomori	1.6	0.6	37.5	0.3	18.8	0.3	18.8	0.1	6.3
Iwate	1.8	0.7	38.9	0.8	44.4	0.3	16.7	0.3	16.7
Miyagi	1.9	0.8	42.1	0.5	26.3	0.4	21.1	0.3	15.8
Akita	1.6	0.7	43.8	0.5	31.3	0.3	18.8	0.2	12.5
Yamagata	1.7	1.0	58.8	0.7	41.2	0.7	41.2	1.2	70.6
Fukushima	2.5	1.4	56.0	0.7	28.0	1.6	64.0	1.4	56.0
Ibaraki	2.7	1.3	48.1	1.1	40.7	1.9	70.4	0.7	25.9
Tochigi	1.9	1.6	84.2	1.1	57.9	0.5	26.3	2.7	142.1
Gumma	2.0	1.9	95.0	1.1	55.0	0.9	45.0	4.4	220.0
Saitama	2.6	2.7	103.8	3.1	119.2	2.3	88.5	3.5	134.6
Chiba	2.7	1.5	55.6	1.4	51.9	1.5	55.6	0.8	29.6
Tokyo	6.7	12.6	188.0	14.8	220.8	20.7	308.9	6.1	91.0
Kanagawa	2.6	4.0	153.8	7.9	303.8	7.3	280.8	1.4	53.8
Niigata	3.2	2.2	68.8	2.6	81.3	2.7	84.4	2.2	68.8
Toyama	1.3	1.4	107.7	1.2	92.3	2.3	176.9	2.0	153.8
Ishikawa	1.3	1.3	100.0	1.1	84.6	0.2	15.4	2.8	215.4
Fukui	1.1	1.2	109.1	0.3	27.3	0.7	63.6	3.4	309.1
Yamanashi	1.0	0.9	90.0	0.2	20.0	0.2	20.0	2.0	200.0
Nagano	2.7	1.9	70.4	1.0	37.0	1.9	70.4	2.6	96.3
Gifu	2.0	2.3	115.0	1.1	55.0	0.9	45.0	2.9	145.0

ᵃ Excluding construction.
ᵇ Primary metals, fabricated metals, machinery and weapons (excluding electrical), transportation equipment, petroleum and coal products.
ᶜ Electrical machinery, precision instruments, and chemicals.

Source: *Population Census of 1950*, Vol. VII, Table 11 in prefectural volumes.

TABLE VI-4 (Continued)

PERCENTAGE OF EMPLOYED IN TOTAL JAPAN

Prefecture	Total Employed	In Manufacturing[a]	$\frac{(2)}{(1)}$	In Heavy Indus.[b]	$\frac{(4)}{(1)}$	In Light Indus.[c]	$\frac{(6)}{(1)}$	In Textiles	$\frac{(8)}{(1)}$
	(1)	(2)	(3)	(4)	(5)	(6)	(7)	(8)	(9)
Shizuoka	2.9	3.4	117.2	2.6	89.7	1.4	48.3	3.8	131.0
Aichi	4.1	7.2	175.6	7.2	175.6	3.9	95.1	10.7	260.9
Mie	1.8	1.9	105.6	1.1	61.1	1.6	88.9	3.0	166.7
Shiga	1.2	1.1	91.7	0.4	33.3	2.0	166.7	2.0	166.7
Kyoto	2.1	2.9	138.1	1.7	81.0	2.9	138.1	5.4	257.1
Osaka	4.1	8.9	217.1	12.9	314.6	10.0	243.9	8.5	207.3
Hyogo	3.8	5.9	155.3	9.2	242.1	6.1	160.5	5.0	131.6
Nara	0.9	0.9	100.0	0.5	55.6	0.5	55.6	1.3	144.4
Wakayama	1.2	1.2	100.0	0.7	58.3	0.7	58.3	1.5	125.0
Tottori	0.8	0.4	50.0	0.2	25.0	0.1	12.5	0.2	25.0
Shimane	1.2	0.6	50.0	0.4	33.3	0.1	8.3	0.6	50.0
Okayama	2.1	2.1	100.0	1.3	61.9	1.4	66.7	4.0	190.5
Hiroshima	2.1	2.8	133.3	3.4	161.9	2.3	109.5	2.8	133.3
Yamaguchi	1.9	1.6	84.2	1.8	94.7	3.6	189.5	0.5	26.3
Tokushima	1.1	0.8	72.7	0.3	27.3	0.8	72.7	0.8	72.7
Kagawa	1.2	1.0	83.3	0.5	41.7	1.2	100.0	1.0	83.3
Ehime	1.8	1.7	94.4	1.1	61.1	1.7	94.4	2.2	122.2
Kochi	1.2	0.6	50.0	0.3	25.0	0.2	16.7	0.4	33.3
Fukuoka	3.9	4.0	102.6	6.1	156.4	4.9	125.6	1.6	41.0
Saga	1.2	0.6	50.0	0.4	33.3	0.4	33.3	0.4	33.3
Nagasaki	1.9	1.3	68.4	2.2	115.8	0.6	31.6	0.2	10.5
Kumamoto	2.3	1.2	52.2	0.4	17.4	1.5	65.2	0.8	34.8
Oita	1.6	0.9	56.3	0.5	31.3	0.4	25.0	0.7	43.8
Miyagi	1.4	0.8	57.1	0.2	14.3	2.3	164.3	0.3	21.4
Kagoshima	2.5	0.8	32.0	0.3	12.0	0.4	16.0	0.5	20.0

incorporated cities. In contrast, the eleven prefectures which have a higher percentage of total employed in industries excluding textiles than they have of the nation's total employed (the prefectures with a ratio of 100 or over in Column 6 of Table VI-4) account for 57.8 per cent of Japan's total employed in manufacturing other than textiles, but 62.0 per cent of the nation's urban population.

Figure VI-1, which shows the geographical location of these two groups of prefectures, indicates clearly the divergence of textile industrial activity from the urbanization pattern. The prefectures

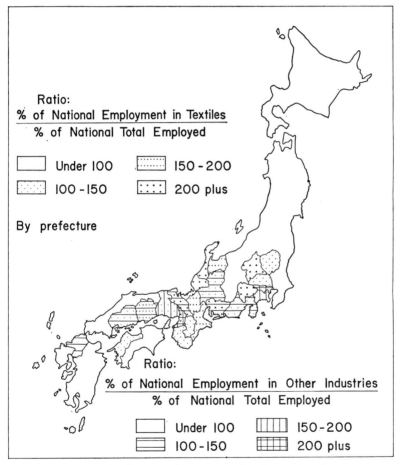

FIGURE VI-1: Distribution of Textile and Other Industrial Employment by Prefecture, 1950 (Source: *Population Census of 1950*, Vol. VII, Table 11)

to the north and west of Tokyo (Tochigi, Gumma, Yamanashi, and Saitama) and those bordering the Japan Sea (Toyama, Ishikawa, and Fukui), which show heavy emphasis in textiles, are prefectures which lack both high levels of urbanization or significant concentrations of other industries. With the exception of Osaka, no prefecture shows a ratio of over 200 for both textiles and other manufacturing activity. It is significant that in the largest urban aggregate of Japan, the Tokyo-Yokohama area, there is no textile emphasis, while the area has a ratio of over 159 for other manufacturing activities.

The rurality of textile processing cited previously in analyzing growth patterns of Japanese cities is again evident. The expansion of nonagricultural activities has been associated historically with urban growth in Japan, but where these nonagricultural pursuits are focused primarily in textiles the urbanization force has been weak. The association of urbanization with nonagricultural employment in Japan has been and is largely an association of city growth with the expansion of activities other than textiles.

The association of high levels of nonagricultural activity with high levels of urban residence by prefecture does not imply, however, that the nonagricultural pursuits are necessarily carried on largely within the administrative boundaries of cities. Table VI-5 shows that not until the post-World War II period was 50 per cent or more of the major urban-oriented employment located within incorporated cities. Two factors largely account for the change in location of nonagricultural activity. First, the growth of large, urban-centered units within Japanese industrial structure has brought some reduction in the number of small, and usually rural, production units. Hence, the city has drawn to it a larger portion of nonagricultural activity. Second, and probably more important, has been the expansion of city boundaries and the incorporation of new cities which absorb many of the smaller centers of nonagricultural pursuits into the urban category.

Certain of Japan's manufactures, however, have been historically associated with urban locations, notably metals-machine production and printing-publishing. Even in 1950 more than half those employed in textiles, ceramics, construction, and lumbering continued to be located outside incorporated cities. Not until 1950 did the chemical, food processing, and gas-electric categories be-

TABLE VI-5. Japan: Percentage Distribution of Major Areas of Nonagricultural Employment by Urban and Rural Location, 1920-1955

Industry	PERCENTAGE OF EMPLOYED POPULATION[a]											
	1920			1930			1950			1955		
	Total	Urban	Rural	Total	Urban	Rural	Total	Urban	Rural	Total	Urban	Rural
Manufacturing[b]	100.0	32.9	67.1	100.0	39.1	60.9	100.0	54.9	45.1	100.0	71.3	28.7
Commerce	100.0	39.3	60.7	100.0	45.7	54.3	100.0	61.0	39.0	100.0	74.4	25.6
Transportation-Communication	100.0	36.6	63.4	100.0	43.5	56.5	100.0	52.4	47.6	100.0	68.4	31.6
Administration-Services	100.0	36.1	63.9	100.0	43.7	56.3	100.0	54.6	45.4	100.0	69.9	30.1
TOTAL	100.0	35.5	64.5	100.0	42.4	57.6	100.0	56.0	44.0	100.0	71.5	28.5

a Total economically active in 1920 and 1930; economically active fourteen years of age and over in 1950 and 1955.
b Including construction.

Sources: Reports of 1920 Census, Vol. III, pt. A-2, Table 5. Japan Statistical Yearbook, 1935, Table 17. Population Census of 1950, Vol. III, pt. 2, Table 14. 1955 Census of Population of Japan, Vol. II, pt. 2, Table 5.

come primarily urban in the location of their employees. By 1955, however, every category in the manufacturing area has at least 50 per cent of its employed in urban areas. The 243 new cities incorporated between 1950 and 1955 largely account for the changes during that period. The conclusion to be drawn is that until 1955 the administrative designation of urban centers had lagged behind the actual growth of areas of nonagricultural emphasis in Japan. At present, most of Japan's nonagricultural activity takes place within areas politically defined as urban.

THE STRUCTURE OF NONAGRICULTURAL EMPLOYMENT

Analysis of the specific areas of Japanese nonagricultural employment from 1920 to 1955 shows a general trend toward a proportional increase in commercial and administration-services activities with a slight proportional decline in manufacturing. Table VI-6 shows the percentage distribution of employed population within the major nonagricultural categories for 1920-55. The world-wide depression which began in 1928-29 is reflected in the fall of manufacturing employment in 1930, but the loss was more than made up by an increase in commercial employment. An increasing proportion of population in these nonagricultural categories is maintained even in 1930 when 49.3 per cent was so employed as against 43.0 per cent for 1920. The effect of World War II can be read from the slight drop in proportion of popula-

TABLE VI-6. Japanese Nonagricultural Employment Composition, 1920-1955

Industry	PERCENTAGE DISTRIBUTION OF TOTAL EMPLOYED				
	1920	1930	1940	1950	1955
Construction	6.3	6.7	5.6	7.8	8.0
Manufacturing	38.3	32.5	39.7	31.9	31.0
Commerce:					
Retail-Wholesale Trade	22.8	28.4	23.8	21.7	24.0
Insurance, Banking	1.2	1.4	1.7	2.0	2.7
Transportation-Communication	9.8	8.9	8.8	10.3	9.0
Services	16.7	17.0	16.9	17.9	19.4
Public Officials	4.9	5.1	3.5	8.4	5.9
TOTAL	100.0	100.0	100.0	100.0	100.0
% Total Employed in Nonagricultural Activities	43.0	49.3	53.4	49.8	57.5

Source: See Table VI-5.

tion in nonagricultural pursuits for 1950 (49.8 per cent in 1950; 53.4 per cent in 1940), but by 1955 the proportion of nonagricultural activities (57.5 per cent) had passed the previous peak of 1940.

A comparison of rural with urban nonagricultural employment composition reveals one paradoxical fact: though the national proportion in nonagricultural employment has shown a trend of consistent increase, the 1920-55 period shows a consistent decrease in the proportion of total urban economically active population in nonagricultural pursuits. In 1920, 92.4 per cent of the urban employed were in the four major nonagricultural categories (manufacturing, commerce, transportation-communications, and administration-services); in 1955, 76.7 per cent of the urban employed were so occupied. This does not indicate a loss in absolute numbers of nonagricultural population by cities, but rather a gain in absolute numbers of agricultural population as city boundaries have been expanded and new cities have been incorporated. For instance, the city of Tokyo had only 0.7 per cent of its male labor force in agricultural pursuits in 1930; extensive boundary expansion in October, 1932 brought within the city areas containing agricultural employment to the extent that the total city area contained 3.4 per cent of its economically active males in agriculture. Itabashi ward, which was annexed to the city at this time, had 27.7 per cent of its male labor force in agriculture.

The influences of boundary changes and new incorporations upon employment composition are logically related to size of the urban place. That is, new cities with their comparatively high agricultural employment are most frequently small at the time of incorporation. Therefore, the smaller the city, the higher the agricultural activity. Conversely, annexations by large cities bring in agricultural population, but in relation to the city's total employed, these additions to the employed population are proportionately small. The larger the city, therefore, the smaller tends to be the proportion of agricultural activity. Table VI-7 shows that for both 1930 and 1950, this relationship holds true. The general level of agricultural activity is higher for 1950, since the number of new cities and the areas of older centers are both larger than in 1930.

In nonagricultural categories, variations in employment struc-

TABLE VI-7. Median Percentage Employed in Japanese Cities by Sex, Industry, and City Size, 1930-1950

City Size and Date[a]	MEDIAN PERCENTAGE EMPLOYED IN INDUSTRIAL CATEGORY									
	Agriculture		Manufacturing		Commerce		Transportation-Communication		Administration-Services	
	Males	Females	Males	Females	Males	Females	Males	Females	Males	Females
500,000+										
1930	1.9	1.0	40.9	24.1	36.8	38.7	7.3	1.1	9.7	10.8
1950	4.0	6.2	43.8	27.7	24.5	33.9	8.6	3.1	16.1	17.0
100-500,000										
1930	4.3	5.5	35.7	17.9	30.6	38.7	7.3	1.0	14.7	12.5
1950	10.2	20.5	35.3	20.7	20.3	27.3	8.8	2.6	15.7	14.3
50-100,000										
1930	7.4	8.0	33.9	27.5	32.6	34.4	7.3	0.7	12.8	9.6
1950	16.3	22.4	33.5	21.1	18.8	23.9	7.8	2.4	14.0	13.2
Under 50,000										
1930	7.7	8.1	35.1	39.8	33.3	34.1	5.5	0.4	10.3	8.5
1950	22.6	35.3	34.1	19.2	15.8	19.0	7.6	1.9	12.4	10.4

a City size as of census date.

Sources: Reports of 1930 Census, Vol. IV, pt. 4, Table 18 from prefectural volumes. Population Census of 1950, Vol. VII, Table 11 from prefectural volumes.

ture according to city size are also to be observed. Male employment in industry shows a tendency to increase with city size in both 1930 and 1950. The same is true for females in 1950, but a decline is evident in the over-all level of female industrial employment between 1930 and 1950 in the cities of less than 100,000 population. In no size category does commerce occupy as high a proportion of males or females in 1950 as in 1930. Further, the trend of a higher proportion of females than males employed in commerce in all size categories is consistent for both dates. An over-all increase in the transportation-communication category is to be noted between 1930 and 1950, with some indication of increases in proportion of both sexes employed in this category as city size increases. The services-administration category parallels transportation-communication in both respects. In summary, between 1930 and 1950, the following trends appear in urban employment composition: 1) an over-all increase in proportion of economically active in agricultural pursuits, 2) a relative stability in male industrial employment coupled with a decrease in female industrial activity in the smaller cities, and 3) over-all decreases in the commercial areas counteracted by increases in the transportation-communication and services-administration categories.

Within the manufacturing category itself, the rurality of textiles and construction is shown in Table VI-8. From 1930 through 1955, the ratios of percentage employed in textiles and construction for urban and rural areas are below 1.00, while these ratios for heavy and other industries are consistently over 1.00. In spite of boundary changes and new incorporations, these latter ratios show a trend of increase throughout the period covered. Again, the point to be emphasized is that Japanese urbanization is associated most closely with industrial activities other than textiles.

SUMMARY

The growth of Japan's urban population has been closely linked to an increase in nonagricultural activity. Until the World War II period, however, significant portions of this activity took place outside the boundaries of incorporated cities. Stringent requirements for city incorporation and heavy dependence upon a rural-oriented textile industry resulted in the designation of many of

TABLE VI-8. Japan: Rural and Urban Employment in Selected Nonagricultural Categories, 1930-55

Manufacturing Category	PERCENTAGE DISTRIBUTION OF TOTAL EMPLOYED								
	1930			1950			1955		
	Urban	Rural	Urban/Rural	Urban	Rural	Urban/Rural	Urban	Rural	Urban/Rural
Construction	12.6	20.7	0.61	15.4	23.5	0.65	17.1	29.5	0.58
Textiles	31.7	33.3	0.95	14.4	20.3	0.71	17.0	19.6	0.87
Heavy Industry	17.1	9.4	1.82	23.1	11.4	2.03	20.5	10.0	2.05
All Other Industry	38.6	36.6	1.05	47.1	44.8	1.05	45.4	40.9	1.11
TOTAL	100.0	100.0	—	100.0	100.0	—	100.0	100.0	—

Sources: *Reports of 1930 Census*, Vol. IV, pt. 4, Table 18 from prefectural volumes. *Population Census of 1950*, Vol. III, pt. 2, Table 14. *1955 Census of Population of Japan*, Vol. II, pt. 2, Table 5.

Japan's industrial labor force as "rural" in official statistics. Revised incorporation procedures and the creation of a more diversified industrial structure underlie the shift of a predominant share of nonagricultural activities into the urban category.

In geographical distribution, Japan's industrial activities closely follow the pattern of urbanization. Traditional areas of heavy population concentration have experienced the major share of Japan's industrialization. The demands of an industrializing society for power and mineral resources have, however, created new population concentrations, notably in northern Kyushu and Hokkaido. Industrialization has meant not only an increasing concentration of industrial activity in large cities, but the creation of large numbers of industrially specialized satellite cities within the regions of the great cities.

Demographic Characteristics of Japan's Urban Population | VII

The geographic selectivity of urbanization in Japan has been documented in Chapter V. Our concern now turns to the demographic selectivity of Japanese urban expansion. The transition from an agrarian to an industrial focus has meant not only the growth of urban agglomerations but a basic shift in the requirements for individual participation in productive activities. To the extent that an industrial system shifts the responsibilities of employment from traditional age and/or sex groups to new groups, the whole network of social relationships within which the society functions will be affected. The demands of urban-industrial employment have historically deviated from those of the agrarian society. In both cases, however, the core of the labor force remains the males in the age groups roughly fifteen to sixty-five years of age, while the variations come with respect to the age at which one enters and leaves the labor force and the magnitude of supplementary labor contributed by females. For example, the mother-housewife, the very young, and the very old find limited opportunities for contributions to the city's employment structure in contrast to those of the village farm community. Further, the specialized skill requirements of urban industry frequently mean longer periods of training which, in turn, create distinctive features of the age structure of the urban employed population.

It is within this general framework that the age and sex structures of Japan's nonagricultural labor force will be explored. In what ways do the age and sex structures of Japan's urban nonagriculturally employed vary from the rural labor force? In what ways can we account for the similarities and differences?

Answers to these questions, however, illuminate the differentiation within a specialized segment of the total urban population—those actually or potentially active in the labor force. These specialized population segments do not constitute the sole concern of one interested in the demographic analysis of Japanese urban structure. Obviously, the economically active population in Japanese cities supports numerous persons who are not part of the urban labor force. The spouse, offspring and aged, who with the economically active population constitute the total urban population, also reveal differentials in demographic traits in response to the selective aspects of urbanization. The *total* population of the city, with its particular distribution of demographic characteristics, is the context within which population changes occur. To the extent that these urban populations differ significantly in demographic traits from rural population components, the character and rates of urban in contrast to rural changes will differ. The differentiation of rural and urban populations is significant, therefore, because the differentiation is causally related to population change. For example, the migration of population in the young labor force ages to Japanese cities gives these cities sex ratios which differ from those found in rural areas. Traditional patterns of marriage are disrupted in the process: the urban migrants marry later than their rural counterparts, contributing to a potential for lower urban fertility. Japanese urban sex ratios can be viewed, therefore, both as an *effect* of the process of urbanization and as one of the underlying *causes* of differential population changes which occur in Japanese rural and urban population segments.

The rural-urban differentials discussed here are recognized as dynamic, shifting contrasts. The social changes inherent in the appearance of urban-industrialism in an agrarian society affect all segments of society, but at different times and rates. To cite rural-urban differences at one point in time is to contrast the penetration of these changes in two segments of the society at that particular time, not to imply that the contrast is a stable one.

The process of rural-urban differentiation has been formulated by Sorokin and Zimmerman as a parabolic relationship.[1] Prior to

1 Pitirim A. Sorokin, and Carle C. Zimmerman, *Principles of Rural-Urban Sociology* (New York: Henry Holt and Co., 1929), p. 610 ff.

the introduction of industrialization, the differences in "city" and rural populations are insignificant. Traditional agrarian social structure is characteristic of the whole of the society, even for those who are town dwellers and not directly engaged in agricultural pursuits. The appearance of industrialism in urban areas brings demands which initiate processes of demographic selectivity. As long as the expanding urban-industrialism remains confined principally to cities, the magnitude of differentiation between rural and urban areas increases. This differentiation reaches a peak, however, and the values and technology of the urban areas begin to penetrate the hinterland. The urban-industrial social structure which previously was dominantly urban now becomes that of the society as a whole. The final phase brings a decline in rural-urban differentiation and ultimately a similarity for the two population groups.

It is the purpose of this chapter to analyze Japanese rural-urban differentiation within this theoretical framework. The principal focus is upon age and sex structures as indices of the differentiation between urban areas and their hinterlands. The implication is that if the pattern of differentiation in these areas can be established, it is valid to assume that other elements of rural-urban differentiation approximate the same pattern. The first problem is to fit the history of Japanese rural-urban differences to the theoretical model suggested by Sorokin and Zimmerman. What is the current level of urban-nonurban differentiation in Japan with respect to age-sex structure? Is the magnitude of differentiation increasing or decreasing; that is, is there evidence to support the point that Japan has passed the peak of rural-urban differentiation and now faces a growing similarity between urban and nonurban populations? And finally, what are the consequences of the changing levels of rural-urban differentiation for Japanese population changes?

Our approach to Japanese urban selectivity will be, first, to analyze the rural-urban differentials with respect to the *employed* population. This analysis will be followed by an exploration of rural-urban differentiation within the *total* population. In this way we follow the causal sequence of urban differentiation. That is, the labor force demands of industrialization, which initially foster urban growth, structure the core city population about which those outside the working population congregate.

SEX STRUCTURE OF THE URBAN EMPLOYED

In contrast to rural agriculture, urban employment, by its very nature, reduces the opportunity for participation on a part-time, home-located basis. The structure of Japanese industrial organization does not, however, exclude entirely the possibility of participation of this sort. Table VII-1 shows that sex ratios (males per

TABLE VII-1. Japan: Median Sex Ratios of Total Employed for Cities by Size and for Rural Areas, 1920-50

Area and Size Category[a]	SEX RATIO OF EMPLOYED POPULATION		
	1920	1930	1950
Total Urban	317.7	312.4	222.2
Cities 500,000+	389.6	358.3	280.1
Cities 100-500,000	323.1	313.1	216.6
Cities 50-100,000	260.6	263.6	193.9
Cities less than 50,000	214.8	216.3	173.7
Total Rural	147.7	164.0	135.6

[a] Size categories as of census date.

Sources: *Reports of the 1920 Census*, Vol. IV, Table I-4 in prefectural volumes. *Reports of the 1930 Census*, Vol. IV, Table 18 in prefectural volumes. *Population Census of 1950*, Vol. VII, Table 11 in prefectural volumes.

100 females) of the urban employed are significantly higher than in the rural areas. The urban influence upon participation of women in the labor force is, however, directly related to the size of the urban area. That is, the traditional pattern of female employment does not show a sharp break between rural and urban areas. The pattern is rather one of a weakening of female labor force activity as the concentration of urban influences increases. Two factors help to explain this pattern. First, both in 1930 and in 1950, the smaller cities had larger proportions of their economically active engaged in agricultural pursuits where female participation is traditionally high. Second, the smaller cities also tended to be those whose industrial emphasis was upon those industries which utilized females extensively, e.g., textiles, ceramics, food processing.

The general trend in female urban employment has been one of increase in relation to male employment. That is, lower sex ratios for the total employed is characteristic of all categories in Table VII-1 for 1950 in comparison with 1930. Table VII-2 shows the areas of the employment structure which have seen the greatest increases in female participation. Three of the four categories which constitute the core of urban employment com-

TABLE VII-2. Japan: Sex Ratios for Employed Population by Industrial Category, 1920-50

Industry	SEX RATIO OF EMPLOYED POPULATION		
	1920	1930	1950
Agriculture-Forestry-Fishing	128.8	129.6	103.9
Mining	339.6	521.5	786.1
Manufacturing	234.6	427.0	313.7
Commerce	209.6	210.6	160.2
Transportation-Communication	1,572.5	1,268.6	816.2
Administration-Services	368.4	487.0	172.3
TOTAL	174.5	188.4	158.5

Sources: *Reports of the 1920 Census*, Vol. IV, pt. A-2, pp. 136-41. *Reports of the 1930 Census*, Vol. III, pp. 9-21. *Population Census of 1950*, Vol. III, pt. 2, Table 16.

position, i.e., industry, commerce, transportation-communication, and administration-services, show increases in the proportion of female employment. Only the industrial area had a higher sex ratio in 1950 than in 1920. The diversification of Japanese industry following World War I, with its movement away from the dominance of textile production, where large numbers of women were employed, largely accounts for the higher sex ratio in this category.

Where nonagricultural employment is located in rural areas, traditional patterns of high female participation and smaller establishments result in lower sex ratios. Table VII-3 shows that in

TABLE VII-3. Japan: Sex Ratios of Employed Population in Urban and Rural Areas by Industry, 1950

Industry	SEX RATIO OF EMPLOYED POPULATION	
	In Incorporated Cities	In Rural Areas
Agriculture-Forestry-Fishing	118.2	102.5
Mining	871.4	776.0
Manufacturing	356.2	271.1
Commerce	171.8	143.8
Transportation-Communication	744.6	911.8
Administration-Services	195.4	295.9
TOTAL	222.2	135.6

Source: *Population Census of 1950*, Vol. III, pt. 2, Table 16.

1950, among the four basic urban activities, only the administrative-services category had a higher sex ratio in the rural areas than in the urban. The lower sex ratio in rural areas holds even in the agriculture-fishing-forestry category, where 118.2 urban males as against 102.5 rural males per 100 females were employed in 1950.

To summarize, since 1920 the Japanese labor force has shown increased female participation. Urban areas have consistently employed proportionately fewer females than males, but even the urban sex ratios have shown decreases between 1920 and 1950. Only the industrial category of employment has tended toward reduced female activity, but the losses here have been more than balanced with gains by females in other areas of employment. Analysis of employed sex ratios by size of cities shows no clear break between rural and urban female employment patterns, but there exists a close association between increasing city size and decreasing sex ratio of employed population. Urbanization can be said to weaken but not destroy traditional Japanese employment patterns.

AGE STRUCTURE OF THE URBAN EMPLOYED

The sex selectivity noted above in Japan's nonagricultural employment composition is paralleled by age selectivity. The demands of urban-oriented employment activities penalize the very young, the very old, and the mother-housewife in contrast to the more mobile segments of the population. This urban age selectivity in Japan is reflected in Figure VII-1 which contrasts urban with rural employed in terms of age and sex for 1950. Largely through migration, the urban areas have drawn into their employment structures heavy concentrations of males in the age groups with the highest labor force potential, i.e., males from twenty to sixty years and especially those from twenty-five to thirty-nine years of age.

Only in the groups of less than twenty years and over sixty years of age do urban females approach rural females in the proportion of the total which is employed. The employed females of over sixty years of age are a relatively insignificant portion of the total in both rural and urban areas (less than 0.1 per cent of the total employed females in either area fell in this age group in 1950). A large portion of the employed females under twenty years of age in both rural and urban areas is engaged in the textile industries. The personnel policies in these industries favor the utilization of young, unmarried girls who are employed by contract with their parents. The girls live in company dormitories throughout the

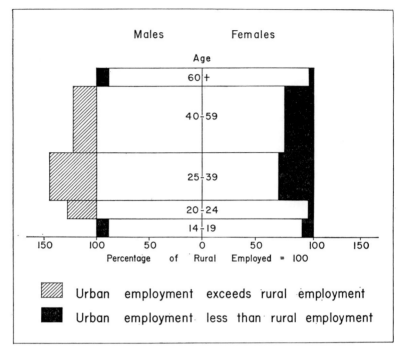

FIGURE VII-1: Urban Employed Population Relative to Rural Employed Population by Age and Sex, 1950 (Source: *Population Census of 1950*, Vol. III, pt. 2, Table 16)

period of their employment with the understanding that they will return to their homes at the time of their marriage.

The importance of textile production in the history of Japanese industrialization has meant that the age structure of the female labor force has deviated sharply from that of males in terms of a utilization of the younger age segments. A striking illustration of this fact is seen in Figure VII-2. The rapid decrease in number of females in the textile industries after nineteen years of age reflects the pattern of termination of employment at the time of marriage. Much the same pattern can be seen for females in industries other than textiles, but on a reduced scale. A further consequence of this pattern is the contrast in length of period of employment between industrially employed males and females. In 1933, for instance, 38.1 per cent of females employed in spinning-weaving mills had been employed for two years or less, while only

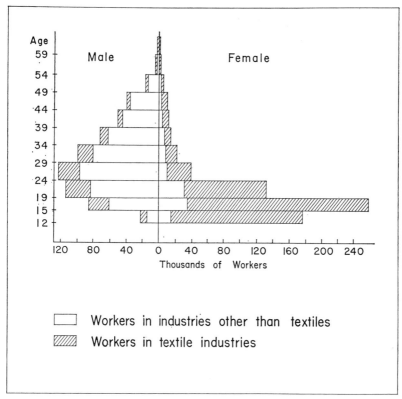

FIGURE VII-2: Age Composition of Industrial Workers, 1930 (Source: Teijiro Ueda, *et al.*, *The Small Industries of Japan: Their Growth and Development* [Shanghai: Kelly and Walsh, Ltd., 1938], p. 90)

5.2 per cent of the males in these industries had terms of service of this length.[2]

The age composition of the total employed has remained relatively stable throughout the 1920-50 period, as measured by median age of employed (Table VII-4). The somewhat higher median ages for 1950 are partially explained by the fact that the 1950 census reports only on persons over fourteen years of age, while the 1920 and 1930 figures are based upon all employed persons.[3] The stability of median ages of employed, however,

[2] Teijiro Ueda, *et al.*, *The Small Industries of Japan* (Shanghai: Kelly and Walsh, Ltd., 1938), p. 91.

[3] In 1950, 4.5 per cent of the total population aged 10-13 years were employed (4.9 per cent of the males and 4.0 per cent of the females).

TABLE VII-4. Japan: Median Age of Total Employed Population by Industry, 1920-50

| | MEDIAN AGE OF EMPLOYED POPULATION[a] | | | | | | | | |
| | 1920 | | | 1930 | | | 1950 | | |
Industry	Total	Males	Females	Total	Males	Females	Total	Males	Females
Agriculture-Forestry-Fishing	35.7	37.3	33.9	36.8	38.2	35.2	36.7	38.2	35.5
Mining	30.1	31.0	27.3	31.0	31.1	31.0	32.5	33.0	35.8
Manufacturing	27.7	29.5	22.7	28.4	29.4	23.4	30.7	32.7	23.7
Commerce	35.0	34.9	35.1	32.9	33.1	32.5	35.4	37.1	32.8
Transportation-Communication	31.0	31.3	24.8	29.4	30.5	19.9	34.1	32.1	22.6
Administration-Services[b]	29.7	31.3	24.2	29.8	30.9	25.0	32.1	34.8	26.4
TOTAL	33.3	34.1	32.0	32.8	33.5	31.5	34.2	35.3	32.3

[a] Figures for 1920 and 1930 are based upon total employed population; figures for 1950 are based upon employed population fourteen years of age and over.
[b] Figures for 1920 and 1930 exclude domestic service; figures for 1950 include domestic service.

Sources: *Reports of 1920 Census*, Vol. VII, Table 34 and 35. *Jinkō tōkei sōran* (Population Statistics Summary), September, 1943, Table 30. *Population Census of 1950*, Vol. III, pt. 2, Table 16.

masks the shifts which have taken place within the labor force, as is shown in Figure VII-3.

Figure VII-3 shows that females in all age groups, with the sole exception of the 20-24 years of age segment, have been decreasing

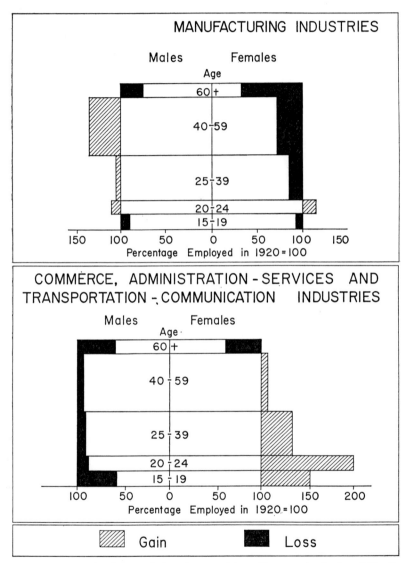

FIGURE VII-3: Age and Sex Composition Changes in Industrially Employed Population, 1920-1950 (Sources: *Reports of 1920 Census*, Vol. IV, pt. A-2, pp. 142-153 and *Population Census of 1950*, Vol. III, pt. 2, Table 16)

proportionately in manufacturing. The youngest and the oldest age groups (under twenty and over sixty years of age) of both sexes show decreased labor force participation from 1920 to 1950. The increase in proportion of the males employed in manufacturing in the forty to fifty-nine year age group is reflected in a rise in median age from 29.5 years in 1920 to 32.7 years in 1950. The only increase in proportion of females in manufacturing took place in the age group which contains the median, with the result that little change occurred in the median age for females from 1920 to 1950 (22.7 years in 1920; 23.7 years in 1950). The net result in manufacturing is a small rise in median age of total employed (from 27.7 years to 30.7 years) from 1920 to 1950, as the male segment aged and female participation, especially in the older age groups, decreased.

In the remaining three urban-oriented employment categories, i.e., commerce, transportation-communication, and administration-services, an opposite trend can be observed for the 1920-50 period (Figure VII-3). In every male age group, and most noticeably in the under twenty and over sixty years age segments, these three employment areas show proportional decreases. Only at ages of sixty years and over do females show a decrease. The aging of the male labor force noted for manufacturing is again evident in the three categories given in Figure VII-3 in that, though losing in every age segment, the smallest decrease is for the older labor force group (forty to fifty-nine years of age). At the same time, the female labor force shows an opposite trend toward a lowering of the median age of employed. The greatest proportionate gain for females was in the twenty to twenty-four years of age group, while the smallest gain was for those forty to fifty-nine years of age. This trend is shown in Table VII-4 where the median ages of females employed in commerce (which contains by far the largest portion of the three categories) and in transportation-communication show decreases from 1920 to 1950.

The trends of changes in labor force age composition are emphasized in the urban vis-à-vis rural populations as shown in Table VII-5. The median age of total employed in cities in every category, with the exception of transportation-communication, is higher than the corresponding figure for rural areas in 1950. The median age for total employed is, however, higher for rural than

TABLE VII-5. Japan: Median Age of Employed Population in Urban and Rural Areas by Industry, 1950

Industry	MEDIAN AGE OF EMPLOYED POPULATION	
	In incorporated cities	In rural areas
Agriculture-Forestry-Fishing	38.9	36.5
Mining	33.0	32.2
Manufacturing	31.2	29.9
Commerce	34.7	36.6
Transportation-Communication	31.9	30.0
Administration-Services	32.3	31.9
TOTAL	33.2	34.7

Source: *Population Census of 1950*, Vol. III, pt. 2, Table 16.

urban areas since the greater portion of rural employed are in the agriculture-fishing-forestry category, which has a higher median age than any other employment category.

The general trend in the age composition of Japan's nonagriculturally employed has been toward an increased concentration of the economically active within roughly the span between twenty and sixty years of age. The very young and the very old of both sexes have shown a decline in labor force participation between 1920 and 1950. In addition, there has been a noticeable aging of the male labor force and an opposite trend for females. Since males dominate the labor force, especially in nonagricultural pursuits, the median age of total employed has increased.

RURAL-URBAN AGE DIFFERENTIALS WITHIN THE TOTAL POPULATION

Turning now to the total population, we again note that the first reliable data on Japanese age structure appeared in the first national census of 1920; therefore, any analysis of this dimension of Japanese population begins well after the onset of Japan's urban-industrialization. During the period since 1920, the roughly 50% increase in Japan's total population has meant relatively little change in the proportional distribution of the major age segments of her total population. If we compare rural and urban age composition by four broad age groupings (0-14, 15-44, 45-64, and 65 years and over) for 1920 through 1950, only slight differences are visible. Within the narrow range of changes, the two segments under 45 years of age show the greatest variation. The youths (0-14 years of age) have varied within 2.8 percentage points, while the young adult segment (15-44 years of age) have varied only one-half this range. The older adults (45-64 years of age) and the aged (65 years and over) show variations of 0.5 of a percentage point or less.

The significance of these comparisons is that they constitute a relatively stable background against which rural-urban comparisons during this period can be made. That is, the increases or decreases in proportional distribution of age groups within urban or rural areas during the 1920-50 period can be assumed largely to be genuine rural-urban differences and not the results of major shifts in the total population which they constitute.

The demands of an expanding urban-centered industrialization attract most effectively that segment of the population with the greatest labor force potential: the young adults. Throughout the 1920-50 period, this age group is more heavily represented in Japan's urban areas than in the rural hinterland (Figure VII-4). Conversely, the age group made up of those adults with the lowest potential contribution to the urban labor force would be those least represented in the urban age structure. The 65 years and over age segment is that showing the greatest rural-urban differential in both 1920 and 1950. The youth and older adult age groups, both showing heavier proportional representation in rural areas, fall below the levels of young adult and the aged in the urban-nonurban contrast.

These generalizations are valid for both 1920 and 1950, but Figure VII-4 shows further that the magnitude of rural-urban differentials for each of the four age segments is less for 1950 than 1920. The differential for the young adult ages in 1950 in contrast to 1920 decreased by one-half: from approximately one-fourth more (126.9) in 1920 urban areas to one-eighth more (112.9) in 1950 urban areas. The differentials favoring rural areas in proportions of the youth and older adult age groups were also cut by one-half or more. Though the differential decreased for the aged, the decrease was the lowest of all the age segments and, in 1950, still gave the urban areas only two-thirds the proportion of population in this age group that was found in the rural hinterland.

The conclusion is that the magnitude of rural-urban differentials in all major age groups has decreased during the 1920-1950 period. However, before it can be assumed that the decrease is characteristic of Japanese urbanization as a whole, it must be noted that the 1950 urban population includes 248 cities constitu-

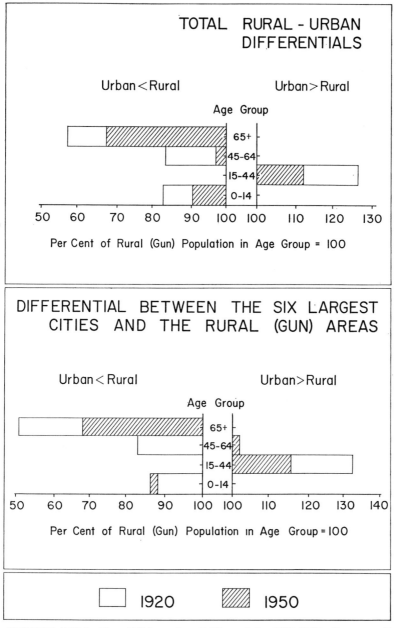

FIGURE VII-4: Rural-Urban Age Differentials, 1920-1950 (Sources: *Reports of the 1920 Census*, Vol. I, Table 3; *Population Statistics, September, 1943*, Table 15; *Population Census of 1950*, Vol. IV, pt. 1 and Vol. VII, Tables 2-3)

ting 37.5% of the total population, in contrast to 1920's 81 cities containing only 18.1% of the total population. It might well be argued that the incorporation of a large number of new cities bringing significant numbers of population into the urban category during the thirty-year span merely "diluted" the urban age structure with rural traits. To test this argument, it is possible to compare the age structures of the six largest cities in 1920 with their 1950 age structures. In this way the influence of administrative changes in urban classification is held to a minimum, and the age structure changes noted can be assumed to reflect more precisely those of Japanese urbanization as such. Figure VII-4 shows the changes in proportion of population in the four age groups in Japan's six largest cities for 1920 and 1950, using the *gun* (nonurban) age distribution as a base. With the exception of the 0-14 years of age group, the directions of age structure shifts are the same as those noted for the total urban population. In fact, and again with the exception of the youngest age segment, the intensity of the changes is greater for the largest of Japan's cities than for the total urban population. For example, the change in the older adult age group (45-64 years of age) in the six largest cities has reversed the total rural-urban relationship. In 1950, Japan's largest cities contained a larger percentage of population in this age category than did the rural population of that census year.

The rural-urban differentials in the 0-14 years of age group will be discussed in detail later in this chapter under the heading of urban influences upon fertility. It is sufficient at this point to note that within the framework of over-all urban-nonurban age structure changes, there is a trend toward homogeneity between the two categories. This homogeneity parallels the spread of industrially oriented occupational demands from the urban centers into the nonurban hinterland, a trend documented in Chapters V and VI above. Fertility patterns, reflected most clearly in the 0-14 years of age group, are at the heart of Japan's still effective familial value structure. The forces for homogeneity in the adult population would appear to be insufficient to erode effectively these fertility values. It is true that the spread of urban-industrialism has brought a trend of falling fertility throughout the nation as a whole, but the trend is most evident in the centers of most intense urbanism (represented by the six largest cities). Of all the rural-urban differentials cited, only that for the proportion of population 0-14 years of age in the six largest cities *increased* during the 1920-1950 period.

RURAL-URBAN SEX STRUCTURE DIFFERENTIALS

The male and female components of Japan's adult population have varied in their contributions to the increasing homogeneity of rural and urban populations since 1920. As was the case with age structure of the total population from 1920 to 1950, there have been only relatively minor shifts in age structure by sex for the Japanese population. The highest variation shown is for females 15-44 years of age, and this is a 2.9 percentage point increase from 1930 to 1950. All other variations are of one percentage point or less for the 1920-50 period. The changes in rural and urban differentials in age structure by sex are, therefore, changes which have occurred within relatively stable over-all age structures.

One of the major characteristics of Japan's urban population is its masculinity. Throughout the 1920-1950 period, males have been more heavily represented in the urban population than in the rural. Table VII-6 shows the sex ratios for total, rural, and urban populations for the 1920-1950 period. For each census year covered, the urban sex ratio exceeds that for the rural population.

TABLE VII-6. Japan: Sex Ratios of Total, Rural, and Urban Populations, 1920-1950

| | Sex Ratio (Males per 100 Females) | | | Excess of Urban over Rural Males per 100 Females |
Year	Total Population	Urban (shi) Population	Rural (gun) Population	
1920	100.4	108.7	98.7	10.0
1930	101.0	106.7	99.2	7.7
1950	96.3	97.0	95.8	1.2
Changes in Males per 100 Females 1920-50	— 4.1	— 11.7	— 2.9	—

Sources: *Jinkō tōkei sōran* (Population Statistics Summary), September, 1943. Table 15, pp. 58-59; *1930 Population Census of Japan*, Vol. I, Tables 12-14, pp. 60-65; *Population Census of 1950*, Vol. IV, Table 2, p. 4.

It is significant, however, that the magnitude of rural-urban differences consistently decreased from 1920 to 1950; the differential in 1950 approached one-tenth of that in 1920 (10.0 vs. 1.2). The trend of sex ratios in the six largest cities of Japan during this period indicates that the decrease in absolute sex ratio as well as the decrease in rural-urban differential characteristic of the total urban population is intensified in the dominant centers of Japan's urban structure (Table VII-7). The change in median sex ratio for the six largest cities from 1920 to 1950 shows a loss of 14.5 males per 100 females, compared to a loss of 11.7 for the total urban population for the same period.

TABLE VII-7. Japan: Sex Ratios for Japan's Six Largest Cities, 1920-1950

City	Sex Ratio (Males per 100 Females)			Changes in Males per 100 Females, 1920-50
	1920	1930	1950	
Tokyo	116.9	112.7	102.1	—14.8
Osaka	116.3	113.4	99.5	—16.8
Kobe	113.8	106.6	95.0	—18.8
Yokohama	113.0	107.5	102.0	—11.0
Nagoya	105.0	106.1	98.4	— 6.6
Kyoto	102.8	107.7	93.8	— 9.0
Median for 6 cities	113.4	107.6	98.9	—14.5

Sources: Prefectural volumes from censuses of respective years.

The decreasing masculinity of the urban as against the rural population is predominantly the result of shifts in the urban male population. Table VII-8 shows the rural-urban differential in age structure by sex for 1920 and 1950. Every age group for each sex showed a rural-urban differential closer to 100 (the rural population age distribution by sex is used as the base) in 1950 than in 1920. This is to say that the growing homogeneity in age and sex structure between the urban and nonurban Japanese populations discussed above is again emphasized. Further, the last column of Table VII-8 shows that in every age group the changes in rural-urban differences between 1920 and 1950 are greater for males than for females. Using the percentage of total population in each age-sex category in the rural population as 100, the smallest change for males is 10.0 points in the 0-14 years of age group. No change in any female age group is of this magnitude. It is noteworthy, how-

TABLE VII-8. Japan: Rural-Urban Differentials in Age Structure by Sex, 1920-1950

| Age Group | PER CENT OF TOTAL POPULATION | | | | RURAL-URBAN DIFFERENTIAL[a] | | |
| | 1920 | | 1950 | | 1920 | 1950 | Change: 1920-50 |
	Urban	Rural	Urban	Rural			
Males							
0-14	30.6	38.0	34.4	38.0	80.5	90.5	10.0
15-44	54.4	41.2	47.6	41.7	132.0	114.1	17.9
45-64	12.5	15.5	15.0	15.3	80.6	98.0	17.4
65+	2.5	5.2	3.0	4.9	48.1	61.2	13.1
Females							
0-14	32.3	37.2	32.3	35.2	86.8	91.8	5.0
15-44	50.0	41.2	48.8	43.6	121.4	111.9	9.5
45-64	13.5	15.5	14.4	14.9	87.1	96.6	9.5
65+	4.2	6.2	4.5	6.3	67.7	61.4	3.7

a Per cent in age and sex group of rural population equals 100.

Sources: *1930 Population Census of Japan*, Vol. I, Tables 13-14, pp. 62-65; *Population Census of 1950*, Vol. III, Part 1, Tables 3-3a, pp. 58-61.

ever, that for both males and females the highest changes are decreases in the urban advantage with respect to the age group of highest labor force contribution: 15-44 years of age.

In summary, the trend in sex structure differentiation between Japan's urban and nonurban areas from 1920 to 1950 has been toward homogeneity. The Japanese urban population has throughout this period been more heavily masculine than the rural population, but the magnitude of this difference has shown a decrease. Analysis shows that this trend is based more heavily upon shifts in male age structure than in female age structure between rural and urban categories.

AGE-SEX DIFFERENTIATIONS WITHIN URBAN POPULATIONS

The rural-urban differentiation apparent thus far in Japanese population has been analyzed on the basis of dichotomizing the population into urban and nonurban categories. Theoretically, this differentiation reflects a continuum from the most traditional, agrarian areas to the areas of most intense urban-industrialism. If we assume city size to be at least a rough approximation of the intensity of urban-industrialism, major demographic characteristics of the urban population categorized by size will tend to reveal the continuous nature of the differentiation.

When analyzed by city size, the higher urban masculinity noted in rural-urban comparisons reveals clearly the relationship of urban differences and magnitude of urban concentration. Table VII-9 shows sex ratios in 1920 and 1950 for cities by size. The differences between size groups are relatively small, especially for 1950, but the direction of differences is consistent: increasing city size equals heavier concentration of males. Level of urban-indus-

TABLE VII-9. Japan: Median Sex Ratios for Urban Areas by Size, 1920-50

	MEDIAN SEX RATIOS	
City Size	1920	1950
Under 50,000	97.8	92.6
50-100,000	98.7	94.1
100-500,000	107.0	95.7
500,000+	115.3	99.0
TOTAL URBAN	108.7	97.0

Sources: *Reports of the 1920 Census*, Vol. IV, Prefectural Volumes; *Population Census of 1950*, Vol. VII, Prefectural Volumes.

trialism as measured by size, therefore, confirms the rural-urban relationship with respect to sex structure.

The age structure by sex lends further support to this conclusion, as shown in Table VII-10. The younger labor force ages, those most sensitive to the demands of urban-industrialism, show not only consistent increases by city size but greater increases for males than for females in both 1920 and 1950. These data again emphasize the significance of male urban age-sex changes in contrast to female changes in the over-all pattern of shifts in Japanese urban structure during the 1920-1950 period.

RURAL-URBAN FAMILY STRUCTURE AND FERTILITY DIFFERENTIALS

The foregoing discussion of age and sex differentials between Japan's rural and urban population has utilized a conception of the city as a focus of functional demands which differ sharply from those of traditional agrarian Japanese life. The age and sex traits of individuals are evaluated differentially by the city in contrast to the agricultural village. Hence, the age and sex structure of the urban population reflects the functional demands of the economic system of the city. The persistent advantage of Japanese urban over rural population in the presence of both males and females in the young adult ages underscores this point. It is also true that this population segment, in addition to its high labor force potential, represents the core of the reproductive capacity of the nation. Any analysis of the relationship of urban-industrialization and fertility rests ultimately upon the convergence of these two maximum potentials within roughly the same age span. It is to be expected, then, that rural-urban differentiation in age-sex structure which reflects a shift in the functional basis of social organization will be paralleled by changes in patterns of reproduction.

The analysis of any phase of Japanese fertility is made difficult by the nature of Japan's pre-World War II vital statistics registration. Unlike the population census, the Japanese vital statistics collection was not revised in 1920. The records of births, deaths, marriages, divorces, and changes of residence continued to be recorded on the basis of place of legal residence (*honseki*). Irrespective of the actual location of the occurrence of the vital phenomenon, it could be legally recorded only by the keeper of the

TABLE VII-10. Japan: Median Percentage of Urban Population in Selected Age-Sex Groups by City Size, 1920-1950

Age-Sex Group	Total Urban	Under 50,000	50-100,000	100-500,000	500,000 +	Percentage point change from "Under 50,000" to "500,000 and over" size groups
				1920		
Total:						
15-24 yrs.	21.6	21.1	21.6	22.0	25.2	4.1
25-44 yrs.	26.7	26.0	26.9	27.8	30.3	4.3
Males:						
15-24 yrs.	21.7	20.9	21.8	23.2	26.5	5.6
25-44 yrs.	27.5	26.7	27.5	29.1	31.2	4.5
Females:						
15-24 yrs.	21.8	21.7	21.6	21.6	23.6	1.9
25-44 yrs.	26.4	25.8	26.5	27.4	29.1	3.3
				1950		
Total:						
15-24 yrs.	20.5	19.3	19.8	20.2	20.8	1.5
25-44 yrs.	27.7	25.6	26.4	27.5	28.4	2.8
Males:						
15-24 yrs.	19.6	18.9	19.7	20.2	21.4	2.5
25-44 yrs.	25.3	24.4	25.3	26.6	28.3	3.9
Females:						
15-24 yrs.	20.0	19.6	20.2	20.4	20.4	0.8
25-44 yrs.	27.5	26.7	27.7	28.6	28.6	1.9

Sources: *Reports of the 1920 Census*, Vol. IV, Prefectural Volumes; *Population Census of 1950*, Vol. VII, Prefectural Volumes.

family records in the *honseki*. These records provide vital statistics only incidentally, since the system was an administrative technique, the purpose of which was to establish legal residence and legal family status. Failure to comply with the requirements meant the loss of legal and inheritance rights. Many of the problems related to an analysis of vital rates in Japan evolve from the essential administrative purpose of the registration system.[4] The Japanese Bureau of Statistics separated legal registration from the collection of vital statistics in 1945.

Prior to 1945, the birth statistics under analysis here contain the weaknesses inherent in the administrative emphasis of their collection. There are, however, advantages to this system which increase the validity of conclusions drawn from analyses of the data collected. First, since there was no legal existence for the Japanese without *honseki* registration, practically all changes were recorded. Taeuber and Beal estimate, for example, that 96% to 98% of all births and deaths occurring in the period 1925-42 were recorded in the year of their occurrence. Secondly, the errors in compilation are fairly consistent, and hence the trends observable are fairly accurate.[5] The birth statistics are in error most frequently not in the recording of births as such, but in the *location* for which they are reported. The widespread practice of married women returning to the home of their own parents for childbirth interferes with the analysis of rural-urban birth rate differentials. The recording of births is by *honseki* in which they occur; therefore, to the degree that women return to rural *honseki* for births, to that degree rural births are over-registered and urban ones are under-registered. Taeuber and Beal further estimate that births for the six largest cities in Japan in 1930 were under-registered by some 7% to 15%.[6]

Qualified as the analyses must be, there are indications that urban-industrialization has influenced significantly the family formation and reproductive patterns of Japan. First, the source of

[4] Irene B. Taeuber, and Edwin G. Beal, Jr., *Guide to the Official Demographic Statistics of Japan,* Supplement, *Population Index,* Vol. 12, No. 4 (October, 1946), pp. 15-19.

[5] *Ibid.,* p. 19.

[6] *Ibid.,* p. 18.

the population constituting the heavier concentration in the young adult ages in Japan's urban areas is internal migration. The movement of this population largely from centers of traditional folk culture to the urban context comes at an age when they would by custom be marrying. Migration, plus the functional requirements of urban labor force participation, delays marriage and hence reduces the opportunities for reproduction.

Table VII-11 shows the percentage of population ever married for rural and urban areas by sex and age for the period 1920-1950. A national trend of later marriage-age is to be noted in comparisons for both rural and urban population of both sexes. The trend was especially effective upon females who for ages 15-19 years decreased from 13.3% ever married in cities in 1920 to 2.9% ever married in cities in 1950, and from 18.9% to 3.8% in rural areas. Roughly 20 percentage-point drops are noted for rural and urban females in the ages 20-24 years. Males also married later in 1950 than in 1920 in both rural and urban areas, but the magnitude of decreases was far less than that for females.

Within this over-all national trend, the data bear out the contention that the major influence of urban residence upon family formation was an increase in age at marriage. For males under 20 years of age in both 1920 and 1950, the urban percentage married was one-half or less that of the rural (though the 1950 rural-urban contrast is between proportions of less than one per cent). For males 20-24 years of age, the 17.3% ever married in urban areas remained approximately one-half the percentage married in rural areas; in 1950, though percentages for both rural and urban areas had fallen, the urban was still only approximately two-thirds that of nonurban areas. The females in this age group (20-24 years), while reflecting the decreasing national trend, maintained a 7 to 10 point rural-urban differential. After the age 25 years, the rural-urban differential in females ever married decreased: the rural-urban ratio for 1920 and 1950 for all ages above 25 years was above 90. The males, however, maintained a rural-urban differential of more than 10 percentage points up to age 30 years, after which the male rural-urban ratio was also over 90. These data support the conclusion of Taeuber and Notestein that the practice of delayed marriage was one of the principal means

TABLE VII-11. JAPAN: Percentage of Rural and Urban Populations ever Married by Age and Sex, 1920-50

PERCENTAGE OF POPULATION EVER MARRIED[a]

| | Males | | | | | | Females | | | | | |
| | 1920 | | | 1950 | | | 1920 | | | 1950 | | |
Age	Urban	Rural	Rural-Urban Ratio[b]	Urban	Rural	Rural-Urban Ratio	Urban	Rural	Rural-Urban Ratio	Urban	Rural	Rural-Urban Ratio
15-19	1.1	3.4	32.4	0.3	0.6	50.0	13.5	18.9	71.4	2.9	3.8	76.3
20-24	17.3	33.5	51.6	12.6	20.8	60.6	60.6	70.9	85.5	40.5	47.5	85.3
25-29	61.8	78.1	79.1	57.6	71.4	80.7	86.3	92.0	93.8	81.8	86.7	94.3
30-34	86.9	93.3	93.1	89.7	93.7	95.7	93.5	96.5	96.9	92.9	95.3	97.5
35-39	93.7	96.4	97.2	96.1	97.3	98.9	95.8	97.7	98.1	96.2	97.5	98.7
40-44	95.9	97.5	98.4	97.9	98.2	99.7	96.7	98.1	98.6	97.4	98.3	99.1
45-49	96.8	97.9	98.2	98.2	98.5	99.7	97.0	98.3	98.7	98.1	98.7	99.4
50+	97.8	98.4	99.4	98.5	98.3	100.2	97.6	98.7	98.9	98.3	98.5	99.7
Total 15+	59.2	73.6	80.4	63.2	67.4	93.8	75.2	82.6	91.0	72.4	75.4	96.0

a Sum of the percentages of population in age-sex groups in marital categories other than single.
b Percentage of rural population ever married equals 100.

Sources: *1930 Population Census of Japan*, Vol. I, Tables 13-14; *Population Census of 1950*, Vol. III, pt. 1, Tables 3-3a.

whereby Japanese birth rates have been lowered since the earliest phases of urban-industrialization.[7]

An urban pattern of later marriage does not, however, indicate a clear break with traditional Japanese family practices. Japanese social structure remains essentially one resting upon a base of strong family ties. The family household head has traditionally had control over the marriage, residence, and occupation of all other members of the family. Setsuko Hani, writing in the post-World War II period, assesses the influence of family dominance in these terms:

It is indeed, the idea or consciousness of the house, either economic or ethical, that has supported the pyramidal monopolistic organization of the Zaibatsu or the political plutocracy of Japan, preserving industrial mysticism which, rejecting national production by machinery, falls back on secret arts handed down from father to son, and justifies the apprenticeship system in regard to handicraft with the attachment of spiritual significance.[8]

Traditional family values remain dominant in the socialization of individuals for participation in modern Japanese society. The widespread existence of household-based commercial and handicraft activities in even the largest cities of an industrialized Japan supports the tenacity of these elements of what is essentially a feudal family system.

Japanese urban-industrialism has weakened this family value framework, but it has failed to destroy its influence. The urban changes noted are largely shifts in the size rather than in the nature of the family structure. As early as 1919, the readjustment of the Japanese family to an urban context is noted by Matsumiya. The range of kinship statuses constituting the household is essentially the same for both rural and urban families, but the numerical strength of status beyond the nuclear family is reduced for urban areas:[9]

[7] Irene B. Taeuber, and Frank W. Notestein, "The Changing Fertility of Japan," *Population Studies,* Vol. I (1947-1948), pp. 27-28.

[8] Setsuko Hani, *The Japanese Family System* (Tokyo: Nihon taiheiyo mondai chōsakai, 1948), pp. 10-11.

[9] Kazuya Matsumiya, "The Family Organization in Present Day Japan," *American Journal of Sociology,* Vol. LIII, No. 2 (September, 1947), p. 109.

Relationship to Household Head	Number of Relatives per 1000 Household Heads	
	Six Largest Cities	Rural Areas
Son's Wife	32	141
Grandchildren	70	277
Wives of Grandchildren	0	3
Great Grandchildren	1	4
Father	34	79
Mother	138	208

A study for a somewhat later date (1925) shows a comparison of the city of Tokyo with Iwate Prefecture, illustrative of the rural agricultural areas:[10]

Percentage Distribution of Households by
Number of Generations Contained

Area	One	Two	Three	Four	Five
Tokyo	25.3	62.6	11.2	0.7	0.0
Iwate Prefecture	3.7	39.3	45.2	11.1	0.7

In 1925, these figures show that 87.9% of Tokyo's households contained members representing no more than two generations. In contrast, Iwate Prefecture had only 43.0% households in this category. The influence of the urban context is clear, but significantly over 10% of Tokyo's families at this time contained three or more generations.

The changes in family structure noted for an urbanizing Japan as a whole are paralleled by an over-all decrease in the national birth rate:[11]

Date	Average Annual Crude Birth Rate	Date	Crude Birth Rate
1920-25	36.7	1947	34.3
1925-30	34.7	1948	33.5
1930-35	32.6	1949	33.0
1935-40	29.3	1950	28.1
		1951	25.3
		1952	23.4
		1953	21.5
		1954	20.0
		1955	19.3

The period following World War II revealed a crude birth rate for Japan equal to that of the early 1920's. This break in the trend

[10] Matsumiya, loc. cit.

[11] Irene B. Taeuber, The Population of Japan (Princeton: Princeton University Press, 1958), pp. 233 and 235.

of decrease was a temporary adjustment to the population dislocations of the war years. It is significant that the eight years from
1947-1955 showed a decrease in crude birth rate which approached
one-half.

Within this trend of national fertility decrease, analysis shows
the urban areas consistently ahead in reproductive decreases.
Though significant traces of traditional familism remain in
Japan's urban-industrialism, the forces represented by growing
city populations and industrial activity brought differentiation in
fertility patterns between rural and urban areas. Taeuber states
that

... if Japanese patriarchial familism were in fact what it should be in
theory throughout the whole of Japanese social structure, the fertility
of married women would have few relations to industrialization or
urbanization. . . . Whatever the relations between marital fertility and
environmental factors may have been in the nineteenth century, by
1925 and 1930 the primary variations in the fertility of married women
within Japan were associated with economic and social rather than
psychological factors. For each age of women, marital fertility was less
in cities of 100 thousand and over than in the remainder of the country. And for each age of women in cities of 100 thousand and over and
outside such cities, fertility was lower in 1930 than it had been in 1925.[12]

A comparison of rural and urban ratios of children 0-5 years of
age with married females in the reproductive ages 15-44 years illustrates clearly this influence of urban residence upon fertility
(Table VII-12). The rural-urban differential for 1920 showed that
the urban areas were below the *gun* population by 14.7 children
per 100 married women in the reproductive ages. The differential
for 1955 had increased to 17.1, but with both rural and urban
populations at ratios approximately 10 below their 1920 levels.
Within the urban population, increasing city size is associated
with decreasing child-woman ratios. The data for 1950 show
higher ratios for all categories, reflecting further the temporarily
high birth rates during the years immediately following the end
of World War II. Even with this fertility readjustment taking
place, the relationship between the categories for 1950 remained
similar to those of 1920 and 1955: the total urban ratio was lower

12 Taeuber, *op. cit.,* p. 264.

TABLE VII-12. Children (0-4 yrs.) Per 100 Married Women (15-44 yrs.) for Selected Population Groups, 1920-1955

Year	MEDIAN NUMBER OF CHILDREN (0-4) PER 100 MARRIED FEMALES (15-44)			City Size Group			
	Total Japan	Rural (gun)	Total Urban	Under 50,000	50-100,000	100-500,000	500,000 +
1920	93.0	97.1	82.4	84.3	83.6	80.7	68.1
1950	102.7	107.4	100.2	100.3	98.1	104.0	92.0
1955	79.8	89.6	72.5	81.0	76.4	72.1	64.1

Sources: *Reports of the 1920 Census*, Vol. IV; *Population Census of 1950*, Vol. VII; *1955 Population Census of Japan*, Vol. V.

than rural, and within the urban population increasing size was associated with decreased child-woman ratios.

It is possible that the presence in urban areas of proportionally larger numbers of the women in the younger reproductive ages, who would not have as yet completed their childbearing, could account for a significant part of the rural-urban fertility differential. There is also the possibility of differential childlessness between ever-married females in rural and urban areas. However, if a comparison is made between urban and nonurban *mothers* by age (in this way, both differential age structure and differential childlessness are held constant), the rural-urban fertility differentials remain essentially as before. Table VII-13 shows that rural-

TABLE VII-13. Number of Children ever Born Per 1000 Mothers by Age, 1950

	NUMBER OF CHILDREN PER 1000 MOTHERS		
Age of Mother	Urban (Shi)	Rural (Gun)	Rural-Urban Ratio (Rural = 100)
15-19	1,278	1,220	104.8
20-24	1,341	1,415	94.8
25-29	1,908	2,045	93.3
30-34	2,859	3,199	89.4
35-39	3,747	4,390	85.4
40-44	4,349	5,299	82.1
45-49	4,621	5,678	81.4
50-54	4,690	5,733	81.8
55-59	4,864	5,717	85.1
60+	4,979	5,434	91.6

Source: Irene B. Taeuber, *Population of Japan* (Princeton, N. J.: Princeton University Press, 1958), p. 266.

urban fertility patterns are more or less comparable through the younger reproductive ages, but that the significant differences develop in the later reproductive years. It is significant that for the ages 15-19 years, the *gun* rate per 1000 mothers is actually 58 less than that for the *shi*, while at ages 55-59 years the urban mothers per 1000 have had 853 fewer children than their rural counterparts.

SUMMARY

The purpose of this chapter has been to specify by major demographic characteristics the historical trend and magnitude of Japanese rural-urban differentiation. Analysis has revealed that from

1920 rural-urban differentiation in age-sex structure has shown a trend of decline. Using the Sorokin-Zimmerman model, we conclude that Japan had passed the peak of rural-urban differentiation prior to 1920, and that since that time there has been a consistent penetration of urban-industrialism into the nonurban areas.

Within this pattern of increasing rural-urban homogeneity, several significant trends are evident. First, population of Japan's cities has been and continues to be more heavily masculine than the rural segments, though rural and urban populations have experienced decreases both in absolute sex ratios and magnitude of rural-urban differences. Further, since 1920 the tendency toward homogeneity in urban and nonurban age-sex differences has been more heavily affected by male age structure shifts than by those of females.

Second, the consequences of a growing rural-urban homogeneity in age-sex differences are reflected in fertility patterns for the two categories. Urban-industrialization of the nation has brought a consistent trend of decline in fertility for all categories of the population. This fact further strengthens the contention that Japan since 1920 has moved along the segment of the parabolic curve of rural-urban differentiation which is beyond the peak of differences between the two population groups. Unlike age-sex differentials, however, there still remains differentiation of a significant magnitude between rural and urban fertility within the trend of over-all decline. The urban environment continues to exert pressures which both increase the age at which marriage occurs and decrease the fertility of the ever-married in contrast to rural areas. There are no indications, however, that proportions of those who never marry are increasing in urban as against rural areas. The Japanese population, therefore, can be characterized as one in which there is an increasing tendency toward a controlled population balance characteristic of the Western nations which earlier experienced urban-industrialization.

A Functional Classification of Japanese Cities | VIII

The employment composition of Japanese cities has thus far been treated largely as a whole, with little emphasis upon the characteristics of individual cities except in terms of broad size and functional groupings. The above discussion serves primarily as a background for approaching the problem of characterizing individual cities in terms of economic structure. The attempt here is to highlight differences in city industrial composition and to classify the cities into groups on this basis. Such groupings become the framework for designating variations in the demographic structure of the cities' populations which are closely associated with variations in industrial composition. Thus the aim of such an analysis is to find factors in the economic structures of Japanese cities which underlie broader demographic variations. For instance, the fact that the city of Yahata is a center for heavy industry or that the city of Izumiotsu is a textile center is of little concern in this study unless it can be shown that there are significant consequences for their respective populations in terms of composition and growth. The labor force demands for heavy industry as against textiles production result in the concentration of population of a different character in these cities. The extent to which women participate in economic activities influences marriage patterns and fertility. The degree to which household production units can be integrated into the major industrial activity of the city influences the family structure. It is in these terms that a functional classification of Japanese cities becomes demographically meaningful. It is the purpose of this chapter to classify functionally the cities of Japan and to discuss their numbers by functional groups, their sizes, geographical distribution, and historical changes in these traits insofar as the data permit.

In developing functional classifications for Japanese cities, the employment structure by industrial categories of the total urban labor force in Japan provides the base data. A particular city's functional characteristics for a given date are determined by contrasting its labor force with that of the total urban labor force for that date.[1] This method removes urban functional classification from the direct influences of shifts in census definitions of labor force activities and in the industrial structure itself.

Ratios of percentage distributions of the economically active by industrial category are calculated for each city, and these in turn are compared to ratios for the total urban population for 1920, 1930 and 1950. The resulting classification indicates the relative composition of each city with respect to the total urban structure. The classification indicates emphasis in employment composition by city rather than by specializations as such. The term specialization implies the absence of or an insignificant amount of activity in areas other than the area of specialization, and is therefore inappropriate in this context. A city classified as industrial by this method may well have a commercial, transport or services activity proportionally equal to or greater than that of the total urban population. A designation as industrial means only that the city's employment structure emphasizes industry, in that its proportion of economically active in industry is greater than that of the total urban population. The method of functional classification of cities utilized here attempts to specify the economic context of each individual city. Such economic characterizations become variables in the causal analysis of intercity variations in demographic structure and growth patterns. From the same source data a hierarchy of Japanese cities can be evolved which specifies the position of each city on the basis of the proportion of the total of a given activity the city contains. This technique is utilized only with respect to the six largest Japanese cities for selected industrial areas. The primary focus is upon explaining intercity variations in demographic composition and growth

[1] For a detailed explanation of the method of functional classification and a listing of all cities by type for 1920 through 1955, see Appendix III.

patterns for *all* Japanese cities, not upon delineating the composition and location of the total urban industrial structure as such.

Table VIII-1 shows the distribution of Japanese cities by size and functional classification for 1920, 1930, and 1950. It is to be noted that the greatest changes from 1920 to 1950 have been in the number of cities with emphases in the industrial, agricultural-fishing, and mining areas. The continued industrialization of the nation, coupled with intensified exploitation of mineral resources, accounts largely for these changes. The expansion of urban boundaries and the incorporation of small, agriculturally-oriented cities noted previously underly the increase in agricultural-fishing cities.[2] One striking trait observable in Table VIII-1 is the relative narrowness of functional emphases found in Japan's largest cities. Not until 1950 do any of the cities of 500,000 or more population have more than two functional emphases. In 1950, Tokyo added the services-administration category to a previous industrial and commercial emphasis, while Yokohama added to a transport emphasis both services-administration and industry. The majority of functionally diversified centers were less than 100,000 population prior to 1950; in 1950, six of the seven cities in this category had passed the 100,000 population level. These small cities of diversified activities serve primarily as centers for commercial servicing and administration of outlying regions, away from areas of high urbanization and industrialization. It is to be noted that these regional centers most frequently fall into the commerce-services-transport category; only one diversified center includes industry in its functional pattern in 1930: the city of Tsu, a city a short distance from the industrial

---

[2] This increase in the number of agriculturally based cities continued at an increasing rate in the census of 1955. A total of 491 cities appear in the 1955 Census of Japan; of these, 306 have 25% or more of the male labor force in extractive activities. Of these 306 cities, 111 have 45% or more in the extractive categories. Further, the percentage of *urban* labor force engaged in extractive pursuits actually increased from 15.2% to 23.4% during 1950-55, though the percentage in the *total* labor force fell from 50.1% to 33.8%. As a result, the delineation of a meaningful rural-urban dichotomy using 1955 Japanese census definitions of cities becomes hazardous, to say the least. Using new criteria, it would be possible to redefine a new urban population for Japan in 1955, but this would necessitate a deviation from the official census definitions, a practice we have avoided thus far in this analysis and one which we will continue to avoid. For this reason we have terminated the analysis of the functional classification of Japanese cities with the 1950 data.

TABLE VIII-1. Functional Classification of Japanese Cities by Size, 1920-1950

Functional Classification	1,000,000+			500-1,000,000			100-500,000			50-100,000			Under 50,000			TOTAL		
	1920	1930	1950	1920	1930	1950	1920	1930	1950	1920	1930	1950	1920	1930	1950	1920	1930	1950
Industrial	—	—	—	—	1	—	1	4	9	1	4	9	4	5	17	6	14	35
Industrial-Commercial	2	1	2	1	1	—	1	—	7	3	2	8	3	6	10	10	10	27
Industrial-Transport	—	—	—	—	—	1	1	4	1	1	6	7	3	1	5	5	11	14
Industrial Services	—	—	1	—	—	—	1	—	—	3	—	3	—	1	—	4	1	3
Commercial	—	1	1	1	—	—	—	—	6	2	3	4	4	3	5	6	7	16
Commercial-Transport	—	—	—	—	—	—	3	2	11	2	2	3	3	6	6	9	10	20
Commercial-Services	—	—	—	1	2	—	—	1	5	3	5	12	7	4	4	10	10	21
Transport	—	—	—	1	2	—	—	1	4	2	1	1	2	—	1	5	4	6
Transport-Services	—	—	—	—	—	—	2	3	7	—	4	6	—	1	2	2	8	15
Services	—	—	—	—	—	—	2	7	—	5	7	5	8	5	—	15	19	5
Agricultural	—	—	—	—	—	—	—	—	2	1	2	19	—	—	46	—	2	67
Mining	—	—	—	—	—	—	—	—	2	1	2	8	—	—	3	1	2	10
Comm-Serv-Trans	—	—	—	—	—	—	—	—	6	1	4	—	6	4	1	7	8	7
Indus-Comm-Trans	—	—	1	—	—	—	—	—	—	—	—	—	—	1	—	—	1	—
Indus-Comm-Serv	—	—	—	—	—	1	—	—	—	—	—	—	1	1	—	1	1	1
Indus-Trans-Serv	—	—	—	—	—	—	—	—	—	—	—	—	—	—	—	—	—	1
TOTAL	2	2	4	3	4	2	11	22	60	24	42	85	41	37	97	81	107	248

^a Size as of census date.

Sources: *Reports of 1920 Census*, Vol. IV, pt. B, Table 1-4 from prefectural volumes. *Reports of 1930 Census*, Vol. IV, pt. 4, Table 18 from prefectural volumes. *Population Census of 1950*, Vol. VII, Table 11 from prefectural volumes.

center of Nagoya. By 1950, however, even this exception disappeared as Tsu became a commercial-services center.

In geographical distribution, industrial emphases in urban employment structures follow closely the pattern of urbanization as a whole. That is, the areas of highest levels of urban residence are also those containing most of the cities with industry as an area of emphasis. Figure VIII-1 and its inserts show the location of cities in 1950 by size and functional emphasis. It is to be noted that the region of high urbanization from the Tokyo-Yokohama

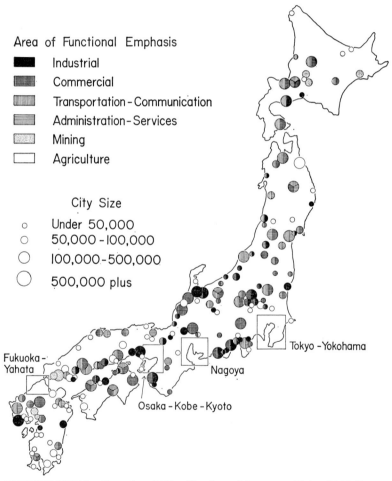

FIGURE VIII-1: Functional Classification of Japanese Cities, 1950 (Source: *Population Census of 1950*, Vol. VII, Table 11 in prefectural volumes)

area southwestward through the Nagoya, Osaka, Hiroshima, and Fukuoka areas contains the majority of Japan's industrial cities. Outside this region of high urbanization and industrialization, the most frequent type of city is that with a commercial or commercial-transport emphasis, e.g., Kanazawa, Kofu, Gifu, Utsunomiya, and Aomori. In addition, the regional center can be clearly seen in Matsuyama, Kochi, and Takamatsu on the southern island of Shikoku, Kagoshima in Kyushu, Sapporo in Hokkaido, and Morioka in northern Honshu. Agricultural cities are to be found throughout the whole nation; the only area in which this type of city becomes numerically dominant is in the southern half of Kyushu.

The Japanese pattern of urban functional distribution has

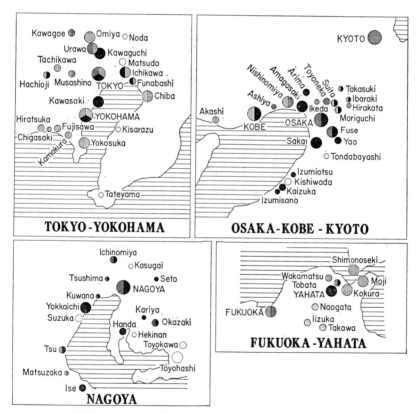

FIGURE VIII-1 (continued): Functional Classification of Japanese Cities, 1950

significant points of similarity to the patterns found in Western Europe and the United States. All the great urban centers in these areas have dominant services-administration functions. Though the "Big Six" cities of Japan show some diversification in function, each of them in 1950 had more than 50 per cent of total nonagricultural labor force in services-administration. This is the criterion utilized by William-Olsson to classify the great cities of Western Europe as "service centers" (e.g., London, Paris, Amsterdam, Rome).[3] The dispersed pattern of small service centers away from areas of high urban-industrialization observed for Japan appears in the European urban functional structure as well. The smaller cities showing specializations in the manufacturing categories are clustered about the larger cities. The William-Olsson maps show clearly, for England and Wales, the specialization in textiles of the smaller cities to the north and east of Manchester, specializations in metals of those around Birmingham, and the heavy concentration of mining-metals cities in the Ruhr around the city of Essen.[4] In the United States, 88.7 per cent of all urban places specializing in manufacturing are in the region north of the Ohio and east of the Mississippi River. The most frequent type of city outside this region is the diversified services-trade center.[5]

In the location of urban industrial functions, the Japanese pattern conforms in major respects to the locational theories evolved from analysis of Western industrial history. That is to say, industrial expansion and the location of new industries tend to concentrate. The economies inherent in the availability of an industrial labor force and sources of raw materials or outlets for finished products make attractive the expansion of existing facilities and the location of new industrial units in already industrialized areas. The paucity of mineral resources within the Japanese home islands has meant that relatively little impetus

3 W. William-Olsson, *Economic Map of Europe* (Stockholm: Generalstabens Litografiska Anstalt, 1953); see also the *Report of the Royal Commission on the Distribution of Industrial Population* (London: His Majesty's Stationery Office, 1940).

4 *Ibid.*

5 Otis D. Duncan and Albert J. Reiss, Jr., *Social Characteristics of Urban and Rural Communities, 1950* (New York: John Wiley and Sons, Inc., 1956), pp. 215-252; Gunnar Alexandersson, *The Industrial Structure of American Cities* (Lincoln, Nebraska: The University of Nebraska Press, 1956).

for industry has existed outside traditional large city locations. Other than the development centered around the northern Kyushu mineral sources, and, to a lesser degree, in central Hokkaido and northwestern Honshu, modern industrial development has remained in the traditional handicraft regions around Tokyo, Nagoya, and Osaka.

Industrial Cities: The cities of Japan which contain emphases in the industrial area fall roughly into two groups. The first group is composed of the large, functionally diversified centers which contain a heavier commitment of male labor force to industry than that of the total urban male labor force.

These large centers are not, however, "specialized" in industry, for they combine emphases in other areas with their industrial commitments. Table VIII-1 has shown that in 1950 no city of 500,000 or more population had an industrial commitment alone. However, such cities, illustrated by Tokyo and Osaka, contain by far the largest concentrations of the industrially employed in Japan. The extent to which industrial activities are concentrated in Japan's largest cities is shown in Table VIII-2. The proportion of industrially employed in the six largest cities of Japan is approximately twice that of their proportion of total employed population. Within the industrial category itself, the proportion of total employed which is in the "Big Six" cities in heavy industries is around one-fourth for both 1930 and 1950. In precision instrument and electrical machinery production, the proportions are over one-half by 1950. Only in textiles and in lumber and wood manufacture do the large centers tend to show reduced concentrations. Osaka and Kyoto are the exceptions in commitment to textiles. Both cities have larger proportions of those employed in textiles than they have of the total Japanese labor force. Osaka's emphasis upon the heavy industries greatly overshadows her textile activity; the city has therefore maintained an industrial classification for the whole 1920-50 period. Kyoto, where textiles is the major industrial commitment, had lost industrial classification by 1950—the only one of the "Big Six" cities lacking an industrial emphasis at this time.

The second group, relatively small cities, show industrial emphases which are more genuinely "specialized" in one or a group of closely related industrial activities. Again, from Table VIII-1

TABLE VIII-2. Percentage of Total Industrial Labor Force Active in Japan's "Big Six" Cities, 1930-1950

Manufacturing Category[a]	PERCENTAGE OF TOTAL JAPANESE INDUSTRIALLY EMPLOYED															
	Tokyo		Yokohama		Kyoto		Osaka		Kobe		Nagoya		Total "6"		Total Japan	
	1930	1950	1930	1950	1930	1950	1930	1950	1930	1950	1930	1950	1930	1950	1930	1950
Textiles	1.5	3.1	0.6	0.4	4.5	4.3	4.6	2.1	0.7	0.4	2.7	1.1	14.6	11.4	100.0	100.0
Apparel	11.0	15.2	1.5	2.2	2.0	2.7	11.1	8.0	1.8	0.7	3.4	3.5	30.8	32.3	100.0	100.0
Food Processing	4.2	8.3	1.3	1.3	1.0	1.7	4.2	3.1	1.2	1.1	1.9	2.5	13.8	18.0	100.0	100.0
Ceramics	2.7	6.2	0.8	1.3	1.6	1.3	8.2	4.2	0.5	0.3	5.5	4.8	19.3	18.1	100.0	100.0
Chemicals	4.3	13.1	1.9	1.8	0.8	1.3	15.0	6.3	8.5	0.8	1.7	1.5	32.2	24.8	100.0	100.0
Paper-Printing	16.4	—	1.2	—	3.0	—	11.9	—	1.8	—	2.6	—	36.9	—	100.0	—
Paper	—	12.7	—	0.5	—	1.7	—	5.3	—	0.3	—	1.9	—	22.4	—	100.0
Printing	—	32.4	—	1.2	—	2.6	—	6.9	—	1.1	—	2.9	—	47.1	—	100.0
Wood Products	4.8	—	1.1	—	1.2	—	5.1	—	1.2	—	3.2	—	16.6	—	100.0	—
Lumber-Wood	—	3.2	—	0.4	—	0.9	—	1.7	—	0.4	—	1.8	—	8.4	—	100.0
Furniture	—	10.1	—	1.3	—	1.3	—	3.1	—	0.7	—	2.6	—	19.1	—	100.0
Precision Insts.	17.3	39.6	1.7	1.4	2.9	4.5	12.9	4.9	1.5	0.6	5.8	4.3	42.1	55.3	100.0	100.0
Machinery	9.3	—	2.1	—	1.6	—	14.7	—	3.6	—	4.0	—	35.3	—	100.0	—
Machinery, Gen'l	—	15.6	—	2.5	—	2.3	—	8.8	—	2.1	—	5.3	—	36.6	—	100.0
Machinery, Elec.	—	26.2	—	6.1	—	3.2	—	6.2	—	1.9	—	2.8	—	46.4	—	100.0
Transportation Eq.	4.7	11.2	4.8	6.6	0.4	0.5	9.7	5.5	10.6	5.6	5.3	4.0	35.5	33.4	100.0	100.0
Metals	6.5	—	1.5	—	1.4	—	14.3	—	2.7	—	2.1	—	28.5	—	100.0	—
Primary Metals	—	9.0	—	2.5	—	0.9	—	6.3	—	3.6	—	2.2	—	24.5	—	100.0
Fabricated Mets.	—	20.4	—	1.7	—	1.5	—	11.2	—	1.0	—	2.9	—	38.7	—	100.0
Construction	5.1	9.6	1.7	1.6	1.6	1.4	4.3	3.3	1.3	1.3	1.6	1.6	15.6	18.8	100.0	100.0
Leather-Bone	10.3	33.9	0.6	1.0	0.9	1.9	29.8	10.2	1.2	1.4	2.0	2.7	44.8	51.1	100.0	100.0
Salt	0.1	—	0.1	—	—	—	—	—	—	—	—	—	0.2	—	100.0	—
Rubber	—	17.9	—	1.6	—	0.6	—	7.9	—	11.8	—	1.0	—	40.4	—	100.0
Tobacco	—	7.2	—	0.1	—	4.2	—	0.7	—	0.2	—	1.8	—	14.2	—	100.0
Other	14.1	20.7	1.0	0.8	4.9	2.3	15.4	6.9	1.7	0.8	4.5	3.1	41.2	34.6	100.0	100.0
Emp'd in Mfg.	5.4	11.1	1.4	1.7	2.3	2.0	7.5	4.6	1.9	1.4	2.8	2.4	21.3	23.6	100.0	100.0
Total Employed	3.4	5.7	0.8	1.0	1.2	1.1	3.7	2.1	1.1	0.8	1.3	1.1	1.5	11.8	100.0	100.0
Total Population	3.2	6.5	1.0	1.1	1.2	1.3	3.8	2.4	1.2	0.9	1.4	1.2	11.8	13.4	100.0	100.0

a Manufacturing categories vary in census reports of 1930 and 1950. No entry for a given date indicates that those employed in this category are included elsewhere at that census date.

Sources: Reports of 1930 Census, Vol. IV, pt. 4, Table 18 from prefectural volumes. Population Census of 1950, Vol. VII, Table 11 from prefectural volumes.

it is to be noted that 17 of the 35 cities which had emphases in the industrial area alone are below the 50,000 population level. Further, these same seventeen cities are more than half the number of cities of less than 50,000 population which have industry either alone or in combination as an employment emphasis.

Not only city size but the type of industrial activity carried on influences the demographic structure of Japan's industrial cities. For instance, an emphasis in textiles with its essentially rural orientation and its traditional utilization of a female labor force contrasts strongly with heavy industry. The continuum of Japanese industrial activity can be broken into three major groups which emphasize such contrasts: textiles, heavy industry, and all other industries. The eighty-one cities with an industrial emphasis either alone or in combination in 1950 are plotted on a three-dimensional graph in Figure VIII-2. The fifteen cities with 20 per cent or more of the male industrial labor force in textiles and less than 30 per cent in heavy industry are categorized as textile cities. The thirty-two cities with 30 per cent or more of the male labor force in heavy industry and less than 20 per cent in textiles form the heavy industry city category. The remaining thirty-four cities fall into the "other industries" group.

The heavy industry cities tend to be larger in size than either textile or other industry centers (Table VIII-3). Further, these cities are heavily concentrated in the two regions historically dominant in urbanization, the Tokyo-Yokohama and Osaka-Kobe areas. These two areas account for sixteen of the thirty-one heavy industry cities (seven in Tokyo and Yokohama prefectures and eleven in the prefectures of Osaka and Kobe). The textile centers cluster first in the three prefectures just north of Tokyo (Saitama, Tochigi, and Gumma) and in the Nagoya-Shizuoka area. These two regions contain nine of the sixteen textile centers. Cities with emphases in the miscellaneous industry category show a more diversified locational pattern than either textile or heavy industry centers. The only region which indicates a concentration is that composed of the Aichi and Shizuoka prefectures which contain seven of the thirty-four miscellaneous industry centers. Considered as a whole, urban industrial activity is centered in three regions: Tokyo-Yokohama, Osaka-Kobe, and Nagoya. These three areas contain thirty-six (44.4 per cent) of Japan's eighty-one cities containing industrial emphases.

Commercial Cities: Sixteen of Japan's 248 cities in 1950 showed an employment composition emphasis in the single area of commerce. In geographical distribution, these cities tend to be located away from regions of high industrialization and urbanization (see Figure VIII-1 and its inserts). Kyoto is the largest of these sixteen cities, with a population of 1.1 million in 1950. The remaining fifteen cities are relatively small (median size: 86,005) and show comparatively low rates of growth.

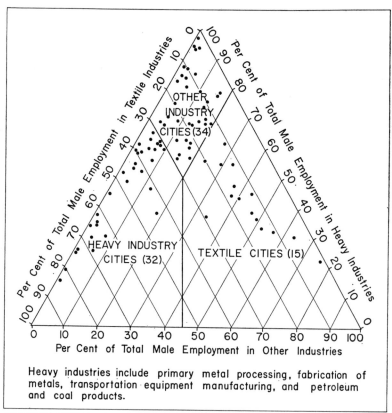

FIGURE VIII-2: Japanese Industrial Cities, 1950 (Source: *Population Census of 1950*, Vol. VII, Table 11 in prefectural volumes)

In the main, the larger commercial cities tend to be old cities which even during the Tokugawa period or earlier served as trade centers. Kyoto and Kanazawa, as well as Kofu, Gifu, and

Fukui, show this pattern clearly. These primarily commercial centers have not been unaffected by the industrialization of the nation, but their location in areas peripheral to industrial developments have tended to intensify and expand their older trade-commerce activities rather than generate new functions.

TABLE VIII-3. Japanese Industrial Cities by Size and Type of Industry, 1950.

		NUMBER OF CITIES BY SIZE GROUP					
Industrial Type	Total	Under 50,000	50- 100,000	100- 500,000	500- 1,000,000	Over 1,000,000	Median Size
Heavy Industry	32	11	6	11	2	2	88,472
Textiles-Apparel	15	5	8	2	—	—	54,297
Other Industries	34	15	14	4	—	1	55,669
TOTAL	81	31	28	17	2	3	58,053

Source: *Population Census of 1950*, Vol. VII, Table 11 from prefectural volumes.

Though the cities with exclusive commercial emphases are located outside the regions of highest urban-industrialism, the major portion of Japanese commercial activities is carried on in these regions. As with industrial activity, the great cities of Japan dominate commercial activity. Of Japan's six largest cities, all except Yokohama and Kobe contained commercial emphases in 1950. The "Big Six" cities contain an even higher proportion of Japan's total employed in commerce (25.6 per cent in 1950) than that employed in industry (23.2 per cent). Table VIII-4 shows the proportion of those employed in commercial activities in each of the "Big Six" cities. Within the pattern of the big city dominance, Tokyo overshadows the other large cities; over one-half of those employed in each category are active in the city of Tokyo.

Transport-Communication and Services-Administration Cities: In Japanese cities an emphasis in the areas of services-administration or transportation-communication is most frequently found in combination with either or both an industrial or commercial emphasis. Of the 93 cities which in 1950 contained emphasis in transport or services only eleven (five in services and six in transport) had an emphasis in either area exclusively. These eleven cities are genuinely specialized cities in their respective categories.

Four of the six cities specializing in transport are located in

TABLE VIII-4. Proportion of Japan's Commercial Labor Force Active in the "Big Six" Cities, 1950

Commercial Activity	PERCENTAGE OF EMPLOYED IN TOTAL JAPAN							Total "6"	Total Japan
	Tokyo	Yokohama	Kobe	Osaka	Nagoya	Kyoto			
Finance	17.9	1.7	2.2	4.7	2.8	2.9		32.2	100.0
Banking	15.8	1.5	2.3	4.5	2.6	2.8		29.5	100.0
Insurance	21.1	2.4	2.4	3.5	2.4	3.3		35.1	100.0
Real Estate	38.5	2.0	3.5	16.7	3.0	3.3		67.0	100.0
Wholesale Trade	17.0	1.5	2.1	7.7	3.9	3.1		35.3	100.0
Retail Trade	11.3	1.5	1.4	4.4	2.2	2.2		23.0	100.0
Total Commerce	12.6	1.5	1.6	4.9	2.6	2.4		25.6	100.0
Total Population	6.5	1.1	0.9	2.4	1.2	1.3		13.4	100.0
Total Labor Force	5.7	1.0	0.8	2.1	1.1	1.1		11.8	100.0

Source: *Population Census of 1950,* Vol. VII, Table 11 from prefectural volumes.

northern Kyushu and at the southern tip of Honshu, i.e., Shimo-noseki, Wakamatsu, Moji, and Kokura. The necessity of moving the products of one of the major areas of heavy industry centered in Yahata northward to the processing plants in the Tokyo, Osaka, and Nagoya areas brought these transport centers into existence early in Japan's industrialization. All four cities were incorporated by 1920, and all four have also, since 1920, had an emphasis upon transport in their respective employment compositions. The other two transport cities, Omiya and Rumoi, were incorporated during the 1930's. Omiya is the railroad marshalling center just north of Tokyo which serves as the rail gateway to the Tokyo-Yokohama region for the whole of northern Honshu and Hokkaido. Rumoi is the western Hokkaido seaport serving as outlet for the mineral resources of central Hokkaido.

The five cities with an exclusive services-administration emphasis are, first, relatively small (between 50,000 and 100,000 population in 1950); and second, in location they are peripheral to large metropolitan areas. Three of the five (Tachikawa, Fujisawa and Haratsuka) are within or contiguous with the Tokyo-Yokohama metropolitan area. The remaining two (Maizuru to the northwest of Kyoto, and the city of Nara) are located in regions dominated by Kyoto and Osaka. The services-administration emphasis in these cities is based upon either a residential suburban relationship to the metropolitan center, i.e., Tachikawa, or a recreational-tourism function, i.e., Hiratsuka, and to some extent Nara.

Mining Cities: The cities showing an employment emphasis in the area of mining are as a group relatively new cities. Omuta of Fukuoka Prefecture was incorporated in 1917 and for 1920, 1930, and 1950 falls into the mining category. Ube of Yamaguchi Prefecture, incorporated in 1922, has likewise maintained a mining emphasis since its incorporation. Kushiro in Hokkaido was incorporated in 1920, but only in 1950 does its employment structure show a functional emphasis in mining. Of the remaining seven mining cities, two were incorporated in the 1930's and five since 1940.

The concentration of Japan's mineral resources in two areas, Hokkaido and northern Kyushu-southern Honshu, means that her mining cities are found exclusively within these regions; Hokkaido contains three of the ten mining centers of 1950 and northern Kyushu-southern Honshu has seven. In size, these centers reflect the recency of their incorporation as well as the limited growth impetus of mining; three of the mining cities were under 50,000 population in 1950 and the remaining seven were all under 100,000.

Agricultural-Fishing Cities: The city with an emphasis in agriculture-fishing is a recent phenomenon in Japanese urban structure. In 1920, no city had more than 25 per cent of its male labor force in agriculture or fishing; by 1930 only two cities fell into this category (Hachinoe in Akita Prefecture and Kushiro in Hokkaido) and both these cities were fishing rather than farming centers. From 1930 to 1950, and especially during the 1940's, requirements for city incorporation were lowered, with the result that a large number of small, essentially rural agglomerations were designated as cities. In the 1950 census, 67 cities qualify as agricultural cities in that they have 25 per cent or more of their male labor force in agriculture, fishing, or forestry. Of these 67 cities, eight were cities which in 1920 or 1930 classifications had functional emphases in nonagricultural areas. In analyzing the agricultural cities the following three groups are meaningful: 1) the farming community, 2) the fishing center, and 3) cities which show a pre-1950 functional emphasis in nonagricultural areas. The eight cities which constitute the third group, agricultural cities with previous nonagricultural functional emphases, are the largest and oldest of the agricultural centers of 1950. All eight cities were incorporated by 1930; Toyohashi, the oldest, was incorporated as early as 1906. The movement of these cities into the agricultural category in the 1950 census is based upon one or a combination of two factors: major boundary expansions which brought into the city's employment structure large numbers of agriculturally employed or the failure of the city's major industrial activity, most frequently textiles. Table VIII-5 lists the eight cities in this group, their pre-1950 functional classifications, and the important factors affecting their 1950 classifications. The city of Kishiwada (Osaka Prefecture), for example, underwent a boundary change in February, 1945 which more than doubled

TABLE VIII-5. Japanese Agricultural Cities of 1950 Which Show Previous Nonagricultural Functional Emphases

City	1950 Population	FUNCTIONAL CLASSIFICATION[a]			Major Economic or Boundary Changes
		1920	1930	1950	
Toyohashi	145,855	CS	CS	A	Loss of textile industry
Kishiwada	98,821	—	IT	A	February, 1945 major boundary change
Yamaguchi	77,759	—	S	A	April, 1944 major boundary change
Miyakanojo	75,114	—	IC	A	April, 1943 major boundary change; loss of textile industry
Uwajima	56,570	—	CT	A	Loss of textile industry
Kurashiki	53,301	—	IC	A	February, 1941 major boundary change
Tsuyama	51,645	—	C	A	January, 1944 major boundary change
Nakatsu	51,410	—	IC	A	August, 1943 major boundary change

[a] I = industrial; C = commercial; S = services; T = transport; A = agricultural.

Source: *Population Census of 1950*, Vol. VII, Table 1 of prefectural volumes.

its population. The textile industry, which employed 37.4 per cent of its male and 90.4 per cent of its female industrially employed labor force in 1930, still accounted for 27.5 per cent of its male and 79.8 per cent of its female industrial labor force in 1950. The 1950 boundaries, however, included large areas peripheral to the city which contained heavy agricultural commitments resulting in the agricultural emphasis for the total city. Much the same is true of the textile centers of Nakatsu in Oita Prefecture and Kurashiki and Tsuyama in Okayama Prefecture. A loss or failure of textile activity in Toyohashi, Yamaguchi, Uwajima and the inability of these cities to create nonagricul-

TABLE VIII-6. Major Industrial Employment in Japan's Agricultural-Fishing Cities, 1950

Industry[a]	Number of Cities	Agricultural-Fishing Cities, 1950
Textiles	9	Nagahama, Saijo, Komatsu, Sano, Ayabe, Kishiwada, Sumoto, Izumo
Food Processing	8	Choshi, Noda, Abashiri, Wakkanai, Makurazaki, Usuki, Yawatahama, Toyokawa
Lumber	4	Hita, Kobayashi, Hitoyoshi, Toyooka
Chemicals	3	Minamata, Naruto, Tokuyama
Ceramics	2	Hekinan, Nanao
Paper	1	Nichinan

[a] Industries in which 20% or more of the male industrially employed were active in 1950.

Source: *Population Census of 1950*, Vol. VII, Table 11 from prefectural volumes.

tural opportunities in other areas for the labor force accounts largely for the classification of these centers as agricultural in 1950. The 1950 farming and fishing centers tend to be new cities of relatively small size. The farming city of Kumagaya (65,487 population) and the fishing center of Hachinoe (104,335 population) are the largest cities in their respective categories.

The agricultural or fishing cities are not totally lacking in non-agricultural activities. Each of these cities has a core population which is urban in its employment structure. Table VIII-6 shows the twenty-seven agricultural-fishing cities which in 1950 had 20 per cent or more of their male labor force in a single industrial area. It is significant that heavy industry as an activity associated with the agricultural-fishing city is absent. The most frequent industrial emphasis in these cities is textiles, closely followed by food processing. Concerned predominantly with the canning of marine products, food processing is the usual industrial activity of the Japanese fishing center. For example, Choshi (Chiba Prefecture) had 49.7 per cent of its male and 75.2 per cent of its female industrially employed in food processing in 1950; at the same time Abashiri in Hokkaido had 39.3 per cent of its male and 80.8 per cent of its female industrial labor force in this category.

In summary, the Japanese cities which possess agricultural or fishing emphases in their employment structures as a whole tend to be relatively new and small cities. The appearance of this type of urban agglomeration in modern Japanese urban structure is to some extent a reflection of the administrative difficulties in keeping abreast of an expanding urban way of life. These areas all contain an essentially urban core, the population of which is functionally urban. The size requirements for incorporation make necessary the pushing of boundaries beyond this core, and hence the anomaly of an "agricultural city." The alternative of not incorporating the area as urban would in turn place the whole of the population in a rural classification.

SUMMARY

This chapter has served to specify the existence of significant functional differentiation among Japanese cities. These differences in functional emphasis are associated with both size of city and location. The industrial city tends to be exclusively a part of the areas of highest urban concentration, usually the great metropolitan settlements. Though not exclusively industrial, the great cities of Japan have industrial emphases within their employment structure, e.g., Tokyo, Osaka. The exclusively industrial cities are smaller in size, but most frequently they are located within the boundaries of the influence of the great cities, e.g., Kawasaki, Amagasaki, Yao. Cities with commercial emphases in combination with industrial emphases are also located within the highly urbanized regions, but this category is supplemented by outlying trade centers, whose functional base is exclusively commercial. The administrative-services center appears most frequently as a city outside the areas of industrial development and extensive urbanization; when this emphasis is present in the large metropolitan area it is as the small, residential suburb for the larger central city. Emphases in transportation-communications and mining are in genuinely specialized cities located at key transportation bridges or at mineral source locations.

Urban Growth and Demographic Differentials by Functional Classification | IX

It is the task of the present chapter to specify the relationship of nonagricultural activity and urban growth for individual cities according to differential functional emphases. The underlying assumption is that although urbanization varies positively with nonagricultural activities, the relationship is qualified by the nature of the nonagricultural activity. That is, because of specific labor force demands, heavy industry, textile production, commerce, or services-administration are each associated with a unique pattern of urban structure and growth. The growth rates and age/sex characteristics of the employed for cities categorized by functional emphases serve as indices bearing out this assumption.

TRENDS OF URBAN GROWTH BY FUNCTIONAL CLASSIFICATION

In general, the Japanese cities showing industrial emphases during the 1920-55 period also show the highest rates of population increase. Sixty-six of the eighty-one cities incorporated by 1920 have consistently had one or more areas of functional emphasis during the period 1920-1950. The sixteen cities with a consistent industrial emphasis have a median average annual rate of increase (1920-55) of 2.8 per cent. Consistent services-administration and transportation-communication emphases show median growth rates of 2.4 per cent each. The lowest rate (1.9 per cent) is present in cities with a commercial emphasis throughout the thirty-year period.

Industry as an urbanizing force in Japan during the 1920-55 period is, however, qualified by locational factors. Significantly, of the five cities with average annual rates of change 1920-55 of 5.0 per cent or more (Sapporo, Amagasaki, Nagoya, Fukuoka, and Takamatsu in Shikoku), only two have industrial emphases. Nagoya and Amagasaki, the two cities with industrial emphases, have two characteristics in common: both fall within areas historically high in urbanization, and both have more than one-third of their male industrial labor force in heavy industries. In contrast, Sapporo and Takamatsu are regional administrative centers serving areas traditionally rural in character. Fukuoka, though located near Kyushu's heavy industry centered in Yahata, is predominantly a regional administration and trade center in function. These illustrative growth patterns indicate that it is largely heavy industry carried on either within large cities or in their satellite areas that underlies the association of industrial functions with urban growth. The urbanizing force inherent in a concentration of commerce and services-administration is most effective in relatively isolated areas which constitute homogeneous regions.

Growth patterns for the 248 cities incorporated by 1950 for the 1950-55 period show industry still slightly ahead of commerce as a force in urban growth, but both are behind transport and services-administration (Table IX-1). The increasing role of services-administration and transport in urbanization is a reflection of

TABLE IX-1. Rates of Growth for Japan's Cities by Functional Classification, 1950-1955

Functional Classification[a]	Median Average Annual Rate of Growth, 1950-55[b] (%)
Transport-Communications	2.2
Administration-Services	2.1
Manufacturing	1.8
Commerce	1.7
Mining	1.2
Agriculture-Fishing	1.1
TOTAL	1.8

[a] All cities with the given emphasis alone or in combination.
[b] Population growth within 1955 boundaries.

Sources: *Population Census of 1950*, Vol. VII, Table 1 from prefectural volumes. *1955 Census of Population of Japan*, Vol. I, Table 12.

maturation in the Japanese economic structure as a whole. The early phase of industrialization emphasizes basic production in the fields of construction and manufacturing. Once these areas become effectively established they create a need for increasingly complex administrative and service activities, e.g., banking and insurance, transport-communication, and wholesale trading units.

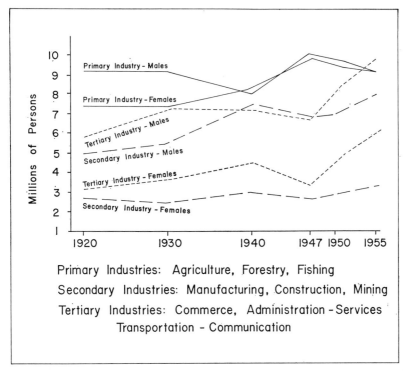

FIGURE IX-1: Employment by Three Industrial Categories, 1920-1955 (Source: *1955 Population Census of Japan*, Vol. II, pt. 2, Introduction)

Until roughly the beginning of World War II, and especially from 1920 onward, the Japanese economy can be characterized as predominantly in the first phase of industrialization. Traits associated with a matured industrialization, that is, one in which administrative functions tend to rise at the expense of productive functions, are evident in post-World War II Japan. Figure IX-1 shows a portion of the evidence for this conclusion. The slope of the curve for both male and female employment in the "tertiary" industries is significantly higher than that of the "secondary" industries from 1947 onward. The intense concern for expanding basic industrial productivity preceding World War II is revealed in the reverse of this relationship from 1930 to 1940.

As dominant foci of the industrialization process, cities reflect in their economic structures the maturation of the national economy. As an illustration of this point, the Japanese cities in 1950 with emphases in employment composition in a single area ranked by functional category (Table IX-2) show the "tertiary" industries of transport and services-administration dominant as factors in urban growth. The broad category commerce is lowest largely because of the inclusion of large numbers of owner-operated household commercial establishments. If the commercial activities associated with urban-industrialism alone are considered, their role in city growth is more clearly seen. For instance, Table IX-3 shows selected aspects of growth for Tokyo and Osaka for 1950-55. It is to be noted from this table that the increases in wholesale trade and banking-insurance-real estate are the greatest increases in any category for both cities. Retail trade, which is dominated by the traditional household commercial unit, shows an increase less than that for the total labor force in both cities.

TABLE IX-2. Growth of Japanese Cities With Single Functional Emphases, 1950-55

Functional Classification[a]	Number of Cities	Median Average Annual Rate of Growth, 1950-1955 (%)[b]
Transport-Communications	6	2.9
Administration-Services	5	2.5
Manufacturing	35	2.0
Commerce	16	1.5

a Cities with functional emphases in given area alone.
b Population growth within 1955 boundaries.

Sources: *Population Census of 1950*, Vol. VII. Table 11 from prefectural volumes. *1955 Census of Population of Japan*, Vol. I, Table 12.

The eight cities with 5.0 per cent or more average annual increase 1950-55 (Table IX-4) further illustrate in their functional emphases the importance of "tertiary" activities in recent urban growth. Six of these cities have a combination of commercial,

TABLE IX-3. Growth and Changes in Employment Composition of Tokyo and Osaka, 1950-55

Population and Labor Force	Per Cent Change 1950-55	
	Tokyo	Osaka
Total Population	29.4	26.4
Total Labor Force	44.4	42.4
Total Employed in		
Manufacturing	51.8	49.2
Construction	26.8	28.1
Total Employed in		
Wholesale Trade	73.8	82.1
Retail Trade	41.9	30.2
Banking, Insurance, Real Estate	78.0	86.3
Transportation, Communications	32.1	4.3
Total Employed in Services	65.3	61.4
Total Employed in Government	19.8	11.7

Sources: *Population Census of 1950*, Vol. VII, pts. 13 and 27, Table 11. *1955 Census of Population of Japan*, Vol. II, pt. 2, Table 5.

services, or transport emphases as against four for industry alone or in combination. Another significant dimension of post-World War II urbanization can be observed from this table. Except for the two cities located in Hokkaido (Obihiro and Tomakomai), the fastest growing cities in the 1950-55 period were either great urban centers (Tokyo, Osaka) or their satellite cities. Musashino

TABLE IX-4. Growth and Functional Classification of Japan's Fastest Growing Cities, 1950-55

City	Population (1955)	Average Annual % Change, 1950-55[a]	Functional Classification
Kawasaki	445,520	7.9	Industrial
Obihiro	70,027	7.0	Commercial-Transport
Tomakomai	51,319	6.2	Industrial
Musashino	94,948	6.0	Commercial-Service
Tokyo	6,969,104	5.9	Industrial-Commercial-Service
Osaka	2,547,316	5.3	Industrial-Commercial
Nishinomiya	210,179	5.0	Commercial-Transport
Toyonaka	127,678	5.0	Commercial

[a] Population growth within 1955 boundaries.

Sources: *Population Census of 1950*, Vol. VII, Table 1 from prefectural volumes. *1955 Census of Population of Japan*, Vol. I, Table 11.

and Kawasaki both have boundaries contiguous to the city of Tokyo; Nishinomiya and Toyonaka are parts of the Greater Osaka area. These growth patterns represent partially a recouping of population losses by large cities during World War II. The increases are, however, more than merely returns to prewar population levels. The concentration of population in large cities and their environs reflects the process of metropolitanization in Japan's urban structure.

Industrial Cities: The association of industry with high rates of urban growth is itself further qualified by the nature of the industrial activity. Utilizing the industrial classification of heavy, textiles, and other, Table IX-5 specifies this qualification. Size of

TABLE IX-5. Growth of Japanese Industrial Cities by Size and Industrial Type, 1950-1955

Industrial Type	Number of Cities	MEDIAN AVERAGE ANNUAL RATE OF GROWTH, 1950-55					
		Under 50,000	50-100,000	100-500,000	500-1,000,000	Over 1,000,000	Total
Heavy Industry	32	0.9	2.2	3.6	4.1	5.0	2.3
Textiles-Apparel	15	0.8	2.0	2.0	—	—	0.9
Other Industry	34	1.6	2.0	2.2	—	5.9	1.6
TOTAL	81	1.4	2.0	3.0	4.1	5.3	1.8

Sources: *Population Census of 1950*, Vol. VII, Table 11 from prefectural volumes. *1955 Population Census of Japan*, Vol. I, Table 12.

city, in addition, influences these differential growth rates in that the over-all pattern from 1920 to 1955 was one in which the larger the industrial city the faster was its rate of increase. Within this broad pattern the cities emphasizing heavy industry led the other two categories with a median of 2.3 per cent average annual rate of growth, a median more than twice that of the textile centers[1] and half again as great as that for the "other" industry cities.

[1] The association of the textile industry with low city growth rates noted in Japan deserves a special comment since this association is in striking contrast to that in the United States and England. Alexandersson finds that the cities specializing in textiles in the United States were the fastest growing of all cities in the decade 1940-50. The United States textile industry has been historically an urban-located activity and has maintained its urban orientation. The early textile centers of New England grew as mill towns which depended upon raw materials as imports; the impetus for urbanization here was the expansion of urban textile production. The growth of cities in England around mechanized production of textiles, dependent

This three-way classification of industrial cities also yields significant variations in demographic characteristics. At this point the concern is with demographic traits of the employed population only, but analyses of age/sex structure and fertility patterns for the total urban population reveal trends which closely approximate the variations emphasized here. Specifically, the extent to which women are economically active and the level of agricultural activity are vital factors in this respect. Table IX-6 shows indices of these factors for the three categories of industrial cities. In all three indices the rurality of the employment structure of textile centers is evident. Though the sex ratio of total employed in textile centers is higher than that of the total rural, the sex

TABLE IX-6. Selected Indices of Employment Composition for Japan's Industrial Cities, 1950

Industrial Type	Number of Cities	Median Sex Ratio Employed Population	Median Sex Ratio Industrially Emp'd	Median Percentage Male Labor Force in Agriculture
Heavy Industry	32	259.4	439.3	9.4
Textiles-Apparel	15	156.2	129.7	15.3
Other Industries	34	192.2	280.7	14.9
Total Urban	248	222.2	362.8	11.0
Total Rural	—	135.6	279.0	57.4

Source: *Population Census of 1950*, Vol. VII, Table 11 from prefectural volumes.

ratio of industrially employed is less than half that of the total rural. The percentage of males in agricultural pursuits in textile centers is 4.3 percentage points higher than that of the urban male population. The cities emphasizing miscellaneous industries are behind the total urban population, but ahead of the total rural in each index cited in Table IX-6. The heavy industry cities are consistently above the total urban in all respects.

The cities of Kiryu (Gumma Prefecture) and Kaizuka (Osaka Prefecture) illustrate well the variations in types of textile centers. First, Kiryu is an inland city located in one of the traditional silk reeling areas of central Honshu. The city was incorporated

upon raw material imports, shows much the same urban focus. In contrast, the early textile industry in Japan was essentially a structure of traditional rural handicraft units. The introduction of modern industrial technology into Japanese textile production did contain elements of urban orientation but other manufacturing activities lacking the rural history of textiles far outranked this industry as an urbanizing force.

in 1921 and serves as an administrative and commercial center for its region. In contrast, Kaizuka is a recently incorporated (1943) sea coast city devoted almost exclusively to cotton weaving and apparel manufacture. Both cities qualify as textile centers, but Kaizuka represents the new specialized, more genuinely industrialized textile center. Kiryu, because of its history as regional center for a predominantly rural area, displays a more traditional economic structure. Kaizuka, for instance, employed only 60.9 males per 100 females in industrial activities in 1950, as against 127.9 males per 100 females in Kiryu. This is to say that the demands of Kaizuka's specialization in textiles emphasized the utilization of a female labor force. Kiryu showed a relatively low sex ratio in industrial employment because of a textile emphasis, but its commercial and administrative functions as a regional center somewhat offset the specialized labor force demands of textile processing. The more diversified economic structure of Kiryu also makes for a lower level of agricultural activity within the city. In 1950, 7.9 per cent of Kiryu's males and 4.4 per cent of the females were in agricultural employment; Kaizuka had 22.1 per cent of its males and 6.6 per cent of its females so employed. These figures highlight one further aspect of employment structure in the textile city: industrial activities associated with textiles serve in many respects the same occupational functions for females as does agriculture. Japanese cities with no textile emphasis in employment structure show consistently higher proportions of males than females in agriculture, while in the textile city the relationship is reversed. This characteristic of Japanese textile production accounts in large measure for the higher over-all levels of agriculture associated with textile cities. To the extent that the city's economic base rests upon textile production, to that extent the opportunities are reduced for males, who make up the greater share of the labor force, to move away from traditional employment in agriculture.

The industrial city emphasizing heavy industries represents the reverse of this pattern. Kawasaki, the industrial center of approximately 200,000 population located between Tokyo and Yokohama, and Aioi, a railroad equipment production center of some 30,000 population in Hyogo Prefecture, exemplify the large and the small heavy industry cities of Japan. In both cities in

1950, the percentage of male labor force in agriculture was less than half that of females so employed (Kawasaki: 12.1 per cent males and 28.7 per cent females; Aioi: 6.9 per cent males and 17.3 per cent females). In the sex ratios of industrially employed for these cities, the demands of a male-oriented economic base are observable. For every 100 females industrially employed in Aioi in 1950, 785 males were active; in Kawasaki 493 males per 100 females were active in industry. Kawasaki, as a comparatively large city, is able to support within its industrial composition significant amounts of industry outside the heavy category. For example, 30.6 per cent of its female labor force is in textiles. Aioi, as a center of genuine specialization in heavy industry, had 80.1 per cent of its males and 60.0 per cent of its females in the single category of transport equipment production, with no other category containing more than 7 per cent of the labor force of either sex. The large diversified city containing an emphasis in heavy industry (e.g., Osaka) tends toward a higher industrially employed sex ratio (432.1 in 1950) than other cities in its size range, but industrial diversification tends to reduce the influence of heavy industry upon labor force composition. Osaka, for instance, had 2.6 per cent of the total of Japan's employed in textiles-apparel activities in 1950, but this area accounted for only 6.9 per cent of her male and 26.1 per cent of her female industrial labor force.

The remaining industrial cities of Japan are those with either a diversified industrial base or specializations in areas other than textiles or heavy industry. Tokyo is the outstanding illustration of the first type. Table VIII-2 has shown that Tokyo contains large portions of Japan's industrially employed. No one specific industrial area, however, is sufficiently strong to have a significant influence upon the composition of the labor force. The employment structure of the second type of industrial city depends largely upon where the city's industrial emphasis lies. The city specializing in chemicals (e.g., Nobeoka) or ceramics (e.g., Seto) in many respects resembles the textile center in that these industries provide opportunities for significant female participation in the labor force. In contrast, a lumbering emphasis (e.g., Noshiro) shows labor force characteristics similar to those present in the heavy industry city.

Commercial Cities: Except where a commercial emphasis is located in a suburban city within an industrial area or where the commercial emphasis is combined with another emphasis of higher growth potential, the Japanese commercial city can be characterized primarily as an isolated, slow-growing city (Table IX-7). The commercial center which brings together both services-administration and transport emphases with its commerce serves as a larger, faster growing regional center. The seven cities with the multiple emphasis pattern, commerce-services-transport in 1950, were all cities incorporated by 1920; they had a median average annual rate of change of 2.3 per cent for 1920-55 and 2.7

TABLE IX-7. Growth of Japan's Commercial Cities, 1950-55

Functional Classification	Number of Cities	Median Average Annual Rate of Growth 1950-55
Commerce	16	1.5
Commerce-Services	21	1.4
Commerce-Industry	28	1.7
Commerce-Transport	20	2.7
Commerce-Services-Transport	7	2.7
TOTAL	92	1.8

Sources: *Population Census of 1950,* Vol. VII, Table 11 from prefectural volumes. *1955 Population Census of Japan,* Vol. I, Table 12.

per cent for 1950-55. The median average annual rate of increase for the eleven commercial cities which were incorporated prior to 1920 is 1.6 per cent (1920-55). The median average annual rate of increase from 1950 to 1955 for the total of sixteen commercial cities is 1.5 per cent (Table IX-7); three of these cities (Marugame, Yamatotakada, and Tochigi) actually lost population during this five-year period. The two commercial cities which diverge from this characterization are Ashiya and Toyonaka. Ashiya (1950 population: 42,951) is a suburb to Kobe, and Toyonaka (1950 population: 86,203) is a northern suburb of Osaka. Their employed populations are predominantly commuters to Kobe and Osaka for commercial activities. In contrast, the employed populations of the other commercial centers are employed largely within their cities of residence. In essence, the growth of Ashiya and Toyonaka represents the growth of the metropolitan areas of Kobe and Osaka rather than independent city growth. Toyonaka increased 24.8 per cent from 1950 to 1955; Ashiya grew by 18.6 per cent during the same period. These were by far the largest increases within the commercial city category.

In terms of the sex structures of employed population, the commercially specialized city employs proportionally more females than do cities of other types. The sixteen cities of 1950 with a commercial emphasis alone had a median sex ratio of total employed of 191.1. Significantly, the two highest employed sex ratios in this group appeared in Ashiya (332.9) and Toyonaka (284.2); these two commercial suburbs were heavily influenced by the industrial emphasis present in the Osaka-Kobe metropolitan area.[2]

Transportation and Services-Administration Cities: In employment structure the transport center is heavily influenced by the male-dominated labor force demands of transportation and transport repair. The six transport cities had a median sex ratio of total employed of 238.5 and an industrially employed sex ratio of 514.4 in 1950. The median size of these cities in 1950 was 122,460; the smallest was the seaport of Rumoi with 32,513 population. The composition of the services-administration category makes difficult any general characterization of the cities specializing in this area. The category includes such diverse groups as hotel employees, medical personnel, and those in military service. Services-administration cities fall into three groups: tourists or resort centers (e.g., Nara and Beppu), military centers (e.g., Yokosuka and Kure), and suburban towns within commuting distance of major cities (e.g., Fujisawa and Kamakura). Sex ratios of the economically active are high in the military centers, low in tourists and resort cities, and high again in the commuters' suburbs. Rates of growth are highest for the commuters' suburbs. For example, the group of towns extending south and west from the Tokyo-Yokohama area, including Kama-

---

[2] High sex ratios for employed population in suburbs of large industrial centers is characteristic of United States urban structure. See Otis D. Duncan and Albert J. Reiss, Jr., *Social Characteristics of Urban and Rural Communities* (New York: John Wiley and Sons, Inc., 1956), pp. 259 ff.; the authors find consistently high sex ratios of employed population in areas around central cities specializing in manufacturing.

kura, Chigasaki, Fujisawa and Hiratsuka, had a median average annual rate of growth of 2.8 per cent from 1950 to 1955. In contrast, the ancient capital city of Nara increased only 3.3 per cent during the whole 1950-55 period, while Yokosuka and Kure had average annual rates of growth of 2.3 per cent and 1.2 per cent respectively.

Mining Cities: The male orientation of the basic economic activity in these cities produced a relatively high sex ratio for total employed: a median of 258.3 for the ten cities in 1950. The manufacturing activities associated with processing mineral resources emphasized still further the utilization of a male labor force; the median sex ratio of the industrially employed in these cities was 557.0 for 1950. The Japanese mining city is one in which female employment is restricted largely to nonindustrial categories; in none of these ten mining cities was as much as 20 per cent of the female labor force in industry in 1950. Conversely, in only two of the mining cities (Naogata and Iizuka) were more than 30 per cent of the male labor force active outside the manufacturing or mining categories. One further characteristic of mining centers is significant: levels of female employment in agriculture are high. In 1950, median percentage of females in agriculture for the ten mining centers was 31.1 per cent.

Agricultural Cities: The labor force composition of Japan's agricultural cities tends toward the traditional rural pattern of high utilization of females. The nonagricultural industries associated with this type of city are also those in which females participate most frequently (e.g., textiles and food processing). The appearance of a large number of cities showing an agricultural-fishing functional emphasis in the post-World War II period is the result of lowered requirements for city incorporation and the expansion of boundaries of previously incorporated cities to include large segments of nonindustrially employed populations.

Utilizing the three classes of agricultural cities presented in the preceding chapter (farming, fishing, and cities with previous nonagricultural emphases), Table IX-8 shows the differentials in growth and structure of economically active population for Japan's 67 "agricultural" cities. By far the largest, fastest growing, and least committed to agriculture are those cities which prior to 1950 showed employment emphases in urban-oriented activities. As a whole this group of cities shows in its employment structure the influence of the labor force demands in textiles. The sex ratio of employed population in this group is below that for either the farming or fishing centers included in Table IX-8.

The populations of Japan's farming and fishing centers show the influences of their nonindustrial emphases: low rates of growth, low sex ratios for employed population, and relatively high commitments to agriculture. Japanese fishing activity is

TABLE IX-8. Employment Structure, Size, and Growth Rates of Japan's Agricultural Cities, 1950-55

Agricultural City Type	Number of Cities	Median Size	Median Average Annual % Change 1950-55[a]	Median Sex Ratio of Employed Population	Median % Males in Agricultural Activities	Median % Males in Industrial Activities
Farming	45	45,085	0.8	156.9	33.7	26.6
Fishing	14	38,560	0.8	177.6	34.5	25.2
Cities with Previous Non-Agricultural Emphasis	8	65,842	1.1	140.2	26.1	31.3

a Growth of population within 1955 boundaries.

Sources: *Population Census of 1950*, Vol. VII, Table 11 from prefectural volumes. *1955 Census of Population of Japan*, Vol. I, Table 12.

male-dominated (the 1950 sex ratio for those employed in marine activities was 807.9), consequently, the fishing centers tend to have higher sex ratios in their labor force than do the other two classes of agricultural cities. However, the heavy commitments to agriculture, where traditionally women find employment, also found in the fishing centers, tend to bring sex ratios of the employed down to levels roughly comparable to those of the other classes of agricultural cities.

The point has been made previously that there is no clear break between Japan's rural and urban populations, and the demographic characteristics of her "agricultural" cities illustrate this point well. The urban agglomerations in this category are essentially neither wholly urban nor wholly rural. To the extent that migrations out of rural areas are short distance moves from the true agricultural community to small, nearby cities of the "agricultural" type and then to larger urban centers, the continued existence of elements of the traditional peasant social structure in a highly urban Japan is partially explained.

SUMMARY

That segment of Japanese urban population associated with industrial activities outside the textile area is that which shows the greatest structural divergence from traditional Japanese population. The highest rates of urbanization during the last three and one-half decades as well as the greatest shifts in the demographic character of the employed population are associated with urban areas showing functional emphases in industrial activities. The more recent maturation of Japan's industrial structure as reflected in expansion of tertiary activities has tended to emphasize this relationship. To the extent that other nonagricultural employment is integrated with industry as an urban base, cities with nonagricultural emphases other than industry have reflected the modernization of Japan in their growth and demographic structure.

Metropolitan Development in Japan | X

Japan's urbanization has expanded both in terms of the proportion of total population living in cities and in the number of urban places. In present-day Japan, residing in a city is characteristic of over one-half the total population. Even the most remote regions of the nation have within their boundaries areas which qualify as urban centers. With this degree of urbanization, however, it becomes increasingly difficult to delimit the genuinely urban population. The population which is functionally urban frequently overflows the administrative boundaries of the politically designated city. Or a group of cities which historically were separate urban units may individually expand and overlap one another so as to become a single urban complex. As a consequence, in a highly urbanized area the administratively defined city becomes less and less useful as the unit of analysis.[1]

A unit which ignores purely politically delimited urban units and which attempts to designate integrated urban agglomerations becomes necessary. The United States Census Bureau's concepts of Standard Metropolitan Area and Urbanized Area and the "conurbation" utilized in the census of England and Wales are illustrative of official recognition of this need. The Japanese have recently utilized a supra-city unit modeled on the Standard Metropolitan Area of the United States Census to designate more realistically the urban structure of Japan.[2]

The criteria upon which any metropolitan unit is based include

[1] For a systematic presentation of the problems involved in metropolitan delimitations, see International Urban Research, *The World's Metropolitan Areas* (Berkeley: University of California Press, 1959), pp. 6-33.

[2] Japan, Prime Minister's Office, *Nihon hyōjun toshi chizu bunri* (The Standard Metropolitan Areas of Japan), Tokyo, March, 1954.

indices designed to bring together all the population in a given area which is integrated occupationally and, through transportation and communication lines, into one urban whole. Formulations of the metropolitan concept stress heavily the functional integration of the population within the area. The metropolitan area is conceived as an urban agglomeration dominated by a central urban core into which flows daily a significant portion of the economically active who reside in contiguous areas and from which emanates the major portion of urban services for the surrounding area. The focus is upon a population which is linked by means of a network of daily activities.[3]

All the data in the form necessary for this type of analysis are rarely, if ever, available. Researchers must be content with indirect, and often incomplete, measures of metropolitan integration. One of the most frequently used criteria for the inclusion of contiguous administrative units with a central city is that a minimum proportion of the economically active persons be in nonagricultural activities. That is, the area must show no break with the economic structure of the urban core. Indices of the extent and direction of commuting and telephone communication are usually included to reveal further the degree of integration with the central city. These items specify the limits of the central city's sphere of interaction. Further, to discern a continuation of the central city's physical structure, a minimum population density is required in the area. No universally accepted set of criteria for metropolitan delimitation is now in use, but the various attempts made to designate such agglomerations represent alternative solutions to a set of common problems.

DELIMITATION OF JAPANESE METROPOLITAN AREAS

Two sets of metropolitan area delimitations exist for Japan; one is the Japanese Census Bureau study cited above, and the other is that evolved by the International Urban Research project of the University of California. The areas designated by the Administrative Control Office of the Japanese Census Bureau

---

[3] For detailed presentations of the metropolitan area concept, see among others, R. D. McKenzie, *The Metropolitan Community* (New York: McGraw-Hill Book Co., Inc., 1933), and Amos H. Hawley, *Human Ecology* (New York: The Ronald Press Co., 1950).

were based upon 1950 population data and incorporated the following criteria:[4]

1. The metropolitan area has as its core an incorporated city of 100,000 or more persons. Cities of less than 100,000 are included when they are prefectural capitals.
2. Surrounding administrative units, e.g., towns (*machi*) and villages (*mura*), are included in the metropolitan area of the central city when all the following traits are present:
   a. The density is at least 170 persons per square kilometer.
   b. At least 50% of the total households are designated as nonagricultural in the agricultural census of 1950.
   c. The average number of telephone calls from the area to the central city for an average month is at least seven per subscriber, or among the total number of passengers in an average month at least 20% are passengers to the central city, and
   d. The area is contiguous with the central city or contiguous with an area which qualifies for inclusion in the metropolitan area.

The study designated 54 metropolitan areas for Japan with a total metropolitan population of 30.3 million in 1950. Five of these are so-called "combined city areas," that is, metropolitan areas with more than one large city within the area. The Tokyo metropolitan area, for example, contains not only the cities within its own administratively defined prefecture, but, among others, Yokohama and Yokosuka from Kanagawa Prefecture to the south, Chiba and Funabashi from Chiba Prefecture to the east, and Kawaguchi and Urawa from Saitama Prefecture to the north. In the same manner the Osaka-Kobe-Kyoto and Nagoya metropolitan areas cross prefectural boundaries to bring together integrated urban agglomerations.

The second set of Japanese metropolitan area delimitations comes from the attempt to delimit metropolitan areas on a world-wide scale made by International Urban Research, University of California. Within the framework of this international study, the criteria for metropolitan delimitations applied to Japan are as follows:

4 *Nihon hyōjun toshi chizu bunri*, pp. 1-4.

1. The metropolitan area must have as its core a city of
   50,000 population or more; the metropolitan area must
   have a total population of 100,000 or more.
2. For inclusion in the metropolitan area, administrative
   districts surrounding the central city must fulfill all the
   following requirements:
   a. A minimum of 65% of the employed population must
      be active in nonagricultural pursuits.
   b. The area must be contiguous to the central city or
      contiguous to an area which qualified for inclusion in
      the metropolitan area, and
   c. The area must be located so as to make commuting
      and communication feasible with the central city.

These criteria resulted in the designation of 63 metropolitan
areas for Japan with a total metropolitan population of 30.2 million in 1950 (the 1950 population is adjusted to the boundaries
of the 1955 census).

The primary value of these studies is that they focus upon the
functionally urban population in contrast to the *administratively*
urban population provided in Japan's national census reports.
By incorporating areas which are administratively rural into
metropolitan areas, the Japanese Census Bureau study increased
by 5.1 million the urban population of 1950, bringing the percentage urban to 59.5% for the nation as a whole. The International Urban Research study added 2.0 million to the total
urban population, making Japan 55.9% urban in 1950. These
delimitations are of further value in that they indicate the degree
of concentration of the urban population within the nation. The
four largest metropolitan areas as delimited by both studies contain well over one-half the total metropolitan population and
over one-third of the total urban population (Table X-1).

Variations in the criteria for metropolitan delimitations between these two studies necessarily result in differences in the
composition of the metropolitan areas. In broad terms, the Japanese Census Bureau designates fewer metropolitan areas, but
their territorial limits are greater. For example, the Japanese
Census Bureau includes Kyoto within the greater Osaka metropolitan area, and Gifu within the Nagoya area; International Urban Research makes both these cities centers of independent
metropolitan areas. International Urban Research delimitations

TABLE X-1. Major Metropolitan Areas of Japan, 1950

Metropolitan Areas	INTERNATIONAL URBAN RESEARCH DELIMITATIONS			JAPANESE BUREAU OF STATISTICS DELIMITATIONS		
	Population (000's)	% of Total Metropolitan Population	% of Total Urban Population	Population (000's)	% of Total Metropolitan Population	% of Total Urban Population
Tokyo-Yokohama	9,049	29.9	19.4	8,567	28.3	17.2
Osaka-Kobe	5,348	17.7	11.5	6,841	22.6	13.7
Kyoto	1,268	4.2	2.7	2,161	7.1	4.3
Nagoya	1,231	4.1	2.6			
Yahata-Kokura-Shimonoseki	1,493	4.9	3.2	1,093	3.6	2.2
Total Major Metropolitan Areas	18,389	60.8	39.4	18,662	61.6	37.4
Total Metropolitan Areas	30,243	100.0	—	30,301	100.0	—
Total Urban Population[a]	46,631	—	100.0	49,798	—	100.0

[a] Population reported as urban by the census definition plus population in unincorporated areas qualifying for inclusion in metropolitan area for each study.

Sources: IUR metropolitan areas compiled from population figures for 1950 adjusted to 1955 boundaries, *1955 Population Census of Japan*, Vol. I. Japanese Bureau of Statistics metropolitan areas delimited in *Nihon hyōjun toshi chizu bunrui* (The Standard Metropolitan Areas of Japan), March, 1954.

include areas containing cities of 50,000 or more where contiguous administrative units of sufficient nonagricultural activity bring the total population of the metropolitan area to 100,000 or more, while the Japanese Census Bureau study includes only those central cities of 100,000 or more. The International Urban Research metropolitan areas, therefore, have a wider and deeper coverage of the total Japanese urban population.

A major factor creating further variations in the metropolitan composition of these two studies is the difference in level of nonagricultural activity required for inclusion of minor civil divisions within a metropolitan area. The Japanese Census Bureau includes areas where 50% or more of the *households* in an area are nonagricultural; International Urban Research bases inclusion upon 65% or more of the area's total *labor force* being in nonagricultural activities. This difference in the occupational criterion creates minor differences in delimitations of relatively small, isolated metropolitan areas. However, in areas where clusters of cities appear, if one uses the Japanese Census Bureau's 50% criterion, broad "bridges" of unincorporated territory appear between the cities. Hence, Kyoto is included in the Osaka-Kobe Metropolitan Area, and Gifu in the Nagoya area. International Urban Research, in contrast, utilizing the 65% cutting point indicates a weak "bridge" between Kyoto and Osaka, and none at all between Nagoya and Gifu. In terms of definition of the metropolitan area concept, cities of the size and functional diversification of Kyoto and Gifu more reasonably qualify as independent metropolitan centers than as subcenters.

These illustrations indicate that a 50% level of nonagricultural activity as utilized in the Japanese Census Bureau study is not sufficient to indicate clear breaks between near-by metropolitan agglomerations. The more conservative 65% cutting point of the International Urban Research study, though not solving all problems of Japanese delimitations, does avoid gross overbounding of metropolitan areas for Japan. For this reason, and the fact that International Urban Research files provide international comparisons in standardized metropolitan delimitations for a large number of countries, the discussion of Japanese metropolitan development which follows will be based upon International Urban Research delimitations of Japanese metropolitan areas.

The growth of metropolitan areas as industrialization expands is yet another respect in which Japan is following the urban experience of the nations which first felt the consequences of an industrial transition. As with urbanization in general, the level of a nation's metropolitanization is closely linked with its level of industrial development. The implication here is that Japan's future urban growth will, following the pattern of the older industrialized nations of the West, continue largely in terms of expansion of existing population centers into larger and larger urban aggregates.[5]

THE GROWTH OF JAPANESE METROPOLITAN AREAS

If metropolitan area delimitations are retrojected to 1920, the broad trends of metropolitan population growth as a whole are revealed. This technique holds 1955 boundaries constant back to 1920, and therefore focuses exclusively upon changes in population. Table X-2 shows the rates of change for the components

TABLE X-2. Japan: Growth of Total, Urban, and Metropolitan Area Population, 1920-1955

Area	POPULATION (000's)[a]		Percentage Change 1920-55
	1920	1955	
TOTAL JAPAN	55,391	89,276	61.2
Total Incorporated Cities[b]	19,855	40,413	103.5
Incorporated Cities Outside Metropolitan Areas	4,166	7,370	76.9
TOTAL METROPOLITAN AREAS	17,001	35,826	110.7
Incorporated Cities of 100,000 and over[b]	15,084	31,038	105.8
Incorporated Cities of Less than 100,000[b]	605	2,006	231.7
Unincorporated Areas	1,312	2,783	112.2

a Population in 1955 boundaries.
b Cities incorporated as of the 1950 census.

Sources: *Population Census of 1950*, Vol. VII, Table 1 from prefectural volumes. *1955 Population Census of Japan*, Vol. I, Table 12.

5 For a more extensive treatment of these international comparisons see Thomas O. Wilkinson, "Urban Structure and Industrialization," *American Sociological Review*, Vol. 25, No. 3 (June, 1960), pp. 356-363.

of Japan's total, urban, and metropolitan populations from 1920 to 1955. One major fact to be noted from this table is that urban growth outside metropolitan areas has been only slightly higher than growth for the total population during the period covered. Japan's urbanization during the last three and one-half decades has been centered primarily within metropolitan areas. Within the metropolitan areas themselves, the major growth has occurred in peripheral regions. That is, the smaller cities (less than 100,000 in 1950) and the unincorporated areas of metropolitan agglomerations show higher rates of growth than the central cities.

TABLE X-3. Population Increase in Tokyo-Yokohama and Osaka-Kobe Metropolitan Areas, 1920-55

Area[a]	POPULATION (000's)[b]		Percentage Change 1920-55
	1920	1955	
TOKYO-YOKOHAMA METROPOLITAN AREA	4,797	11,349	136.6
Cities over 100,000	4,479	9,936	121.9
Cities under 100,000	121	551	355.3
Unincorporated areas	197	862	336.9
OSAKA-KOBE METROPOLITAN AREA	2,822	6,405	127.0
Cities over 100,000	2,297	4,842	110.8
Cities under 100,000	204	826	305.0
Unincorporated areas	321	737	129.5

[a] Cities incorporated as of the 1950 census.
[b] Population in 1955 boundaries.

Sources: See Table V-3.

The centrifugal or decentralizing pattern of expansion found in total metropolitan growth is emphasized in Japan's largest metropolitan areas. Table X-3 summarizes for the Toyko-Yokohama and Osaka-Kobe metropolitan areas the growth of metropolitan components for the 1920-55 period. Again, the smaller cities and unincorporated areas lead in increases, but at rates up to three times as high as those for the corresponding total metropolitan area components. This pattern of centrifugal population growth for Japan's metropolitan areas does not imply a withering away of the central cities. The central city still functions as the dominant core of the metropolitan area, but rather than depending largely upon population resident within its boundaries, the modern urban center draws heavily upon a population which commutes daily from regions outside the city's boundaries. This change is reflected in an increase in the proportion of population residing outside the central city which is employed in the central city.

Table X-4 shows the daily per cent changes in labor force for Japan's six major cities in 1930 and 1955, holding the administrative boundaries constant. With the exceptions of Kyoto and Yokohama, the volume of labor force commuting has in-

TABLE X-4. Percentage Change from Resident to "Daytime" Labor Force for Japan's Six Largest Cities, 1930 and 1955

| City[a] | Percentage Change from Resident Employed Population to "Daytime" Employed Population | |
	1930	1955
Tokyo	0.7	10.9
Yokohama	−1.8	−2.2
Nagoya	1.6	13.0
Kyoto	0.4	−0.9
Osaka	4.7	30.5
Kobe	0.1	3.2

a Boundaries of 1930 are adjusted to approximate those of 1955.

Sources: *Roku dai toshi: Sangyo betsu chukan jinkō* (Six Major Cities: Industrial Breakdown of Daytime Population), Tokyo, 1936. *1955 Population Census of Japan,* Vol. II, pt. 2, Table 11.

creased appreciably for these cities. Kyoto, a city with little suburban development, shows insignificant changes between resident and "daytime" labor force for both 1930 and 1955. Yokohama, though a city of over one million in 1955, continues to be dominated by the metropolis of Tokyo. The daily loss of labor force is accounted for largely by the movement of population from the extensive residential wards in the western and northern sections of the city into Tokyo's central districts.

Analysis of density patterns for the two largest metropolitan developments (Tokyo-Yokohama and Osaka-Kobe) shows that although the central cities in these areas have increased in density, the greatest gains have been in the smaller cities and in the unincorporated areas surrounding the central cities. For example, excluding the central cities of Tokyo and Yokohama, only eight administrative units had densities greater than 2,000 persons per square mile in 1920 in the metropolitan area; by 1955, only three units fell below this density level. The same general pattern holds for the Osaka-Kobe metropolitan area.

The centrifugal growth within metropolitan areas is also evident *within* the central cities themselves. For example, shifts in density within the 1955 boundaries of the city of Tokyo from 1920 to 1955 show that the central sections of the city have actually lost in residential density although the density for the total city has risen during this period. No section of the city contained a density of 100,000 or more persons per square mile in 1955, while in 1920 five of the central wards showed densities of this magnitude. It is to be emphasized that these figures refer to *residential* density only; the "daytime" population of Tokyo's central wards has shown a consistent pattern of increase. To illustrate: the three wards at the center of Tokyo show the following percentage increases of "daytime" over permanent residents from 1930 to 1947:[6]

Per Cent Gain in Daytime Population Over Permanent Population

Ward	1930	1940	1947
Chiyoda	88.0	129.0	249.7
Chuo	33.8	53.2	128.4
Minato	12.3	21.0	53.0

In summary, the highest levels of population growth in Japanese metropolitan areas take place in regions peripheral to the central cities, with rising levels of daily commuting to the central cities. The Japanese pattern is essentially the deconcentration found in Western metropolitan growth. For example, "Since 1861, the first date that comparison can be made, the Outer Ring of Greater London has been growing more rapidly than London itself." Before 1900, French writers had noted the "dispersive tendency" in metropolitan growth of France.[7] Early studies of American cities show more rapid increases for areas surrounding large cities than for the cities themselves. For example, as early as the late nineteenth century, the suburban areas of Boston, Massachusetts were

---

[6] *Tōkyō-to no jinkō ni kansuru tōkei shiryo* (Statistical Materials Relating to the Population of the Metropolitan Prefecture of Tokyo), March, 1955, Table 60.

[7] Kingsley, Davis, "The Origins and Growth of Urbanization in the World," *American Journal of Sociology*, LX (March, 1955), pp. 435-436.

experiencing rates of growth from three to eight times as high as that for the city of Boston.[8] More recent studies of United States urbanization utilizing the Standard Metropolitan Areas delimited by the U.S. Bureau of the Census show clearly a pattern of centrifugal growth for metropolitan areas whose central cities are over one million in population:[9]

Per Cent Change in Population

Area	*1900-10*	*1910-20*	*1920-30*	*1930-40*	*1940-50*
Central City	32.2	19.3	24.0	5.6	9.4
Satellite Area	36.7	28.5	43.8	11.8	33.0

A further parallel to the Japanese pattern of metropolitan growth is found in an increasing magnitude of daily movement toward the centers of United States metropolitan areas.[10]

The major difference between the Japanese and United States patterns of metropolitan growth is a difference in the extent of decentralization. Deconcentration is found primarily in the largest of Japan's metropolitan areas alone. Outside the Tokyo-Yokohama and Osaka-Kobe areas, the metropolitan area of Japan is typically a single city with limited, if any, metropolitan development outside its administrative boundaries. The typical United States city has a significant proportion of the population in contiguous areas in nonagricultural activities; hence the functionally urban population more frequently overflows administrative boundaries in the United States than is the case for Japan. Growth of peripheral regions of Japan's metropolitan areas has been closely linked to the expansion of public transportation facilities; the areas showing the highest levels of metropolitanization are those in which interurban lines are most highly developed (e.g., Tokyo and Osaka). The smaller Japanese cities depend upon limited public transportation and the bicycle for commuting. It is to be expected, then, that the administrative boundaries of numerous Japanese cities can and do encompass the greater proportion of the urban-oriented population of the area. For instance, the relatively large

8 Adna F. Weber, *The Growth of Cities in the Nineteenth Century* (Studies in History, Economics and Public Law, Vol. XI, New York: Macmillan Co., 1899), pp. 38-39.
9 Amos H. Hawley, *The Changing Shape of Metropolitan America* (Glencoe, Ill.: The Free Press, 1956), p. 36.
10 Donald L. Foley, "The Daily Movements of Population into Central Business Districts," *American Sociological Review*, 17 (October, 1952), pp. 538-553.

cities of Sendai (375,844 population in 1955) and Matsuyama (213,457 population) have no contiguous areas which qualify for inclusion with the central cities in metropolitan delimitations. Further, the industrial center of Nagoya has only seven administrative units covering 49.3 square miles and only 164,871 population which qualify as part of its metropolitan area.

Deconcentration can be said to be characteristic of Japanese metropolitan growth only because the major portion of metropolitan population is located in a few large metropolitan areas. That is, 49.6% of Japan's metropolitan population resided in the Tokyo-Yokohama and Osaka-Kobe metropolitan areas in 1955, and these two areas were experiencing deconcentration. Little, if any, evidence exists of deconcentration in the remaining sixty-one metropolitan areas. It is well to note, however, that the frequent annexations of contiguous areas which is common for the smaller cities reflect a limited centrifugal growth.

JAPANESE METROPOLITAN STRUCTURE

It has been frequently noted in historical treatments of urban growth that levels of technological development are associated with uniquely adapted community organizations. The peasant-agricultural society creates the agricultural village to serve primarily as market center. The specialized industrial city appears with the development of an advanced productive and transportation technology. As urban specialization develops, the city expands not only in absolute population and area but in its dominance of control and service functions over its surrounding areas. The concept of the metropolitan area refers to this most recent type of urban agglomeration. The extent to which the metropolitan area exercises dominance, is, however, directly related to the social and economic structure of the society in which it exists. The United States, for example, is the limiting case in which a high standard of living, a relatively small population in a large area, and a high level of technological development provide a context for the appearance of specialized urban areas surrounded by numerous sub-areas. Transportation and communication facilities are developed to the degree that the major urban centers can draw from an extensive hinterland the population and knowledge necessary for their maintenance. Metropolitanization of this character is largely the result of the specific combination of socio-economic factors active in the development of the United States. Any consideration of Japanese metropolitan structure must also recognize particular aspects of the nation's social structure which exercise significant influences upon the concentration and integration of population.

Japanese metropolitanization is part of the whole fabric of Japanese society and as such can be isolated from the whole for analytical purposes only. The following list is, therefore, an illustrative rather than an exhaustive survey of socio-economic influences upon Japanese metropolitan structure:

1) A limited private ownership of transportation facilities, specifically automobiles, restricts the development of extensive suburban areas. Only areas served by developed public transportation systems are capable of supporting large commuting populations.
2) The paucity of cultivatable land creates severe competition between expanding urban land usage and agricultural production in areas peripheral to cities.
3) Industrial and commercial systems incorporate large numbers of dispersed production and trade units. Though most often integral parts of a complex "putting out" system, household establishments employing family members only are the most numerous type of establishment in Japan. The result is a degree of a real self-sufficiency which mediates against a high level of direct metropolitan integration.

Given these factors, the metropolitan areas of Japan tend to be more compact in area than, for instance, those of the United States. Further, the degree of direct functional integration within the metropolitan areas can be expected to be of a lower order in Japan than in the United States.

The 1920 census provides the first reliable data on Japanese metropolitan development. The territory surrounding a few major cities showed in occupational characteristics the expansion of urban-oriented population beyond administrative urban boundaries. For instance, there are clear indications of the development of a population essentially urban in character in the area between the cities of Tokyo and Yokohama. The expansion of boundaries for these two cities, plus the incorporation of the city of Kawasaki in 1924, created a solid urban settlement from the north of Tokyo

Bay southward to Yokosuka. The early development of this metropolitan settlement is clear in that the "rural" administrative units directly surrounding the city of Tokyo in its 1920 boundaries contained levels of nonagricultural employment even greater than

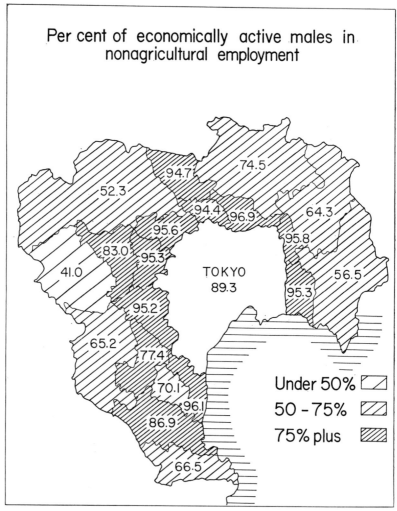

FIGURE X-1: Tokyo and Environs Nonagricultural Employment, 1920 (Source: *Reports of the 1920 Census*, Vol. IV, pt. 1)

that of the city itself (Figure X-1). Much the same is true of the city of Osaka and its contiguous area. Annexation of these areas to the central cities or incorporation of the areas as independent cities has been frequent since 1920. The city of Tokyo now has within its incorporated boundaries the total area shown in Figure X-1. The appearance of such cities as Fuse, Suita, and Toyonaka as incorporated cities contiguous with Osaka is also indicative of metropolitanization.

Though the large metropolitan areas of Japan, composed of several cities and contiguous unincorporated areas, contain a major portion of Japan's total urban population, this type of metropolitan area accounts for only twelve of Japan's total of 63 metro-

TABLE X-5. Japanese Metropolitan Structure, 1955

Composition of Metropolitan Areas	Num- ber	TOTAL METRO- POLITAN AREAS		TOTAL INCOR- PORATED CITIES[a]		UNINCOR- PORATED AREAS	
		Popula- tion (000's)	Per Cent	Popula- tion (000's)	Per Cent	Popula- tion (000's)	Per Cent
One Incorporated City	32	5,907	16.7	5,907	18.1	—	—
Two or More Incorporated Cities	7	1,581	4.5	1,581	4.8	—	—
One Incorporated City, plus Unincorporated Areas	12	3,272	9.2	2,833	8.8	440	15.8
Two or More Incorporated Cities, plus Unincorporated Areas	12	24,627	69.6	22,284	68.3	2,343	84.2
TOTAL	63	35,387	100.0	32,605	100.0	2,783	100.0

[a] Cities incorporated at the time of the 1950 census.

Source: *1955 Population Census of Japan,* Vol. I.

politan areas. Table X-5 shows for 1955 the major structural characteristics of Japan's metropolitan population. Over one-half of all Japan's metropolitan areas are made up of single incorporated cities; seven others contain two or more incorporated cities only. Of the total metropolitan population, only 7.8% is located outside incorporated city boundaries.

The characteristics of Japanese metropolitan structure noted here are to some extent the product of the techniques of delimitation. Japanese censuses provide data for minor civil divisions which are relatively small in area; additions of contiguous area to central cities can, therefore, be made in small increments, i.e., *machi* and *mura.* This is noted in contrast to the United States where metropolitan areas are composed of central cities and contiguous counties.[11] In order to encompass a settlement of urban-oriented population within a United States metropolitan area, a comparatively large area must be added to the central city. In Japan, parallel metropolitan delimitations would be based upon *gun* inclusions in contrast to the *machi* and *mura.* Any comparisons of Japanese metropolitan structure with that of other nations must be qualified to some degree by the specific techniques of drawing metropolitan boundaries.

However, not all of the structural differences in such comparisons can be accounted for in these terms. In contrast to Japan, residential patterns and levels of private transportation ownership in the United States are such that more dispersed metropolitan structure exists in actual fact in the United States. It is perhaps overstating the contrast to cite the fact that 85.9% of Japan's metropolitan population in 1950 resided in incorporated cities of 100,000 and over in contrast to 55.9% of the United States metropolitan populations residing in central cities of this size in 1950,[12] although the direction of the contrast is valid.

The compact nature of Japanese metropolitan areas is closely linked to the absence of widespread use of private automobiles. In 1955, for instance, Japan had 7.8 passenger cars per 1000 total population in contrast to the United States where there were 329.5 automobiles per 1000 total population. Not only is private transportation limited in Japan, but that which is available is heavily concentrated in a few urban prefectures. The six most urban prefectures account for approximately one-half of all Japan's passenger cars. The rapid growth of population in peripheral urban areas in the United States can be dated quite clearly from the mass production of automobiles following World War I.[13] Japan, on the other hand, has had an urban structure closely linked to railroad and interurban transport patterns.

---

[11] For details of 1950 United States metropolitan area delimitations, see *1950 Census of Population, Population of Standard Metropolitan Areas,* April 1, 1950 (U. S. Bureau of Census: Washington, D. C.), Series PC-3, pp. 1-3.

[12] Hawley, *op. cit.,* p. 22.

[13] Leo F. Schnore and Gene B. Petersen, "Urban and Metropolitan Development in the United States and Canada," *The Annals* of *The American Academy of Political and Social Sciences,* 316 (March, 1958), pp. 60-68.

One major consequence of this orientation is the tendency, except in the largest of metropolitan areas, for settlements around central cities to be satellite rather than suburban in character. A satellite area is one which through proximity and broad economic channels is integrated to the central city, but also it is an area which contains sufficient employment activity to occupy the major portion of its residential labor force within its own boundaries. In contrast, the population in a suburb is linked to its area largely through residence alone; it tends to be occupationally dependent upon the central city. The key variable in this distinction is the magnitude of commuting by the labor force to the central city. The satellite area shows little, if any, change between "daytime" and resident labor force; the suburb typically shows a significant loss of economically active population during working hours. The data do not exist for a precise classification of the component populations of Japanese metropolitan areas in these terms, but they are sufficient to be indicative of broad trends.

In addition to commuting data, several other variables are available for use in making the distinction between satellites and suburbs. First, the occupational structure of the suburban area will show a predominance of urban-oriented activities, especially in the "white collar" categories of commerce and administration-services; conversely, agricultural activities will tend to be limited. Second, the sex ratio of employed population will be high in suburbs since this ratio varies directly with the size of city in Japan and the population of the suburb will be influenced more by the central city's size than by the size of the suburb itself. Third, the rate of growth of the suburb in contrast to the satellite will be higher since the impetus for suburban growth comes from the large, diversified central city rather than from the limited activities available in the suburb itself.

Table X-6 shows a classification of cities within the largest Japanese metropolitan areas utilizing the above criteria. Characterization along the satellite-suburb continuum is, of necessity, an approximation. Few cities on the basis of all criteria fall distinctly into one of the two categories. Nishinomiya and Ashiya in the Osaka-Kobe metropolitan area and Musashino in the Tokyo-Yokohama area provide the clearest suburban patterns: high rates of growth, high employed sex ratio, occupational em-

TABLE X-6. Central Cities, Satellites, and Suburbs of Japan's Major Metropolitan Areas, 1950-55

City	Population (1955)[a]	% Change (1950-55)[a]	Functional Classification (1950)[b]	Sex Ratio of Employed Population (1950)[b]	% Male Labor Force in Agriculture (1950)[b]	% Daily Change in Labor Force[c]	Monthly Per Capita Commuters to Central City (1950)[d]	City Classification
TOKYO	6,969,104	29.4	ICS	276.2	2.4	10.9	—	Central City
YOKOHAMA	1,143,687	20.2	IST	284.4	9.3	− 2.2	—	Central City
Kawasaki	445,520	39.6	I	317.1	9.4	3.7	9.1	Satellite
Yokosuka	279,182	11.4	ST	322.8	7.6	− 0.5	2.4	Satellite
Chiba	197,962	17.9	ST	203.3	18.0	− 4.7	2.5	Satellite
Omiya	144,540	15.6	T	232.5	10.2	−23.6	3.3	Suburb
Urawa	143,044	15.0	CS	250.6	10.0	−25.9	1.8	Suburb
Hachioji	133,447	13.6	IS	192.6	7.0	− 7.3	1.9	Satellite
Kawaguchi	130,599	17.1	I	259.4	12.1	2.0	2.6	Satellite
Ichikawa	129,700	13.6	IC	207.2	11.1	−32.2	6.5	Suburb
Funabashi	114,921	14.8	CS	223.7	19.8	−21.4	7.3	Suburb
Fujisawa	109,101	12.6	S	240.5	17.6	−18.5	6.9	Suburb
Kawagoe	104,612	4.2	CS	208.7	10.9	− 8.7	1.4	Satellite
Musashino	94,948	29.8	CS	315.2	3.4	N.A.	15.1	Suburb
Kamakura	91,328	7.0	ST	278.1	9.5	N.A.	3.5	Satellite
Matsudo	68,363	14.6	A	187.6	31.6	N.A.	N.A.	Satellite
Hiratsuka	67,022	19.7	S	317.5	7.2	N.A.	3.3	Suburb
Tachikawa	63,644	23.2	S	276.3	3.1	N.A.	6.8	Suburb
Chigasaki	56,895	13.5	ST	252.4	23.3	N.A.	2.8	Satellite

Sources:

[a] *1955 Population Census of Japan*, Vol. I, Table 12.

[b] *Population Census of 1950*, Vol. VII, Table 11. See Appendix III for functional classifications of Japanese cities. I = industrial, C = commercial, S = services-administration, T = transportation-communication, A = agriculture, M = mining.

[c] *1955 Population Census of Japan*, Vol. II, pt. 2, Table 11.

[d] *Nihon hyōjun toshi chizu bunrui* (The Standard Metropolitan Areas of Japan), Tokyo, March, 1954.

TABLE X-6 (Continued)

City	Population (1955)[a]	% Change (1950-55)[a]	Functional Classification (1950)[b]	Sex Ratio of Employed Population (1950)[b]	% Male Labor Force in Agriculture (1950)[b]	% Daily Change in Labor Force[c]	Monthly Per Capita Commuters to Central City (1950)[d]	City Classification
OSAKA	2,547,316	26.4	IC	284.0	1.2	30.5	—	Central City
KOBE	979,305	20.4	IT	289.1	5.5	3.2	—	Central City
Amagasaki	335,513	20.1	I	311.9	3.9	−11.1	7.5	Suburb
Sakai	251,793	17.8	I	307.2	10.1	0.4	4.7	Satellite
Nishinomiya	210,179	24.9	CT	303.3	5.4	−36.8	9.4	Suburb
Fuse	176,052	17.3	IC	297.6	6.0	−4.3	9.6	Suburb
Toyonaka	127,678	24.8	C	284.2	9.1	−34.0	9.8	Suburb
Akashi	120,200	7.3	ST	269.7	12.9	−5.7	8.2	Suburb
Yao	95,825	11.4	I	283.9	12.3	N.A.	5.9	Satellite
Suita	88,458	11.1	IT	300.5	5.9	N.A.	5.9	Satellite
Itami	68,982	15.3	I	261.7	11.6	N.A.	4.5	Satellite
Moriguchi	68,204	17.5	IT	277.3	2.7	N.A.	9.0	Suburb
Takasuki	54,208	9.2	IT	215.3	20.1	N.A.	6.4	Satellite
Ibaraki	51,014	12.7	IT	238.4	18.3	N.A.	8.4	Satellite
Ashiya	50,960	18.6	C	332.9	3.8	N.A.	12.3	Suburb
Ikeda	50,073	10.8	CT	253.6	11.1	N.A.	6.6	Satellite
Hirakata	49,940	13.6	ST	220.2	22.6	N.A.	5.6	Satellite
Tondabayashi	32,107	5.6	A	245.1	34.7	N.A.	5.0	Satellite

TABLE X-6 (Continued)

City	Population (1955)a	% Change (1950-55)a	Functional Classification (1950)b	Sex Ratio of Employed Population (1950)b	% Male Labor Force in Agriculture (1950)b	% Daily Change in Labor Force c	Monthly Per Capita Commuters to Central City (1950)a	City Classification
NAGOYA	1,336,780	23.4	IC	237.7	3.1	13.0	—	Central City
Kasugai	53,311	10.7	A	168.2	33.7	N.A.	5.7	Satellite
Moriyama	45,451	18.5	I	226.8	13.0	N.A.	6.3	Satellite
KYOTO	1,204,084	8.9	C	227.6	4.8	− 0.9	—	Central City
Otsu	107,498	4.5	IS	193.7	6.5	11.2	8.6	Satellite
Uji	40,061	4.8	S	291.4	15.9	N.A.	2.7	Satellite
YAHATA	286,241	21.6	I	310.4	3.0	13.7	—	Central City
SHIMONOSEKI	230,503	13.4	T	231.4	16.6	6.4	—	Central City
KOKURA	242,240	21.6	T	232.4	12.8	5.4	—	Central City
Takawa	100,071	5.8	M	209.3	6.6	2.0	0.1	Satellite
Moji	145,027	16.6	T	264.0	6.4	6.6	4.0	Satellite
Wakamatsu	97,310	8.6	T	254.0	8.4	N.A.	7.9	Satellite
Tobata	97,214	10.6	IT	281.2	5.0	N.A.	8.5	Satellite
Naogata	62,520	8.3	M	225.9	3.6	N.A.	0.5	Satellite
Iizuka	61,650	5.8	M	290.3	6.6	N.A.	0.2	Satellite

phases in commerce and administration-services, and high levels of commuting to central cities. Amagasaki and Sakai in the Osaka-Kobe area and Kawasaki in the Tokyo-Yokohama area illustrate the satellites: heavy commitments to industrial activities, little or no loss of labor force during working hours, and higher commitments of male labor force to agricultural activities than is the case with suburban communities.

The smaller the city, the more difficult the classification because of the lack of data on labor force commuting. Where these data are missing, the over-all commuting index and the growth rate for 1950-55 serve as the primary basis for classification. In terms of functional classification, the rapidly growing city with an emphasis in commerce and/or administration-services tends to be suburban; an emphasis in industry or agriculture coupled with a relatively lower rate of growth is most frequently characteristic of the satellite.

The conclusions to be drawn from this analysis emphasize the narrowness of suburban as against satellite development in Japanese metropolitan areas. The Tokyo-Yokohama and Osaka-Kobe areas are the only regions of significant suburbanization. These areas contain more extensive interurban transportation systems and appreciably higher levels of passenger car ownership than Japan's other urban agglomerations. Even in these two metropolitan areas, however, the satellite pattern is predominant. The Kyoto and Nagoya metropolitan areas with central cities of over one million population each contain minor peripheral populations, the overwhelming portion of which is satellite in character. The Yahata-Kokura-Shimonoseki metropolitan area is a region of genuine specialization in heavy industry, mining, and transportation which serves to integrate a group of highly specialized satellite cities.

INTERNAL DIFFERENTIATION IN JAPANESE METROPOLITAN AREAS

The metropolitan area by definition contains a population whose economic activities are essentially urban in character. The area functions as a specialized urban core for the hinterland which it serves. Within the metropolitan area itself, however, the intensity of specialization is subject to variation. The component units of a given metropolitan area are differentiated in terms of contributions to the over-all metropolitan structure. Such terms as residential suburb, industrial satellite, and central business district are created to designate this differentiation. One of the major indices of internal differentiation in metropolitan areas is the employment composition of component populations. This section focuses specifically upon contrasts in employment composition between the central cities and outlying or ring areas[14] in Japanese metropolitan areas.

The narrowness of fringe or ring development in Japanese metropolitanization, however, makes central city with ring comparisons significant for only a limited number of metropolitan areas. Only three metropolitan areas had more than 20% of their total population residing outside the central cities in 1950:

Metropolitan Area	% of M.A. Population in Ring Area	% of Total Japanese Ring Population
Yahata-Kokura-Shimonoseki	64.4	15.4
Osaka-Kobe	47.8	35.0
Tokyo-Yokohama	27.6	34.0
Total Japanese Metro. Areas	25.0	100.0

These three metropolitan areas account for 84.4% of all Japan's metropolitan ring population. Differentiation between the central cities and rings of these areas, therefore, provides the most meaningful basis for the analysis of internal structure of Japan's metropolitan areas.

Table X-7 and Figure X-2 show the employment composition by sex for the total metropolitan areas of Japan and for the three areas with significant ring development. These data reveal that the major distinction between the central city and the ring is in level of commercial activity. For the total metropolitan areas, for Tokyo-Yokohama, and for Osaka-Kobe, the commercial category is the one in which the greatest variation occurs between central city and ring. The heavy emphasis upon mining and mineral processing surrounding Yahata results in a low level of commercial activity for both the central cities and the ring, but even here the central cities have a higher commitment to commerce than does the ring.

---

[14] The term "ring" as used here refers to all population or area composed of cities and unincorporated territory outside the central city of a metropolitan agglomeration.

Employment in services shows a lower level of central city-ring variation than that found in commerce. In general, the central city shows a slightly higher commitment to services than the ring, as revealed for the total metropolitan population in Table X-7 and Figure X-2. The exception in this respect is for male employ-

TABLE X-7. Japan: Employment Composition of Metropolitan Areas, 1950.

Metropolitan Area and Employment Category	Central Cities				Ring Areas			
	Total	Males	Females	Sex Ratio	Total	Males	Females	Sex Ratio
		Percentage				Percentage		
TOTAL METRO-POLITAN AREA	100.0	100.0	100.0	237.0	100.0	100.0	100.0	239.2
Extractive[a]	9.9	8.2	14.0	138.2	23.6	22.1	27.2	197.7
Manufacturing[b]	34.6	38.9	24.2	381.0	33.8	36.4	27.4	323.4
Commerce	24.2	21.9	29.7	174.6	16.1	14.4	20.2	173.4
Services	22.3	19.7	28.3	164.8	18.3	16.9	21.6	190.4
Transport	8.9	11.1	3.6	732.2	8.1	10.0	3.5	699.8
Other[c]	0.2	0.2	0.2	291.4	0.2	0.2	0.2	317.7
TOKYO-YOKOHAMA	100.0	100.0	100.0	277.4	100.0	100.0	100.0	258.4
Extractive	4.4	3.6	6.4	156.4	17.0	13.3	26.7	129.5
Manufacturing	37.8	42.7	24.4	486.4	32.9	37.6	20.8	466.2
Commerce	25.6	23.0	32.8	194.1	16.9	15.0	21.6	178.8
Services	24.3	21.2	32.9	178.1	24.5	23.6	27.0	225.8
Transport	7.6	9.2	3.2	807.7	8.5	10.3	3.8	704.7
Other	0.3	0.3	0.3	306.3	0.2	0.2	0.2	315.1
OSAKA-KOBE	100.0	100.0	100.0	285.4	100.0	100.0	100.0	253.0
Extractive	2.6	2.4	3.4	198.0	14.2	13.7	15.5	223.8
Manufacturing	41.2	45.5	28.8	449.9	42.3	44.0	37.8	294.2
Commerce	27.6	24.8	35.6	199.0	18.9	17.6	22.2	200.5
Services	18.0	14.7	27.1	155.2	16.2	14.3	20.9	172.8
Transport	10.2	12.1	4.7	733.2	8.1	10.0	3.3	758.5
Other	0.4	0.5	0.4	416.7	0.3	0.4	0.3	461.1
YAHATA-KOKURA-SHIMONOSEKI	100.0	100.0	100.0	256.1	100.0	100.0	100.0	272.0
Extractive	15.2	11.9	23.8	127.3	49.0	51.6	42.0	334.1
Manufacturing	40.1	47.1	22.1	548.2	17.4	19.6	11.4	467.4
Commerce	17.4	13.8	26.5	133.1	12.8	9.7	21.4	122.7
Services	15.4	12.7	22.4	145.0	12.2	9.0	20.7	118.9
Transport	11.8	14.4	5.1	728.4	8.5	10.0	4.4	623.3
Other	0.1	0.1	0.1	175.2	0.1	0.1	0.1	248.8

a Includes agriculture, forestry, fishing, and mining.
b Includes construction.
c Includes miscellaneous and not stated.

Source: *Population Census of 1950*, Vol. VII, Tables 11 and 12 from prefectural volumes.

ment in Tokyo-Yokohama. The services category here includes government officials as well as professional and white collar personnel. The Tokyo-Yokohama area as national capital and world center has a predominance of Japan's population active in these categories. These are the populations most capable of residing in suburban areas, and the higher level of male service employment in the Tokyo-Yokohama ring is at least partially the result of this type of residential suburb development. In contrast, female

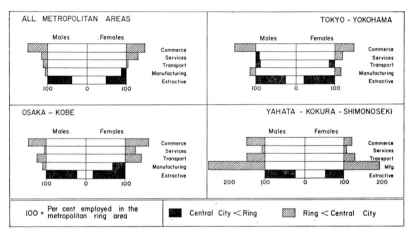

FIGURE X-2: Employment Structures of Central Cities and Metropolitan Rings, 1950 (Source: *Population Census of 1950,* Vol. VII, Tables 11 and 12 in prefectural volumes)

service activity is more heavily committed to traditional service areas. Total Japanese metropolitan areas, as well as the three metropolitan areas shown, show a concentration of females so employed in the central city where opportunities in these fields are most frequent. The contrast here is between male service activity in which professional and white collar employment can provide a standard of living capable of supporting residence in suburbs and commuting to the central city, and female service activities in which domestic employment links the employee closely to place of work. Tokyo-Yokohama is the area in Japan most developed in the professional and white collar occupations, and therefore it shows the only indication of central city-ring differentiation in this respect.

A sex differential associated with manufacturing activity in the central city as against the ring is also present. Manufacturing employment shows only slight differentiation between central city and ring, but the direction of the difference is toward increased male activity and decreased female activity in the central cities. Central cities generally contain the large factory types of industry which favor male employment, as against the outlying areas where the most frequent activity is in the textile and household industries which show increased levels of female labor force participation. For total metropolitan areas and the Osaka-Kobe area the proportion of female labor force active in manufacturing in rings actually rises above that of the central cities. The extensive development of light industries within the central cities of Tokyo-Yokohama reverses the relationship for this area; the heavy commitment to mining and minerals processing in the ring of the Yahata area also gives a larger portion of female labor force to manufacturing in the central cities than in rings.

The point for emphasis here, however, is the dispersed nature of manufacturing within the Japanese metropolitan area. This contrasts sharply with metropolitan manufacturing activities in the United States. Bogue finds a rapid decrease in manufacturing from the central city outward in United States metropolitan areas.[15] The dependence of Japanese industry upon the small production unit, in contrast to the dominance of the large factory pattern found in the United States, highlights a key difference in economic organization. This difference has dynamic consequences for metropolitan development in Japan vis-à-vis the United States. The introductory portions of this chapter suggested a type of economic integration within Japanese metropolitan areas different from that of the United States. It is primarily in terms of the contrast between Japan's small, dispersed production system and the United States system that differences in metropolitan integration become apparent. Though the Japanese industries dependent upon the production by small establishments and household units have efficient warehousing and marketing combines which control production, the fact remains that manufacturing activity as such is

15 Donald J. Bogue, *The Structure of the Metropolitan Community* (Ann Arbor, Mich.: University of Michigan Press, 1950), pp. 153-192.

dispersed. The result is a degree of functional homogeneity within Japanese metropolitan areas which contrasts vividly with metropolitan structure in the West, and particularly in the United States.

A further indication of this relative metropolitan homogeneity is shown in Table X-8. There are only minor differences in the levels of male and female participation in the labor force between central cities and their rings in Japanese metropolitan settlements. As a whole, both sexes increase labor force activity outside the central cities. In contrast, Duncan and Reiss show that in

TABLE X-8. Percentage of Population Fifteen Years of Age and over Employed in Central Cities and Rings of Japanese Metropolitan Areas, by Sex, 1950

| Area | % OF EMPLOYED POPULATION 15 YRS. OF AGE AND OVER | | | |
| | Central Cities | | Rings | |
	Males	Females	Males	Females
TOTAL METRO-POLITAN AREAS	80.2	32.0	83.2	34.1
TOKYO-YOKOHAMA	79.9	29.3	79.6	30.4
OSAKA-KOBE	81.3	27.8	79.0	29.3
YAHATA-KOKURA-SHIMONOSEKI	82.0	31.5	82.2	30.2

Sources: *Population Census of 1950*, Vol. VII, Tables 11 and 12 from prefectural volumes.

United States metropolitan areas labor force participation decreases from the central city outward, and especially for females.[16]

The final area of central city-ring comparison is extractive employment. If the dominant trait of central city employment composition is commerce, that of the ring is surely extractive activities. The growth of metropolitan populations has placed larger and larger numbers of urban dwellers in the former agricultural areas contiguous to central cities. The value of scarce cultivatable land in Japan, however, makes for a tenacious agriculture even when urban land usage competes for the same territory. Further, the excess labor force in urban areas frequently turns to subsistence agriculture on the periphery of cities. Nearly one-fourth of the labor force in the rings of Japan's metropolitan areas is employed

[16] Otis D. Duncan, and Albert J. Reiss, Jr., *Social Characteristics of Urban and Rural Communities, 1950* (New York: John Wiley and Sons, Inc., 1956), p. 128.

in extractive pursuits; even in Tokyo-Yokohama, 17% of the ring labor force is so employed.

In summary, Japanese metropolitan areas have a low level of differentiation in employment structure between central cities and rings. The major contrasts exist between proportional commitments of labor force to commerce and extractive pursuits. The central cities consistently have higher proportions of labor force in commerce and lower proportions in extractive activities than do their ring populations. Manufacturing employment shows only a slight tendency to decrease from central city to ring. The basic shifts in employment which take place outward from the central city are essentially changes in female labor force participation; sex ratios for the two key categories of commerce and manufacturing show a trend of decrease from the central city to the ring.

SUMMARY

This chapter has shown the degree to which Japan's urbanization has moved toward the large, functionally diverse urban agglomeration or metropolitan area. The first national census of 1920 indicated metropolitan development, but it was confined principally to the largest cities. Urban expansion since 1920 has tended to emphasize this trend. The Tokyo-Yokohama and Osaka-Kobe areas currently contain the major portions of Japan's urban-oriented population who are residents of areas outside the boundaries of administratively defined cities. Within these areas the process of deconcentration, familiar to students of United States metropolitan growth, is apparent.

The evidence of metropolitanization in Japanese urban structure indicates, however, that the characteristics of Japanese socio-economic organization contribute to the unique features in her metropolitan growth. The continuation of the small, household-based production and commercial unit results in the dispersal of manufacturing and trade activities throughout the whole of the urban agglomeration. A higher level of homogeneity of labor force activity characterizes Japanese metropolitan population than in the United States. This is not to say that internal differentiation is wholly absent in Japanese metropolitan structure. Commercial activities show a distinct decrease from the central city outward, whereas manufacturing activities are relatively stable throughout the area. Even the largest metropolitan areas show significant levels of agriculture in ring areas, and this activity rapidly decreases toward the central cities.

Japanese metropolitanization, therefore, can be characterized as relatively narrow in areal terms, but sufficiently high in density to account for a significant portion of Japan's total urban population. Further, Japanese social, and specifically economic, organization militates against the high level of functional heterogeneity characteristic of Western metropolitan structure.

Japanese Urbanization: An International Comparison   XI

The differences between the patterns of Japanese urban growth and those of the industrialized nations of the West have been emphasized. It is well to note, however, that there are numerous basic similarities in these patterns of city development. Such similarities are the consequences of what may be termed the functional prerequisites of urbanization as a process, irrespective of its specific cultural context.

It is possible to see the roots of these prerequisites in the development of man's earliest permanent settlements.[1] The Neolithic domestication of plants and animals and the invention of tools which significantly expanded raw manpower meant essentially that man could control his food supply. Groups larger than nomadic familial units could settle more or less permanently in one area. Historically these settlements can be viewed as the first link in a chain of material and social creations culminating in the city as we know it today. The improvements in agricultural and metallurgical technology which followed these early beginnings made possible the emergence of the townsmen: artisan, trader, ruler and religious functionary. This is to say that expansion of individual productivity in agriculture made possible the freeing of a segment of society for activities not directly connected with the production of food. The first functional prerequisite of urbanization is, then, a minimal social "specialization" or division of labor based upon the development of an agricultural

[1] See Kingsley Davis, "The Origin and Growth of Urbanization in the World," *The American Journal of Sociology*, LX, 5 (March, 1955), pp. 429-438.

technology. An agricultural "revolution" must precede an urban-industrial revolution.

The extent to which an agricultural "revolution" can support city growth is evidenced by the existence of large cities in the period prior to a genuine industrial revolution. Fifteenth century Venice and London, or the earlier cities of Egypt, Greece and India, are illustrations that immediately come to mind. However, compared to contemporary urban settlements these earlier cities are not particularly impressive either in size or number. Until the advances in industrial technology of the eighteenth and nineteenth centuries, urban populations were effectively limited by the capacity of their agricultural hinterlands to support them. The revolution in industrial techniques for the first time made it possible for city dwellers to begin to contribute significantly to their own support. It became possible for the townsman to produce to such capacity that he could begin to supply the agriculturalist with mass produced items at a lower time cost as well as monetary cost than the agriculturalist could supply himself. There is visible here the beginning of the modern symbiotic relationship of rural and urban specialists. The second functional prerequisite of urbanization as illustrated here is an industrial technology of such magnitude as to supplant effectively nonagricultural subsistence production by agriculturalists. Modern society is a complex system of relationships between specialists; genuine self-sufficient subsistence production by individuals or small familial units cannot be maintained as part of the larger system.

Indices of the working out of adaptations to these functional prerequisites can be observed in the structures of contemporary urban-industrial societies. If we accept an approximate minimum of one-half of total population living in cities as designating urbanized countries, we can expect at least two types of relationships: 1) proportion of economically active outside the agricultural category will correlate positively with level of urbanization, and 2) the contribution of agriculture to total national production will have an inverse relationship with level of urbanization.

Table XI-1 shows recent data for these two relationships. A simple Spearman rank correlation (r_r) for per cent of total population defined urban and per cent male labor force in nonagricultural pursuits is .74; the r_r for per cent urban and per cent of gross domestic product originating in agriculture, forestry and fishing is —.50. These gross indicators of the urbanization process as postulated here tend to bear out the validity of this approach.

The process of urbanization itself exercises a range of functional demands upon a population. With a shift from an agricultural

TABLE XI-1: Indices of Urbanization and Level of Economic Development for Nations More Than 50% Urban, *circa* 1950

Country	Per Cent Total Population Defined Urban[a]	Per Cent Males in Nonagricultural Employment[b]	Per Cent Gross Domestic Product from Agriculture, Forestry, Fishing[c]
United Kingdom	80.3[d]	93.6	4
Israel	71.3[d]	88.9	12
Germany	71.0[d]	82.2	7
Australia	68.9	80.9	N.A.
Denmark	67.3	71.0	15
United States	64.0[d]	91.5	5
Belgium	62.7	86.4	7
Argentina	62.5	70.3	22
Canada	61.6	76.5	7
New Zealand	61.3	77.8	22
Cuba	57.0[d]	53.1	N.A.
France	55.9	73.8	10
Netherlands	54.6	80.0	11
Venezuela	53.8	52.3	N.A.
Japan	53.5	59.8	15

a Unless otherwise designated the urban population is that reported in the *Demographic Yearbook, 1955*, Tables 7 and 8.

b Unless otherwise designated the source for figures is *Demographic Yearbook, 1956*, Table 12.

c United States, Bureau of the Census, *Statistical Abstract of the United States, 1962*, p. 915.

d From official census reports and yearbooks.

focus to an industrial one, the way of life within a given society changes significantly in terms of the qualifications for participation in that society. The evaluation of individual traits vis-à-vis social status, for example in the labor force, is altered to meet the new requirements of an emerging specialization. This is to say that the urbanization process is selective of demographic characteristics; urban populations differ measurably from their surrounding rural populations. This generalization, however, must be qualified by the level of urbanization involved. Mature urban societies show little rural-urban differentiation since the major portion of the population has become "urbanized" in way of life even if geographically it does not fall within administrative boundaries of cities. Rogoff and associates[2] have investigated the hypothesis that the greater the concentration of persons in large cities, the greater the diffusion of urban functional demands for participation in the society. Hence the higher the level of urbanization the smaller should be the discrepancy between urban and rural age composition. To test this hypothesis, per cent of total population in cities of 100,000 persons and over was correlated with an index of rural-urban age structure differentiation:

$$\frac{\text{Per Cent of Non-Urban Population Aged 15-65 Years}}{\text{Per Cent of Urban Population Aged 15-65 Years}} \times 100.$$

The resulting coefficient of linear correlation (r) for thirty-two countries was —.71, indicating that some one-half the variation among countries in rural-urban age structure differences is accounted for by the variation in their level of urbanization.

Again, the conclusion to be drawn is that there are significant elements of universality in the urbanization process. One more illustration will suffice to emphasize this point. Throughout Japan's modern era, the same cities have tended to be her largest cities; newer urban increases have tended to come to the older larger cities. We term this process one of urban size begetting size. Davis has shown the same to be true of Indian cities for the past seventy years.[3] The history of the relative sizes of New York and Chicago for the United States, of London and Birmingham in the United Kingdom, and of Paris and Marseilles for France reveals much the same pattern. These comparisons suggest a further hypothesis relative to the universals of urbanization: a nation's urban structure tends to take the form of a relatively stable *system* of cities. This system is the result of the manner in which a series of urban growth factors are distributed among the nation's cities. The location of such functions as national

[2] Natalie Rogoff, *et al.*, *Demographic Indices of the World's Urban Population*, (Columbia University, Bureau of Applied Social Research, 1953). (Processed).

[3] Kingsley Davis, *The Population of India and Pakistan* (Princeton: Princeton University Press, 1951), pp. 130-131.

capital, the major commercial and/or transportation center, and access to a deep water port form singly or in combination a relatively permanent base of urban growth for specific cities. The dominance by London of the United Kingdom's urbanization or the position of Paris in French urban growth, as well as Tokyo's historical leadership among Japanese cities, all reveal aspects of this type of urban system.

The recognition of national systems of cities with a concomitant process of increasing urban concentration is further supported when data for metropolitan areas are brought to bear. Though our initial concern was with designating similarities in urbanization throughout the world, metropolitan structure comparisons make it possible to lead into the unique aspects of urban growth and, more specifically, to focus upon the variations which Japan's urbanization incorporates.

To begin, previous studies have established the existence of a high positive association between urbanization and economic development. In computing levels of urbanization, these studies have utilized officially reported populations in all administratively defined cities or segments thereof. For instance, a correlation between percentage of economically active males in nonextractive employment for all countries of over one million total population (circa 1945) has a significantly high positive index of correlation (see Chapter VI).

The availability of metropolitan data with relatively complete world coverage[4] makes possible further investigations of the structure of urban population in its association with economic development. The proportion of population residing in politically defined cities provides an index of the *extent* of a nation's urbanization; the proportion of population residing in metropolitan areas highlights the *depth* or concentration of that urbanization. Here the essential question is whether or not both of these facets of the urban process bear the same relationship to industrialization. A simple ratio of the metropolitan population to the total urban population gives a rough index of metropolitan concentration. This index, in turn, can be correlated with nonextractive

---

[4] International Urban Research, *The World's Metropolitan Areas* (Berkeley: The University of California Press, 1959).

TABLE XI-2: Indices of Urbanization, Metropolitanization, and Economic Development for Selected Countries, *circa* 1950

Country	Date	Per Cent Total Population Defined Urban[a] (1)	Per Cent Total Population in Metropolitan Areas[b] (2)	Metropolitan Index: Col. (2) / Col. (1) (3)	Per Cent Males in Non-agricultural Employment[c] (4)
50% or More Urban					
United Kingdom	1951	80.3[d]	77.0	0.959	93.6
Israel	1949	71.3[d]	55.9	0.784	88.9
Germany	1950	71.0[d]	46.7	0.658	82.2
Australia	1947	68.9	55.4	0.804	80.9
Denmark	1950	67.3	45.5	0.676	71.0
United States	1950	64.0[d]	55.9	0.873	91.5
Belgium	1947	62.7	41.4	0.660	86.4
Argentina	1947	62.5	43.8	0.700	70.3
Canada	1951	61.6	45.5	0.739	76.5
New Zealand	1951	61.3	33.6	0.711	77.8
Cuba	1953	57.0[d]	26.0	0.456	53.1
France	1954	55.9	34.4	0.615	73.8
Netherlands	1947	54.6	45.6	0.835	80.0
Venezuela	1950	53.8	26.2	0.487	52.3
Japan	1950	53.5	36.9	0.716	59.8
25-50% Urban					
Austria	1951	49.2	38.9	0.791	75.1
Sweden	1950	47.5	31.8	0.669	74.7
Mexico	1950	42.6[d]	20.3	0.477	42.2
Union S. Africa	1951	42.6	31.5	0.739	53.0
Ireland	1951	41.5	23.4	0.564	54.0
Italy	1951	40.9[d]	27.3	0.667	57.5
Spain	1950	37.0	24.2	0.654	46.6
Greece	1951	36.8	22.0	0.598	50.5
Switzerland	1950	36.5	41.2	1.129	78.5
El Salvador	1950	36.5	11.9	0.326	26.7
Columbia	1951	36.3	18.6	0.512	36.8[d]
Brazil	1950	36.2	17.6	0.486	37.3
Peru	1940	36.1	10.4	0.288	33.7[d]
Panama	1950	36.0	23.9	0.664	40.8
Nicaragua	1950	34.9	13.3	0.381	23.1
Paraguay	1950	34.6	15.6	0.451	35.1[d]
Iraq	1947	33.8	17.5	0.518	45.0[d]
Costa Rica	1950	33.5	19.9	0.594	37.4
Finland	1950	32.3	17.0	0.526	53.9
Norway	1950	32.2	21.8	0.677	68.6
Portugal	1950	31.2	19.6	0.628	47.9
Honduras	1950	31.0	7.3	0.235	16.9

TABLE XI-2: (*Continued*)

Country	Date	Per Cent Total Population Defined Urban[a] (1)	Per Cent Total Population in Metropolitan Areas[b] (2)	Metropolitan Index: Col. (2) / Col. (1) (3)	Per Cent Males in Nonagricultural Employment[c] (4)
Egypt	1947	30.1	19.6	0.651	47.6
Ecuador	1950	28.5	14.9	0.523	38.1
Malaya	1947	26.5	12.7	0.470	39.2
25% or Less Urban					
Guatemala	1950	25.0	10.6	0.424	24.0[d]
Philippines	1948	24.1	10.3	0.427	36.4
Dominican Rep.	1950	23.8	11.2	0.471	34.7
Turkey	1950	21.9	14.0	0.639	30.6
India	1951	17.3	7.8	0.451	30.6
Ceylon	1946	15.4	9.5	0.617	49.4
Haiti	1950	12.2	6.0	0.492	13.4
Pakistan	1951	11.4	5.1	0.447	23.7
Thailand	1947	9.9[d]	6.8	0.687	18.3

a Unless otherwise designated the urban population is that reported in the *Demographic Yearbook, 1955,* Tables 7 and 8.

b Metropolitan area delimitations prepared by International Urban Research, University of California, Berkeley.

c Unless otherwise designated the source for these figures is the *Demographic Yearbook, 1956,* Table 12.

d From official census reports and yearbooks.

employment as a practical test of the association of metropolitanization and industrial activity.

Table XI-2 shows the 49 nations for which data on urbanization, metropolitanization, and economic activity are available circa 1950. The index of metropolitan concentration is shown in Column 3. A linear correlation of this index and the percentage of males in nonextractive employment results in an index of correlation (r) of +.776 for the total sample. Metropolitanization therefore bears a relatively close association to industrialization, but not so close as that between the extent of urbanization, as measured by population in cities of 100,000 and over, and industrial activity.

Of primary significance is the fact that the association of metropolitanization and economic development becomes closer as the extent of urbanization increases. This is to say that as the proportion of population in administratively defined cities increases, the concentration of urban population in metropolitan areas reflects more clearly the level of industrial development. The 15 countries with more than 50 per cent of their total population defined as urban have a coefficient of correlation of +.841 between metropolitan concentration and industrial activity, as shown in Table XI-3. This association decreases to +.828 for the 41 countries with more than 25 per cent population defined as urban. Both these associations are closer than the +.776 cited above for the total sample of 49 nations.

TABLE XI-3: Correlations of Metropolitanization Index and Economic Development for Selected Countries, *circa* 1950

Percentage Urban[a]	Number of Countries	Coefficient of Correlation (r)[b]
Over 50%	15	+.841
Over 25%	41	+.828
TOTAL	49	+.776

[a] Per cent of total population residing in administratively defined cities.

[b] Linear correlation computed for percentage of economically active males in nonextractive employment and index of metropolitanization:

$$\frac{\text{Per cent of total population in metropolitan areas}}{\text{Per cent total population urban}}$$

Sources: See Table XI-2.

These results confirm the linkage of metropolitanization and economic development, but the association is a qualified one. High levels of urbanization and industrial activity are positively associated with metropolitanization, but the development of population agglomerations which are metropolitan in character is not invariably linked to these two traits. Metropolitan growth is characteristic of some countries of relatively low urbanization and industrial development. Table XI-4 shows that the average

TABLE XI-4: Distribution of Metropolitan Areas of One Million Population or More by Level of Urbanization for Selected Countries, *circa* 1950

Percentage Urban	Number of Countries	Number of M.A.'s One Million Plus	Average Number M.A.'s
Over 50%	15	44	2.9
25%-50%	25	14	0.6
Under 25%	9	9	1.0

Sources: See Table XI-2.

number of metropolitan areas of over one million population for countries of less than 25 per cent urban is almost twice that for countries between 25 per cent and 50 per cent urban. India, for example, although low in total level of urban residence (17.3 per cent) and in male nonextractive employment (30.6 per cent), contains some of the world's largest metropolitan areas among her five urban agglomerations of over one million population.

Preliminary historical analyses in Western nations suggest that even where levels of urbanization and metropolitanization are both currently high, significant differentials existed during earlier periods. Manchester, England, a far from rare example, quite early in the industrialization process reached a size in excess of 100,000 population. Even before the coming of modern transportation facilities in the form of the steam railway, Manchester would appear to have reached metropolitan size and to have done so when the national level of urbanization in England was relatively low. This suggests the possibility that in the earlier phases of urban-industrialism in Western nations relatively low urbanization was coupled with relatively high metropolitanization. It is significant that even in Western nations such as England the appearance of areas of metropolitan size *preceded* the major developments in transportation and communication technology.

It is clear that understanding the development of metropolitan concentrations historically in Western nations and currently in non-Western nations will require the search for factors other than technological or those associated with the technological expansion closely identified with Western industrialization.

The deviant cases in the metropolitan-industrial relationship discussed above show certain regularities. In Latin American nations, for instance, comparatively higher levels of over-all urbanization are associated with lower metropolitanization, irrespective of nonagricultural employment levels. Table XI-2 shows that Cuba and Venezuela have the lowest metropolitan indices of all nations with more than 50 per cent urban populations. At the other extreme, Guatemala has the lowest metropolitan index of all nations 25 per cent or less urban; while the lowest metropolitan index of the total sample is that for Honduras, though her total population is nearly one-third urban. In contrast, a group of Eastern and African nations which are low in economic development and extent of urbanization show comparatively high metropolitan levels. The following summary is illustrative of the major regional differences:

	Western Europe and Anglo-America	Latin America	The East and Africa
Industrialization	High	Moderate/Low	Medium/Low
Urbanization	High	High	Low
Metropolitanization	High	Low	High

Analysis of all the nations falling within these categories is beyond the scope of the present study. However, a summary of the major elements underlying Japanese urbanization as contained in the present study can serve to confirm the earlier contention that within the framework of conforming to the functional prerequisites of urbanization, a wide range of organizational alternatives exists.

Japan has the lowest percentage of total population defined as urban and the third lowest percentage of males in nonagricultural employment of the 15 nations with more than half their total populations defined as urban (Table XI-2). Nevertheless the metropolitan index places her above many of the highly industrialized nations of the West. The contrast between Japan and Germany or France, for example, shows Japan to be less urbanized and less industrialized, but more metropolitan. Japan therefore illustrates again the lack of a direct association of urban-industrialism with metropolitan growth. Japan's industrial transition, with respect to both the nature of her economic organization and her population movements, was and continues to be of a kind that makes understandable her deviation from Western experience.

First, the paucity of cultivatable land within the home islands coupled with an industrial system which has never been able to reduce significantly the agricultural labor force, creates a constant pressure toward areal compactness of urban settlements. The agricultural density of Japan (males working in agriculture per square mile of cultivated land) is over 400, as against an average of 79 for Europe and ten for the United States and Canada. Although nonagricultural employment and urban population show consistent increases throughout the last century, the absolute number of Japanese agricultural households has remained relatively stable: 5.6 million in 1872 and 6.1 million in 1951. The competition from agricultural land usage and high rural densities means that urban population increases are apt to take place within existing urban boundaries or in minimal annexations of contiguous territory. Therefore, Japan's rapid increases in urban population have tended to increase city sizes to the metropolitan level rather than to create extensive suburbanization around the cities.

In addition to these spatial pressures toward metropolitanization, Japanese economic organization tends to concentrate even further the urban population. Two basically dissimilar productive systems make up Japanese industrial structure. The so-called strategic industries—shipbuilding, chemicals, armaments, and the like—have been developed through governmental sponsorship and subsidy, and have since their beginning utilized the most advanced industrial technology. The development of this segment of the Japanese economy was intended principally to implement Japan's early nationalistic political aims, rather than as a policy to improve standards of living for the population as a whole. Production of goods for home consumption has been largely left to household-handicraft industry. The "putting out" system is widely used in this type of production, even in the largest cities, and exists side by side with large-scale factories. The result of this dual productive system is to increase greatly the proportions of the industrial labor force and the number of industrial establishments which fall into the "small" industry category.

With a limited number of large-scale industries, and these centered in a few major urban regions, the employment opportunities associated with an expanding Japanese industrialization tend to channel urban population increases toward already existing urban areas. The industrial labor force engaged in subsistence production of the handicraft-household type functions in combination employment-residence locations within the cities or blends into rural areas where agriculture can become a secondary occupation. This fact helps to explain the significantly high proportion of agriculturalists within the administrative boundaries of even the largest of Japan's cities. Nerima ward, an outlying area of the city of Tokyo, for example, had 14.5 per cent of its economically active males in agriculture as late as 1950.

Only the two largest of Japan's metropolitan areas have developed sufficiently to counteract the pressures toward concentration cited here. Tokyo-Yokohama and Osaka-Kobe show significant peripheral urbanization outside the administrative boundaries of the cities falling within these metropolitan areas. The remaining 61 of Japan's metropolitan areas emphasize the pattern of concentration within the cities. In only 24 of Japan's 63 metropolitan areas in 1955 did persons live outside the administrative boundaries of incorporated cities, and 84.2 per cent of this suburban population was contained in 12 of the 24 metropolitan areas. Moreover, 49 per cent of these 2.8 million suburbanites resided within either the Tokyo-Yokohama or Osaka-Kobe metropolitan area.

This summary of the factors underlying the emergence of Japan's metropolitan structure has served to highlight two elements contributing to the uniqueness of Japan's urbanization as a whole. First, the sheer lack of geographical area relative to total population has led to a "tighter" urban settlement pattern. This is to say more than that both rural and urban densities in Japan are high compared to other nations. There is a higher *functional* density as well. Differentiated activities which in most Western industrial nations tend to be spatially separated are, in Japan, frequently found close together. This is especially true when one observes the interpenetration of agrarian and nonagrarian activities within the ecological structure of Japanese cities.

Second, the economic processes whereby Japan's industrial transition was accomplished were heavily influenced by governmental participation. This participation was nationalistic rather than economic in purpose. Japan's early modern leaders were concerned that they create a Japan strong politically on the international scene, and national economic development was a major means to that end. Any improvements in individual standards of living and consumption patterns were largely fortuitous. The bifurcated economic system noted above was the result; export, and other internationally significant production, felt the impact of technological modernization while consumer production tended to remain largely in traditional forms. The result of these economic factors for Japanese urbanization is seen largely in the nature of the industrial labor force which combines both the highly skilled and the handicraft worker.

The maintenance of a viable segment of the economic structure which is essentially handicraft in organization places the Japanese family system in a unique role vis-à-vis the industrialization of the nation. In facing the difficulties of modernizing their nation, the leaders of early modern Japan recognized the effectiveness of the traditional family system. Their approach essentially was to alter the overt, material aspects of Japan through industrialization, while preserving significant elements from the covert, non-material system as mechanisms of social control. Individual life was to become subordinate to the family unit (*ie*); the *ie* was to be the essential institution in a way of life that would maintain the social structure and values of an agrarian past in an industrializing present.

The relevance of these facets of Japanese family structure to the urban-industrialization of the nation lies in their creation of channels for the shift of individuals from agrarian to industrial pursuits. Given the family organizational traits cited above, this shift represented for the individual worker a change in means of earning a living which entailed a rather narrow range of reorientation in his mode of existence. Even after his migration to the city for new employment, all significant changes in his social status (e.g., marriages, births, divorces, and deaths) were referred to the family register in his place of origin. The urban-industrial labor force thus expanded, but it carried with it significant ties to traditional social groupings. The dislocations of World War II and the Occupation-sponsored revisions of the civil code weakened traditional family attitudes. However, there remains sufficient evidence to continue to regard Japan as essentially familistic in outlook.[5]

The economic organization created to administer Japan's modern industrialization reflects clearly this basic familism. The emergence of an industrial elite was not so much the result of

[5] Attitude surveys in contemporary Japan reveal a continuation of traditional outlooks especially in the area of family relationships; see, for example, Shio Sakanishi, "Women's Position and the Family System," *The Annals of the American Academy of Political and Social Science,* 308 (November, 1956), pp. 130-140.

a rational, competitive sorting of individuals as it was the co-operation of strategically placed family units. The great commercial houses (*zaibatsu*) bear the family names of the kinship groups who own and administer them. The principal channels for participation at the upper levels in these enterprises are birth and marriage into the controlling family units. These powerful kinship units are the descendants of the group of energetic former members of the warrior class (*samurai*) who were largely responsible for initiating the opening of Japan and administering the early steps toward modernization. Meiji policies of modernization were evolved largely through the cooperation of the government and these economically powerful familial groups.[6]

Abegglen's post-World War II study[7] traces recruitment policies for the executive levels of Japanese industry and shows that young candidates for employment at these levels are the products of particular schools and professors who have maintained placement relationships with specific companies for decades. Once the man is employed, his tie to the company is a permanent one both with respect to his loyalty to the employer and the employer's loyalty to him. Occupational advancement is conceived as possible exclusively within the channels of the particular company of one's original employment. The permanence of employment is recognized as a lasting commitment assumed by the employer for the laborer as well. In times of falling production, the employee is furloughed at a reduced wage, but with the understanding that he is to be recalled when labor force needs again rise. There are striking echoes of the relationships of the pre-Restoration feudal lord with his warrior staff and his agrarian workers in those of the modern Japanese employer and his employees.

Even this brief summary of the interplay of Japanese family organization and industrial development supports the recognition of Japanese familism as a channel for the flow of feudal-tinged outlooks and organizational techniques from the agrarian past

---

6 Thomas C. Smith, *Political Change and Industrial Development in Japan: Government Enterprise, 1868-1880* (Stanford: Stanford University Press, 1955), and William W. Lockwood, *The Economic Development of Japan* (Princeton: Princeton University Press, 1954).

7 James G. Abegglen, *The Japanese Factory: Aspects of Its Social Organization* (Glencoe, Ill.: The Free Press, 1958).

into the industrial present. Our task now is to verify these traditional elements through the use of specific indices.

First, let it be noted that the tenacity of traditional familial elements was not fostered merely by a nostalgic attachment to the past; there were valid economic reasons for their retention. From the beginnings of Japan's modernization her most abundant resource has been manpower, and her scarcest resource has been investment capital. An economic organization which could substitute labor for capital was the one most likely to be successful. If traditional industry, with its emphasis upon hand labor, could be turned from subsistence to market production, the profits could be invested in new heavy industries which demand large capital outlay. At the risk of oversimplification, this describes, in large measure, the policy followed in Japanese industrial development. The traditional handicraft production unit, which significantly was also a strong family unit, was made an integral part of Japan's industrial structure.

The industrial and commercial organization of modern Japan shows clearly the consequences of these policies: in 1954, 50% of Japanese industrial establishments, employing 12% of her industrial labor force, had less than five workers. In the same year, 87% of her trade establishments with 55% of the labor force in trade were of this size. The census of 1955 shows that a significant proportion of these small economic units were family units. This census reports "unpaid family workers" as "persons who work without pay in the business, farm, trade or professional enterprise operated by a member of the household in which they live. Persons helping their relatives in their works without pay are included in this category, even if they do not belong to the proprietor's household." These, then, are persons doing not merely housework but engaging rather in a more genuine occupational activity. Approximately one-third (30.5%) of Japan's 1955 labor force were in this category. In contrast, the United States had 2.5% (1959) and Great Britain 0.2% (1950) in this category.

The figures for unpaid family workers refer to the total labor force, including those in agriculture, where this type of employment is to be expected. Our primary concern, however, is with that segment of the employment structure specifically associated with urban-industrialism. If we consider the two largest urban concentrations in Japan, Tokyo-*to* and Osaka-*fu*, we note that the proportion cited for the nation as a whole decreases, but also that the role of unpaid family workers is still a significant one, especially in the commercial area (Table XI-5).

TABLE XI-5: Percentage Distribution of Unpaid Family Workers by Industry, Tokyo-*to* and Osaka-*fu*, 1955

Industrial Category	Per Cent of Total Employed in Industry Who Are Unpaid Family Workers		Per Cent Distribution of Total Unpaid Family Workers in Area	
	Tokyo	Osaka	Tokyo	Osaka
Extractive (Agriculture, For., Fish., Min.)	55.1	48.8	28.7	37.8
Mfg. (incl. Const.)	3.9	4.4	20.5	18.5
Wholesale Trade (inc. Fin., Ins. & R.E.)	3.8	5.6	3.9	4.8
Retail Trade	16.7	22.4	36.7	30.1
Transp. & Communication	0.2	0.6	0.3	0.5
Services	3.7	6.2	9.9	8.3
TOTAL	7.3	10.2	100.0	100.0

Source: *1955 Population Census of Japan*, Prefectural Volumes V-13, V-27, Table 10.

The contribution of unpaid family employment to the economic structure of urban areas is shown in more detail in Table XI-6. Here, the proportion of unpaid family workers active in

TABLE XI-6: Median Percentage of Labor Force Employed as Unpaid Family Workers by Sex and City Size, 1955

		UNPAID FAMILY WORKERS			
		Males		Females	
City Size	No. of Cities	Median	Range	Median	Range
Under 50,000	253	17.6	2.1-30.5	67.9	11.5-80.2
50,000-74,999	103	12.2	2.1-27.7	49.8	11.2-76.5
75,000-99,999	37	17.3	2.1-20.8	46.2	12.0-69.7
100,000-249,999	73	8.4	2.3-21.1	38.2	17.5-62.4
250,000-499,999	18	5.6	2.6-12.4	25.7	15.7-41.4
500,000-749,999	1	5.0	—	21.4	—
750,000-999,999	1	3.9	—	20.3	—
1,000,000 & over	5	4.5	3.1- 6.1	20.8	13.6-22.7

Source: *1955 Population Census of Japan*, Prefectural Volumes V-1 through V-46, Table 10.

administratively defined cities is presented by size of city. There is a clear inverse relationship between city size and participation of unpaid family workers in the labor force. We conclude that an increasing rate of urbanization, as measured by size, tends to weaken the force of familial production units in Japanese industrial organization. However, urban-industrialization does not destroy these channels for agrarian traditions, for historical and present necessities keep them as basic to Japanese industrial structure. This does not mean that Japanese economic organization is therefore inefficient. A distinction between organizational efficiency and technological efficiency is useful here. Japanese industry is certainly in some segments technologically inefficient—machine tools could vastly increase production of those goods and services now produced by hand and hand tools. The organizational efficiency of Japanese industry, however, is just as certainly of a high order. The utilization of hand labor absorbs much of the oversupply of laborers who otherwise would be unemployed. By integrating them into the economic system, modern Japanese industry quite efficiently substitutes labor for scarce capital. In the process, the social environment of Japan's urban centers evolves a unique blending of the present and the past.

SUMMARY

We have approached the urbanization and industrialization of Japan with a twofold purpose: to reveal the nature of Japan's conformity to the universal demands of modernization and to explore the unique means whereby Japan has selected from structural alternatives in evolving her own urban-industrial social system.

In terms of the universals of the urbanization process, Japanese experience conforms to the theoretical model. Growth of urban population paralleled the shift from an agrarian centered system to an industrial one. A developed division of labor emerged which in demographic terms differentiates population along a rural-urban continuum. The maturation of Japan's urban-industrial process has seen the development of metropolitan complexes. The specific organizational forms which are present in Japan's urban-industrialism, however, are uniquely Japanese. This, of course, is true in comparisons among Western nations as well. Once one leaves the level of univeral generalization with respect to urban-industrialization, for example, the particular French, Dutch, or German elements in their respective modern histories become visible. A case study of Japan re-emphasizes this point and, in turn, heightens sensitivity to variations in the transitions of nations within the Western group.

The unique elements in the Japanese urban-industrial transition can be summarized under three major headings: political, economic, and familial. Each of these areas reveals the adaptations of a primary social institution to the prerequisites of an urban-industrial transition. The "raw materials" of past history were molded and edited to fit newly introduced requirements of social organization. The migration of the agrarian peasant from his rural location to Japan's growing cities meant a great deal more functionally than a mere shift in the geographical distribution of national population. In essence, Japanese social organization had to deal with the penetration of goals and values which at their base were international in scope. The world view of the Japanese was expanded in recognition of the interdependence of their own system and that of other nations. The stresses and strains generated in this process were largely absorbed by the upper levels of the Japanese politico-economic hierarchy, in significant contrast to the rather widespread social disorganizations which characterized the transitional periods of most Western European societies.

This last point is a convenient bridge to a summary of the first of the three areas of Japanese adaptation noted above. The role of Japan's political leadership in goal formulation and utilization of resources toward the accomplishment of these goals in Japan's early modern period stands in sharp contrast to that of the West. The wealth of Japan at the time of her opening to international activities was in the hands of a merchant class oriented wholly to an internal economic system (see Chapter II). The economic power available had been evolved in terms of adaptations to a single political structure. The wealth and power generated from international sources through foreign commercial activities which characterized Western European merchants were absent in Japan in the initial phases of her modernization. As a consequence, the role of Japanese political administration took on a large share of the entrepreneurial functions both with respect to foreign commercial and industrial activities and the development of that segment of the indigenous economy relevant to foreign activities.

Within this framework Japanese economic and industrial development served the specific political purposes of those primarily concerned with the international political standing of Japan. In this sense Japan's early modernization was a "planned" transition. The results for the concomitant urbanization lay largely in the forms of economic organization upon which city growth was based.

Governmental sponsorship through subsidies and outright ownership of those segments of the economy which were relevant to fostering Japan's international standing meant that these industries felt rapid technological change and expansion. Those industries largely devoted to consumer production were left to traditional means of production. Here, again, we stress the source of the combination of the mechanical and the handicraft noted even in contemporary Japanese economic organization. The pressures of efficiency in manpower utilization characteristic of an industrializing system would be expected to destroy the remnants of traditional productive techniques. However, Japan's relatively large population at the onset of her industrialization and the continuous increase in population during her modern period have created an "oversupply" of labor force which is absorbed into those segments of the economy where the ratio of manpower to production is high. There is, therefore, an efficient substitution of a plentiful manpower for a less plentiful investment capital.

The demographic characteristics of Japan's urban populations clearly reveal this background. The penetration of agricultural activities into the administratively defined urban population's labor force shows the narrowness of the line between urban and rural labor force differentiation. Further, the significant proportions of unpaid family workers in urban employment categories indicate a dependence upon the handicraft, family based production and commercial unit.

The utilization of the familial unit in these activities has consequences beyond the form of economic organization. The maintenance of groupings which have as their primary basis for unity elements of kinship creates a channel for the flow of tradition-tinged values and social mechanisms. These values and mechanisms are of necessity modified by an urban context and especially by Japan's experiences of World War II and after, but the crucial point is that the channels are not destroyed. The urban-industrialization of employment does not necessarily mean the disbanding of the Japanese family as a functioning productive unit. This is in sharp contrast to the family unit in the urban industrial context of most of the Western European nations, where economic activities are almost exclusively outside the home and where the familial group functions as a consumption unit, not as a productive unit.

It is in this sort of generalization that the analysis of Japanese urban experience takes on its greatest significance. The unique ways in which a Japanese urban system evolved, utilizing modified elements from its traditional social organization, underscore the theoretical contention that there exists a wide range of alternatives to the patterns of adaptation present in Western urban systems. The Japanese urban experience adds little, if at all, to the *general* theory of urban-industrialization. The growth of urban areas as a concomitant of the introduction of manpower-expanding technologies and production for markets beyond indigenous consumer needs occurred in Japan as the same generalized process had occurred in previously developed nations. In this sense, Japan falls uneventfully into the category of urban-industrialized nations.

Once beyond this level, however, the history of Japan's transition provides those nations currently at earlier stages with stimulating clues to the possibilities inherent in the transition to industrialization. Again, this is not to say that Japan is the prototype of non-Western urban industrialization. Rather, those who are exercising leadership in the modernization of the non-Western nations can in their policy decisions draw upon a vastly expanded range of alternatives. For if there is one overriding conclusion to be drawn from the Japanese experience, it is that the technological and organizational means necessary for urban-industrialization can be utilized in such a way as to create a unique system which carries the stamp of the particular society's goals and values, both past and present.

Appendix I

Population of Japan
During the Tokugawa Period

Year	Population*
1721	26,065,425
1726	26,548,998
1732	26,921,816
1744	26,153,450
1750	25,917,830
1756	26,061,830
1762	25,921,458
1768	26,252,057
1774	25,990,451
1780	26,010,600
1786	25,086,466
1792	24,891,441
1798	25,471,033
1804	25,517,729
1816	25,621,957
1828	27,201,400
1834	27,063,907
1846	26,907,625

* This chart does not include those of the rank of lord (*tono*) or above, *samurai*, or those attached as serving persons to *samurai* houses. The inclusion of persons below fifteen years of age depended upon the custom of each feudal domain. Honjo concludes that it is justifiable to estimate the total population of Japan for the latter half of the Tokugawa period as being between 28,000,000 and 30,000,000.

Source: Honjo, Eijoro, *Jinkō oyobi jinkō mondai* (Population and Population Problems) (Tokyo: Nihon Hyoronsha, 1930), p. 38.

Appendix II

Populations of Japanese Cities During the Tokugawa Period (1600-1868)

Population figures for cities in Japan under the Tokugawa of necessity must be estimates. The primary sources of these estimates are surveys conducted within the feudal domains by the lords for purposes of taxation. Warriors and persons less than fifteen years of age were usually excluded from these counts since rarely did they fall under the tax laws. In many cases records of even these incomplete counts were not preserved by the local lords. The following list of Tokugawa cities, therefore, is complete neither as to the number of cities nor the total resident populations.

The three largest cities of Edo (Tokyo), Osaka, and Kyoto are those for which the greatest amount of data exists. Each of these cities is presented below in some detail. The sources for these population figures are Eijiro Honjo, *Jinkō oyobi jinkō mondai* (Population and Population Problems) (Tokyo: Nihon Hyoronsha, 1930), pp. 91-103, and Bonsen Takahashi, *Nihon jinkōshi no kenkyū* (Study of the History of Japan's Population) (Tokyo: Sanyusha, 1941), pp. 235-60. Following these are listed the cities for which only scattered data at infrequent intervals are available. Takeshi Toyoda, *Nihon no hōken toshi* (The Feudal Cities of Japan) (Tokyo: Iwanami Zenshu, 1956), pp. 148-58, is the source of these data.

TABLE A. The Population of Edo (Tokyo) under the Tokugawa

		POPULATION	
	Date	Townsmen[a]	Others[b]
1721,	November	501,394	
1722,	March	526,211	44,014
	April	483,355	
	September	476,236	
1723,	April	459,842	
	May	526,212	44,013
	May	526,317	
	September	473,840	
1724,	April	464,577	
	July	537,531	38,127
	September	469,343	
1725,	April	460,102	
	June	472,496	
	September	537,531	
1726		471,988	
1731		525,700	29,980
1732		533,518	
1735		525,700	29,980
1737		526,212	33,173
1742		515,122	50,815
1744		526,612	8,062
1746		515,122	
1750		509,708	
1756		505,858	
1762		595,858	
1768		508,467	
1774		482,747	
1780		489,787	
1786		457,083	
1786,	October	1,285,300[c]	64,240
1791		535,710	30,071
1792		481,669	
1798,	May	492,449	
1804		492,053	
1810		497,085	
1816		501,161	
1822		520,793	
1828		527,293	
1832		545,623	
1834		545,623	
1841		563,689	
1842		447,349	73,714
1842		479,103	74,154
1843		477,076	70,876
1844		491,905	67,592
1845		557,698	

TABLE A. (*Continued*)

Date		Townsmen[a]	Others[b]
		POPULATION	
1854,	April	573,619	
	October	570,898	
1855,	April	573,619	
	October	564,544	
1867		539,618	
1867		528,463	
1867		457,066	

[a] Nonsamurai residents (*machigata*).
[b] Persons in special enumeration categories (e.g., priests, the blind, prostitutes).
[c] Estimated total population.

TABLE B. The Population of Kyoto under the Tokugawa

Date	Population	Dwellings
1634	410,089	37,087
1637		38,220
1661	362,322	
1665	352,344	
1669		39,230
1674	408,723	
1681	577,548	47,000
1688	429,792	39,072
1696	375,232	34,112
1700	372,856	33,896
1711	350,986	39,649
1711	302,755	
1716	350,367	
1719	341,494	
1729	374,449	
1732	526,222	
1750	526,225	
1753	526,222	
1873	238,663	

TABLE C. Population of Osaka under the Tokugawa

Date	Population	Priests	Outcasts
1625	279,610		
1665	268,760		
1679	287,891		
1689	330,244		
1699	364,154		
1709	381,626		
1715	374,684	900	
1721	382,472	1,009	
1725	369,161	995	
1736	389,866	960	
1743	501,166		
1756	409,984		3,372
1760	411,639		3,380
1765	419,863		3,590
1770	405,481		3,578
1775	408,293		3,606
1780	404,818		3,686
1785	380,416		3,791
1790	382,641		3,976
1795	384,652		4,243
1800	379,121		4,423
1805	381,410		4,423
1810	381,169		4,448
1815	374,008		4,562
1820	374,368		4,572
1825	377,928		4,883
1830	371,252		4,980
1835	361,434		4,956
1840	337,215		4,306
1845	339,545		4,548
1850	326,187		4,450
1855	316,919		4,247
1861	308,192		
1868	381,306		
1873	271,992		

TABLE D. The Population of Secondary Cities under the Tokugawa

City	Date	TOWNSMEN House-holds	TOWNSMEN Popula-tion	SAMURAI House-holds	SAMURAI Popula-tion	TOTAL Popula-tion
Kagoshima	1770		59,728			
	1800		61,482			
	1826		72,350			
Kanazawa	1664	9,878	55,106			
	1697	12,850	68,636			
	1710	12,558	64,987			
	1755	13,443		1,365	7,553	
	1789	14,909	56,355	1,086		
Nagoya	1654		54,932			
	1669		55,849			
	1692		63,734			
	1868				30,000	
Hiroshima	1663	3,504	36,142	1,350	6,680	42,822
	1750					75,000
Sendai	1813	2,385	23,098	8,900	44,000	67,098
Takada	1680	3,333	21,567			
Akita	1747		21,313		17,650	38,963
Tokushima	1717	1,558	20,590			
Kochi	1665		17,154			
Fukuoka	1690		15,009			
Kofu	1690		14,344			
Matsue	1763		13,995			
	1763		13,908		15,268	29,263
Yamagata	1697	2,157	13,662		16,484	30,392
Tottori	1748–50		13,125			
Okayama	1667					28,669
	1707		10,228		25,000	35,228
	1717					27,950
Kurume	1629	1,423				
	1699		8,764			
	1858		11,208			
Utsunomiya	1695		9,744			
Matsumoto	1725	1,233	8,206			
Tsuruoka	1770	2,006	7,822			
Okazaki	1716	1,854	6,137			
	1833	1,586	6,566			
Ogaki	1720	810	5,543			
Hagi	1667	1,580	5,300			
Ueda	1710	361	2,424			
Matsuyama	1711–15	1,700				
Mito	1680	1,777				

Appendix III

A Functional Classification
of Japanese Cities

The technique presented here for the categorization of cities in Japan is an attempt to highlight areas of emphasis in the employment composition of individual cities relative to the total urban employment structure.

Male employment data are utilized in the classification for two reasons: first, females account for less than one-fourth of the employment within incorporated cities during the period 1920-55; a significant portion of this female employment is in either household industries or domestic service. Second, since the methods of recording female employment vary from country to country much more widely than is the case for male employment, male data are more useful in international comparisons.

As a first step, the 1920, 1930, 1950, and 1955 percentage distributions of employed males for total urban and for individual cities were calculated for the following broad categories:

a) Agriculture-Fishing-Forestry
b) Mining
c) Industry (including Construction)
d) Commerce
e) Transportation-Communication
f) Administration-Services (including Government, Military; excluding Domestic Service)
g) All other employment

All cities with 25 per cent or more males employed in the first category were classified as "agricultural" cities. "Mining" cities are those which had 25 per cent or more in the second category.

From the percentage distribution of total males employed in incorporated cities, ratios were computed to show the commitment to each of the four major urban employment areas in relation to the total in the other three areas, as follows:

Industrial:

$$\frac{\%\ \text{in Industry}}{\%\ \text{in Commerce} + \%\ \text{in Transportation-Communication} + \%\ \text{in Administration-Services}}$$

Commercial:

$$\frac{\%\ \text{in Commerce}}{\%\ \text{in Industry} + \%\ \text{in Transporation-Communication} + \%\ \text{in Administration-Services}}$$

Transportation-Communication:

$$\frac{\%\ \text{in Transportation-Communication}}{\%\ \text{in Industry} + \%\ \text{in Commerce} + \%\ \text{in Administration-Services}}$$

Administration-Services:

$$\frac{\%\ \text{in Administration-Services}}{\%\ \text{in Industry} + \%\ \text{in Commerce} + \%\ \text{in Transportation-Communications}}$$

The resulting base ratios for each of the four years are as follows:

	1920	1930	1950	1955
Industry	.82	.69	.84	.58
Commerce	.44	.58	.31	.38
Administration-Services	.15	.16	.25	.31
Transportation-Communication	.13	.09	.12	.14

These ratios for the *total* urban male labor force were used as bases for determining functional classification as follows: if an individual city had a ratio for one or more of the industrial categories *above* those of the total urban male labor force, the city was recorded as having functional emphases in these areas. For example, the industrial ratio for 1955 was .58; the city of Tomakomai in Hokkaido had an industrial ratio of 1.04 and therefore was designated as industrial. A city classified as industrial by the method used here may well have a commercial, transport or service activity proportionally equal to or greater than that of the total urban population, and, hence, show a multiple emphasis. Chigasaki of Kanagawa Prefecture, for example, had ratios for transport and services-administration in addition to industry above those of the total urban population in 1955; the city was classified as industrial-transport-services in functional emphasis for this year. An individual city may have one, two, or three (but never four) areas of functional emphasis. In the following table functional emphases are indicated: I = Industrial, C = Commercial, T = Transportation-Communications, S = Services-Administration, A = Agricultural-Forestry-Fishing, and M = Mining.

APPENDIX III

Functional Classification

Area	1920	1930	1950	1955
HOKKAIDO				
Sapporo	ST	ST	CST	CTS
Asahikawa	S	S	CT	CTS
Otaru	CT	CT	CT	CT
Hakodate	CT	CT	CT	TS
Muroran	IT	IT	IT	IT
Kushiro	CT	A	M	T
Obihiro	—	—	CT	CTS
Kitami	—	—	A	A
Yubari	—	—	M	M
Iwamisawa	—	—	A	A
Abashiri	—	—	A	A
Rumoe	—	—	T	TS
Tomakomai	—	—	I	IT
Wakkanai	—	—	A	A
Bibai	—	—	M	M
Ashibetsu	—	—	—	M
Ebetsu	—	—	—	A
Akabira	—	—	—	M
Mombetsu	—	—	—	A
Shibetsu	—	—	—	A
AOMORI				
Aomori	CT	CT	CT	CTS
Hirosaki	CS	S	CS	A
Hachinoe	—	A	A	A
Kuroishi	—	—	—	A
Goshogawara	—	—	—	A
Sambongi	—	—	—	A
IWATE				
Morioka	CST	ST	CST	CTS
Kamaishi	—	—	I	I
Miyako	—	—	A	A
Ichinoseki	—	—	A	A
Ofunato	—	—	—	A
Mizusawa	—	—	—	A
Hanamaki	—	—	—	A
Kitakami	—	—	—	A
Kuji	—	—	—	A
Tono	—	—	—	A
Rikuzentakata	—	—	—	A
MIYAGI				
Sendai	ST	ST	ST	CTS
Ishinomaki	—	—	CS	C

APPENDIX III (*Continued*)

Area	Functional Classification			
	1920	*1930*	*1950*	*1955*
MIYAGI (*Cont.*)				
Shiogama	—	—	CT	CTS
Furukawa	—	—	—	A
Kesennuma	—	—	—	A
Shiroishi	—	—	—	A
AKITA				
Akita	S	ST	ST	TS
Noshiro	—	—	IT	A
Yokote	—	—	—	A
Odate	—	—	—	A
Honjo	—	—	—	A
Oga	—	—	—	A
Yuzawa	—	—	—	A
Omagari	—	—	—	A
YAMAGATA				
Yamagata	S	S	CS	A
Yonezawa	I	I	IC	A
Tsuruoka	—	CS	CS	A
Sakata	—	—	IT	A
Shinjo	—	—	A	A
Sagae	—	—	—	A
Kaminoyama	—	—	—	A
Murayama	—	—	—	A
Nagai	—	—	—	A
FUKUSHIMA				
Fukushima	CST	CST	ST	CTS
Aizuwakamatsu	S	IS	C	CT
Koriyama	—	IC	CT	CTS
Taira	—	—	CT	A
Shirakawa	—	—	CT	A
Haramachi	—	—	—	A
Sukagawa	—	—	—	A
Kitakata	—	—	—	A
Joban	—	—	—	M
Iwaki	—	—	—	A
Soma	—	—	—	A
Uchigo	—	—	—	M
Nakoso	—	—	—	A
IBARAKI				
Mito	CST	CST	CS	CTS
Hitachi	—	—	I	I
Tsuchiura	—	—	A	A
Koga	—	—	IC	CT
Ishioka	—	—	—	A

APPENDIX III (*Continued*)

Area	Functional Classification			
	1920	1930	1950	1955
IBARAKI (*Cont.*)				
Shimodate	—	—	—	A
Yuki	—	—	—	A
Ryugasaki	—	—	—	A
Nakaminato	—	—	—	A
Shimozuma	—	—	—	A
Mitsukaido	—	—	—	A
Hitachiota	—	—	—	A
Katsuta	—	—	—	A
Takahagi	—	—	—	AM
TOCHIGI				
Utsunomiya	CST	CST	CT	CS
Ashikaga	—	I	IC	IC
Tochigi	—	—	C	A
Sano	—	—	A	A
Kanuma	—	—	IC	A
Nikko	—	—	—	I
Imaichi	—	—	—	A
Oyama	—	—	—	A
Moka	—	—	—	A
Otahara	—	—	—	A
GUMMA				
Maebashi	IC	IC	CS	A
Takasaki	C	CST	CT	CT
Kiryu	—	I	IC	I
Isesaki	—	—	IC	A
Ota	—	- -	A	A
Numata	—	—	—	A
Tatebayashi	—	—	—	A
Shibukawa	—	—	—	A
Fujioka	—	—	—	A
Tomioka	—	—	—	A
SAITAMA				
Kawagoe	—	I	CS	A
Kumagaya	—	—	A	A
Kawaguchi	—	—	I	I
Urawa	—	—	CS	CS
Omiya	—	—	T	T
Gyoda	—	—	I	A
Chichibu	—	—	IC	I
Tokorosawa	—	—	—	A
Hanno	—	—	—	A
Kazo	—	—	—	A
Honjo	—	—	—	A
Higashimatsuyama	—	—	—	A

APPENDIX III (*Continued*)

Area	1920	Functional Classification 1930	1950	1955
SAITAMA (*Cont.*)				
Iwatsuki	—	—	—	A
Kasukabe	—	—	—	A
Sayama	—	—	—	A
Hanyu	—	—	—	A
Konosu	—	—	—	A
Fukaya	—	—	—	A
CHIBA				
Chiba	—	—	ST	TS
Choshi	—	—	A	A
Ichikawa	—	—	IC	IC
Funabashi	—	—	CS	S
Tateyama	—	—	A	A
Kisarazu	—	—	A	A
Matsudo	—	—	A	A
Noda	—	—	A	I
Sawara	—	—	—	A
Mobara	—	—	—	A
Narita	—	—	—	A
Sakura	—	—	—	A
Togane	—	—	—	A
Asahi	—	—	—	A
Yokaichiba	—	—	—	A
Narashino	—	—	—	TS
Kashiwa	—	—	—	A
TOKYO				
Tokyo	IC	C	ICS	IC
Hachioji	I	I	IS	IS
Tachikawa	—	—	S	S
Musashino	—	—	CS	CS
Mitaka	—	—	—	S
Ome	—	—	—	IS
Fuchu	—	—	—	S
Akishima	—	—	—	S
Chofu	—	—	—	IS
KANAGAWA				
Yokohama	CT	T	IST	TS
Yokosuka	S	S	ST	S
Kawasaki	—	IT	I	I
Hiratsuka	—	—	S	S
Kamakura	—	—	ST	CTS
Fujisawa	—	—	S	TS
Odawara	—	—	IT	IT
Chigasaki	—	—	ST	ITS
Zushi	—	—	—	S

APPENDIX III *(Continued)*

Functional Classification

Area	1920	1930	1950	1955
KANAGAWA *(Cont.)*				
Sagamihara	—	—	—	A
Miura	—	—	—	A
Hatano	—	—	—	A
Atsugi	—	—	—	A
NIIGATA				
Niigata	T	IT	ST	TS
Nagaoka	IC	CT	IC	A
Takada	S	S	CS	A
Sanjo	—	—	IC	IC
Kashiwazaki	—	—	IC	A
Shibata	—	—	CS	A
Niitsu	—	—	—	A
Ojiya	—	—	—	A
Kamo	—	—	—	A
Tokamachi	—	—	—	A
Mitsuke	—	—	—	A
Murakami	—	—	—	A
Tsubame	—	—	—	A
Naoetsu	—	—	—	A
Tochio	—	—	—	A
Itoigawa	—	—	—	A
Arai	—	—	—	A
Gosen	—	—	—	A
Ryotsu	—	—	—	A
TOYAMA				
Toyama	CS	CS	IC	C
Takaoka	I	I	I	I
Shimminato	—	—	—	A
Uozu	—	—	—	A
Himi	—	—	—	A
Namerikawa	—	—	—	A
Kurobe	—	—	—	A
Tonami	—	—	—	A
ISHIKAWA				
Kanazawa	S	S	C	CS
Nanao	—	—	A	A
Komatsu	—	—	A	A
Wajima	—	—	—	A
Suzu	—	—	—	A
FUKUI				
Fukui	C	C	C	C
Tsuruga	—	—	IT	A
Takefu	—	—	IC	A

APPENDIX III (*Continued*)

Area	Functional Classification			
	1920	*1930*	*1950*	*1955*
FUKUI (*Cont.*)				
Obama	—	—	—	A
Ono	—	—	—	A
Katsuyama	—	—	—	A
Sabae	—	—	—	A
YAMANASHI				
Kofu	C	C	C	CS
Fujiyoshida	—	—	—	I
Enzan	—	—	—	A
Tsuru	—	—	—	A
Yamanashi	—	—	—	A
Otsuki	—	—	—	A
Nirazaki	—	—	—	A
NAGANO				
Nagano	CST	CS	CST	TS
Matsumoto	CS	CS	C	A
Ueda	C	C	CS	CS
Okaya	—	—	I	I
Iida	—	—	C	CS
Suwa	—	—	A	A
Suzaka	—	—	—	A
Komoro	—	—	—	A
Ina	—	—	—	A
Komagane	—	—	—	A
Nakano	—	—	—	A
Omachi	—	—	—	A
Iiyama	—	—	—	A
GIFU				
Gifu	IS	C	C	C
Ogaki	I	I	I	I
Takayama	—	—	A	A
Tajimi	—	—	IC	IC
Seki	—	—	—	A
Nakatsugawa	—	—	—	A
Mino	—	—	—	A
Mizunami	—	—	—	A
Hashima	—	—	—	A
Ena	—	—	—	A
Minokamo	—	—	—	A
Toki	—	—	—	I
SHIZUOKA				
Shizuoka	IS	I	IC	IC
Hamamatsu	IS	I	IC	IC

APPENDIX III (*Continued*)

Area	1920	Functional Classification 1930	1950	1955
SHIZUOKA (*Cont.*)				
Numazu	—	CT	CT	IT
Shimizu	—	IT	IT	IT
Atami	—	—	CT	CS
Mishima	—	—	I	T
Fujinomiya	—	—	A	A
Ito	—	—	A	A
Shimada	—	—	I	A
Yoshiwara	—	—	I	A
Iwata	—	—	IC	A
Yaizu	—	—	—	A
Fuji	—	—	—	I
Kakegawa	—	—	—	A
Fujieda	—	—	—	A
Gotemba	—	—	—	A
AICHI				
Nagoya	IC	I	IC	I
Toyohashi	CS	CS	A	A
Okazaki	IC	I	IC	I
Ichinomiya	—	IC	IC	I
Seto	—	I	I	I
Handa	—	—	I	I
Kasugai	—	—	A	A
Toyokawa	—	—	A	S
Tsushima	—	—	IC	I
Hekinan	—	—	A	I
Kariya	—	—	I	I
Koromo	—	—	—	I
Anjo	—	—	—	A
Nishio	—	—	—	A
Gamagori	—	—	—	I
Inuyama	—	—	—	A
Tokoname	—	—	—	I
Moriyama	—	—	—	IT
Konan	—	—	—	A
Bisai	—	—	—	I
Komaki	—	—	—	A
MIE				
Tsu	ICS	IT	CS	CS
Yokkaichi	IT	CS	I	I
Ise	—	—	—	TS
Matsusaka	—	—	CT	A
Kuwana	—	—	IC	I
Ueno	—	—	A	A

APPENDIX III (Continued)

Area	1920	Functional Classification 1930	1950	1955
MIE (Cont.)				
Suzuka	—	—	A	A
Nabari	—	—	—	A
Owase	—	—	—	A
Kameyama	—	—	—	A
Toba	—	—	—	A
Kumano	—	—	—	A
SHIGA				
Otsu	CST	CST	IS	ITS
Hikone	—	—	I	IT
Nagahama	—	—	A	A
Omihachiman	—	—	—	A
Yokaichi	—	—	—	A
Kusatsu	—	—	—	A
KYOTO				
Kyoto	IC	IC	C	IT
Fukuchiyama	—	—	A	A
Maizuru	—	—	S	S
Ayabe	—	—	A	A
Uji	—	—	—	ITS
Miyazu	—	—	—	A
Kameoka	—	—	—	A
OSAKA				
Osaka	IC	IC	IC	IC
Sakai	I	I	I	I
Kishiwada	—	IT	A	I
Toyonaka	—	—	C	IC
Fuse	—	—	IC	I
Ikeda	—	—	CT	C
Suita	—	—	IT	IT
Izumiotsu	—	—	I	I
Takatsuki	—	—	IT	IT
Kaizuka	—	—	I	I
Moriguchi	—	—	IT	IT
Hirakata	—	—	ST	TS
Ibaraki	—	—	IT	IT
Yao	—	—	I	I
Izumisano	—	—	I	A
Tondabayashi	—	—	A	A
Neyagawa	—	—	—	TS
Kawachinagano	—	—	—	A
Hiraoka	—	—	—	I
Kawachi	—	—	—	I
Matsubara	—	—	—	I

APPENDIX III (*Continued*)

Functional Classification

Area	1920	1930	1950	1955
HYOGO				
Kobe	T	T	IT	T
Himeji	S	S	I	I
Amagasaki	IT	IT	I	I
Akashi	T	CT	ST	IT
Nishinomiya	—	CT	CT	ICT
Sumoto	—	—	A	A
Ashiya	—	—	C	C
Itami	—	—	I	IS
Aioi	—	—	I	I
Toyooka	—	—	A	A
Kakogawa	—	—	A	A
Tatsuno	—	—	—	A
Ako	—	—	—	I
Nishiwaki	—	—	—	I
Takarazuka	—	—	—	CS
Miki	—	—	—	A
Takasage	—	—	—	IT
Kawanishi	—	—	—	I
Ono	—	—	—	A
NARA				
Nara	CS	S	S	CTS
Yamatotakada	—	—	C	C
Yamatokoriyama	—	—	—	A
Tenri	—	—	—	A
WAKAYAMA				
Wakayama	IC	I	IC	I
Kainan	—	—	I	I
Tanabe	—	—	A	A
Shingu	—	—	CT	A
Hashimoto	—	—	—	A
Gobo	—	—	—	CT
TOTTORI				
Tottori	CS	CS	CS	A
Yonago	—	CT	ST	A
Kurayoshi	—	—	—	TS
SHIMANE				
Matsue	CS	CS	CS	CS
Hamada	—	—	A	A
Izumo	—	—	A	A
Masuda	—	—	—	A
Oda	—	—	—	A
Yasugi	—	—	—	A
Gotsu	—	—	—	A
Hirata	—	—	—	A

APPENDIX III (*Continued*)

Area	*Functional Classification*			
	1920	*1930*	*1950*	*1955*
OKAYAMA				
Okayama	CT	CS	CT	CTS
Kurashiki	—	IC	A	A
Tsuyama	—	C	A	A
Tamano	—	—	I	I
Kojima	—	—	A	I
Tamashima	—	—	—	A
Kasaoka	—	—	—	A
Saidaiji	—	—	—	A
Ibara	—	—	—	A
Soja	—	—	—	A
Takahashi	—	—	—	A
Niimi	—	—	—	A
HIROSHIMA				
Hiroshima	S	S	CT	CTS
Kure	IS	S	ST	S
Mihara	—	—	IT	I
Onomichi	CT	CT	C	A
Fukuyama	S	S	IC	A
Innoshima	—	—	—	A
Matsunaga	—	—	—	IC
Fuchu	—	—	—	I
Miyoshi	—	—	—	A
Shobara	—	—	—	A
Otake	—	—	—	I
YAMAGUCHI				
Shimonoseki	CT	CST	T	T
Ube	—	M	M	IT
Yamaguchi	—	S	A	A
Hagi	—	—	A	A
Tokuyama	—	—	A	A
Hofu	—	—	ST	A
Kudamatsu	—	—	I	I
Iwakuni	—	—	IS	ITS
Onoda	—	—	M	M
Hikari	—	—	A	A
Nagato	—	—	—	A
Yanai	—	—	—	A
Mine	—	—	—	AM
TOKUSHIMA				
Tokushima	IC	ICS	C	CS
Naruto	—	—	A	A
Komatsushima	—	—	—	A

APPENDIX III *(Continued)*

Functional Classification

Area	1920	1930	1950	1955
KAGAWA				
Takamatsu	CST	ST	CST	CTS
Marugame	CS	S	C	A
Sakaide	—	—	IT	A
Zentsuji	—	—	—	A
Kanonji	—	—	—	A
EHIME				
Matsuyama	S	S	CST	CTS
Imabari	IC	IC	IC	A
Uwajima	—	CT	A	A
Yawatahama	—	—	A	A
Niihama	—	—	I	I
Saijo	—	—	A	A
Ozu	—	—	—	A
Iyomishima	—	—	—	A
Kawanoe	—	—	—	A
Iyo	—	—	—	A
KOCHI				
Kochi	C	CST	CST	CTS
Aki	—	—	—	A
Susaki	—	—	—	A
Nakamura	—	—	—	A
Sukumo	—	—	—	A
Tosashimizu	—	—	—	A
FUKUOKA				
Fukuoka	CS	S	CS	CS
Wakamatsu	T	T	T	T
Yahata	I	IT	I	I
Tobata	—	IT	IT	I
Naogata	—	IT	M	CTS
Iizuka	—	—	M	M
Kurume	C	—	C	CS
Omuta	M	S	M	I
Kokura	S	M	T	TS
Moji	T	IT	T	T
Takawa	—	T	M	M
Yanagawa	—	—	—	A
Yamada	—	—	—	M
Amagi	—	—	—	A
Yame	—	—	—	A
Chikugo	—	—	—	A
Okawa	—	—	—	A
Yukuhashi	—	—	—	A
Buzen	—	—	—	A

APPENDIX III (*Continued*)

| Area | *Functional Classification* | | | |
	1920	1930	1950	1955
SAGA				
Saga	CS	CS	CS	CS
Karatsu	—	—	CT	A
Tosu	—	—	—	A
Taku	—	—	—	AM
Imari	—	—	—	A
Takeo	—	—	—	A
Kashima	—	—	—	A
NAGASAKI				
Nagasaki	IT	IT	I	CS
Sasebo	S	S	ST	TS
Shimabara	—	—	A	A
Isahaya	—	—	A	A
Omura	—	—	A	A
Fukue	—	—	—	A
Hirado	—	—	—	A
Matsuura	—	—	—	AM
KUMAMOTO				
Kumamoto	S	S	CS	CTS
Yatsushiro	—	—	I	A
Hitoyoshi	—	—	A	A
Arao	—	—	M	M
Minamata	—	—	A	I
Tamana	—	—	—	A
Hondo	—	—	—	A
Yamaga	—	—	—	A
Ushibuka	—	—	—	A
OITA				
Oita	S	ST	ST	CTS
Beppu	—	C	CS	CS
Nakatsu	—	IC	A	A
Hita	—	—	A	A
Saiki	—	—	A	A
Usuki	—	—	A	A
Tsukumi	—	—	—	A
Taketa	—	—	—	A
Tsurusaki	—	—	—	A
Bungotakada	—	—	—	A
Kitsuki	—	—	—	A
MIYAZAKI				
Miyazaki	—	S	CS	A
Miyakonojo	—	IC	A	A
Nobeoka	—	—	I	I
Nichinan	—	—	A	A

APPENDIX III (*Continued*)

Area	Functional Classification 1920	1930	1950	1955
MIYAZAKI (*Cont.*)				
Kobayashi	—	—	A	A
Hyuga	—	—	—	A
Kushima	—	—	—	A
KAGOSHIMA				
Kagoshima	CT	ST	CST	CTS
Sendai	—	—	A	A
Kanoya	—	—	A	A
Makurazaki	—	—	A	A
Kushikino	—	—	A	A
Akune	—	—	—	A
Izumi	—	—	—	A
Okuchi	—	—	—	A
Ibusuki	—	—	—	A
Kaseda	—	—	—	A
Kokubu	—	—	—	A
Naze	—	—	—	A

Bibliography

The following items are those used as sources or background materials for this study. This listing obviously is not intended as a general bibliography for either the history of Japan or the whole of Japanese demographic development. For those interested in a more extensive general compilation, the standard work is *A Selected List of Books and Articles on Japan in English, French and German* by Hugh Borton, Serge Elisséeff, William W. Lockwood and John C. Pelzel (Cambridge, 1954). Irene B. Taeuber's *The Population of Japan* (Princeton, N.J., 1958) contains the most complete and detailed demographic bibliography available in English.

In listing the items below, those which are exclusively in Japanese are followed by English translations in brackets. Where the titles are bilingual, the English titles are given without brackets.

Abbeglen, James G. *The Japanese Factory*. Glencoe, Ill., 1958.

Ackerman, E. A. *Japan's Natural Resources and their Relation to Japan's Economic Future*. Chicago, 1953.

————. "The Commercial and Industrial Prospect," in Douglas G. Haring, editor, *Japan's Prospect*. Cambridge, Mass., 1946.

Alexandersson, Gunnar. *The Industrial Structure of American Cities*. Lincoln, Neb., 1956.

Allen, G. C. *Modern Japan and Its Problems*. New York, 1937.

————. *Japanese Industry: Its Recent Development and Present Condition*. New York, 1940.

————. "Japanese Industry: Its Organization and Development to 1937," in E. B. Schumpeter, editor, *The Industrialization of Japan and Manchukuoa, 1930-1940: Population, Raw Materials and Industry*. New York, 1940.

————. *A Short Economic History of Modern Japan, 1867-1937*. London, 1951.

————. *Japan's Economic Recovery*. London, 1958.

Asakawa, K. "Some Aspects of Japanese Feudal Institutions," *Transactions of the Asiatic Society of Japan*, first series, 46 (1918).

Ashida, Ijin. *Dainihon dokushi chizu* [Historical Maps of Japan]. Tokyo, 1935.

Ayanori, Okazaki. *Nihon jinkō no jisshoteki kenkyū* [A Factual Study of the Population of Japan]. Tokyo, 1950.

Beardsley, Richard K., John W. Hall, and Robert E. Ward. *Village Japan.* Chicago, 1959.

Bendix, Reinhard. *Work and Authority in Industry.* New York, 1956.

Bogue, Donald J. *The Population of the United States.* Glencoe, Ill., 1959.

————. *The Structure of the Metropolitan Community.* Ann Arbor, Mich., 1950.

Borton, Hugh. *Japan Since 1931.* New York, 1940.

————. "War and the Rise of Industrialization in Japan," in Jesse D. Clarkson and Thomas C. Cochran, editors, *War as a Social Institution.* New York, 1941.

————. *Japan's Modern Century.* New York, 1955.

Boxer, C. R. *Jan Compagnie in Japan, 1600-1850.* The Hague, 1950.

Brown, Delmer M. *Money Economy in Medieval Japan.* New Haven, Conn., 1951.

Chaddock, Robert E. "Age and Sex in Population Analysis," in Joseph J. Spengler and Otis D. Duncan, editors, *Demographic Analysis.* Glencoe, Ill., 1956.

Cohen, Jerome B. *Japan's Economy in War and Reconstruction.* Minneapolis, Minn., 1954.

————. "Problems in Foreign Trade and Investment," *The Annals of the American Academy of Political and Social Sciences,* 308 (1956).

Crocker, W. R. *The Japanese Population Problems: The Coming Crisis.* London, 1931.

Davis, Kingsley. *Human Society.* New York, 1949.

————. *The Population of India and Pakistan.* Princeton, N. J., 1951.

————. "The Origin and Growth of Urbanization in the World," *American Journal of Sociology,* LX (1955).

————. "Institutional Patterns Favoring High Fertility in Underdeveloped Areas," *Eugenics Quarterly,* 2 (1955).

————. "The Sociology of Demographic Behavior," in Robert K. Merton, and Leonard Broom, and Leonard S. Cottrell, Jr., editors, *Sociology Today.* New York, 1959.

———— and Hilda Hertz. "The World Distribution of Urbanization," in Joseph J. Spengler and Otis D. Duncan, editors, *Demographic Analysis.* Glencoe, Ill., 1956.

Diamond, William. "On the Dangers of an Urban Interpretation of History," in E. F. Goldman, editor, *Historiography and Urbanization.* New York, 1941.

Dickinson, Robert E. *City, Region and Regionalism: A Geographic Contribution to Human Ecology.* New York, 1947.

Dore, Ronald P. *City Life in Japan: A Study of a Tokyo Ward.* Berkeley, Calif., 1958.

Duncan, Otis D. and Albert J. Reiss, Jr. *Social Characteristics of Urban and Rural Communities: 1950.* New York, 1956.

Eldridge, Hope Tisdale. "The Process of Urbanization," in Joseph J. Spengler and Otis D. Duncan, editors, *Demographic Analysis.* Glencoe, Ill., 1956.

Embree, John F. *Suye Mura, A Japanese Village.* Chicago, 1939.

————. *The Japanese Nation, A Social Survey.* New York, 1945.

Endo, Motoo. *Nihon chūsei toshiron* [A Study of Japanese Cities in the Middle Ages]. Tokyo, 1940.

Erselcuk, Muzagger. "Iron and Steel Industry in Japan," *Economic Geography,* 23 (1947).

Eyre, John D. "Post-Occupation Conditions in Rural Japan," *The Annals of the American Academy of Political and Social Sciences,* 308 (1956).

Fisher, Harold M. and Clyde F. Kohn. *Readings in Urban Geography.* Chicago, 1959.

Fisher, Robert Moore, editor. *The Metropolis in Modern Life.* Garden City, N. Y., 1955.

Foley, Donald L. "The Daily Movements of Population into Central Business Districts," *American Sociological Review,* 17 (1952).

Gibbins, H. de B. *The Industrial History of England.* London, 1926.

Gibbs, Jack P. and Walter T. Martin. "Urbanization and Natural Resources: A Study in Organizational Ecology," *American Sociological Review,* 23 (1958).

Ginsburg, Norton, editor. *The Pattern of Asia.* Englewood Cliffs, N. J., 1958.

Grad, Andrew J. *Land and Peasant in Japan.* New York, 1952.

Greenberg, Joseph H. "City Size and Sex Distribution," *American Sociological Review,* XIV (1949).

Gubbins, J. H. *The Progress of Japan, 1853-1871.* Oxford, 1911.

————. *The Making of Modern Japan.* London, 1922.

Haig, Robert M. and Roswell C. McCrea. "Major Economic Factors in Metropolitan Growth and Arrangement," *Quarterly Journal of Economics,* 40 (1926).

Hall, Robert B. "Some Rural Settlement Forms in Japan," *Geographical Review,* 21 (1931).

————. "The Yamato Basin, Japan," *Annals of the Association of American Geographers,* XXII (1932).

————. "The Cities of Japan: Notes on Distribution and Inherited Forms," *Annals of the Association of American Geographers,* XXIV (1934).

————. "Tokaido: Road and Region," *Geographical Review,* 27 (1937).

————. "The Road in Old Japan," in Percy W. Long, editor, *Studies in the History of Culture.* Menasha, Wis., 1942.

Hallenbeck, Wilbur C. *American Urban Communities.* New York, 1951.

Hamilton, C. Horace. "Population Pressure and Other Factors Affecting Net Rural-Urban Migration," in Joseph J. Spengler and Otis D. Duncan, editors, *Demographic Analysis.* Glencoe, Ill., 1956.

Hani, Setsuko. *The Japanese Family System.* Tokyo, 1948.

Harada, Shinichi. *Labor Conditions in Japan.* New York, 1928.

Harada, Tomohiko, *Chūsei ni okeru toshi no kenkyū* [Study of Cities in the Middle Ages]. Tokyo, 1942.

Haring, Douglas G., editor. *Japan's Prospect.* Cambridge, Mass., 1946.

Harris, Chauncey D. "Suburbs," *American Journal of Sociology,* 49 (1943).

Hatt, Paul K. and Albert J. Reiss, Jr. *Cities and Society: The Revised Reader in Urban Sociology.* Glencoe, Ill., 1957.

Hawley, Amos H. *Human Ecology: A Theory of Community Structure.* New York, 1950.

————. *The Changing Shape of Metropolitan America: Deconcentration since 1920.* Glencoe, Ill., 1956.

Hoffman, Laurence A. "Japan: Main Population Concentrations," *Journal of Geography,* 46 (1947).

Honda, T. "Historical Analysis of Population Problems in Japan," *Jinkō mondai kenkyū* [Journal of Population Problems], 6 (1950).

Honjo, Eijiro. *Jinkō oyobi jinkō mondai* [Population and Population Problems]. Tokyo, 1930.

————. "The Population and Its Problems in the Tokugawa Era," *Bulletin de l'Institution Internationale de Statistique,* 25 (1931).

————. *The Social and Economic History of Japan.* Kyoto, 1935.

————. "Economic Ideas in Tokugawa Days," *Kyoto University Economic Review,* 13 (1938).

————. "A Survey of Economic Thought in the Closing Days of the Tokugawa Period," *Kyoto University Economic Review,* 13 (1938).

————. *Nihon jinkōshi* [History of Japan's Population]. Tokyo, 1941.

————. *Economic Theory and History of Japan in the Tokugawa Period.* Tokyo, 1943.

————. *Hyakushō chōnin no rekishi* [History of Farmers and Townsmen]. Tokyo, 1949.

Hoover, Edgar M. *Location of Economic Activity.* New York, 1948.

Hubbard, G. E. *Eastern Industrialization and its Effect on the West.* London, 1938.

Ike, Nobutaka. "The Pattern of Railway Development in Japan," *Far Eastern Quarterly,* XIV (1955).

Imai, Toshiki. *Toshi hattenshi kenkyū* [Studies in the Development of Cities]. Tokyo, 1951.

Imori, Rikuhei. *Toshi to nōson* [City and Village]. Tokyo, 1944.

International Labor Office. *Industrial Labor in Japan.* Geneva, 1933.

International Urban Research. *The World's Metropolitan Areas.* Berkeley, Calif., 1959.

Ishii, Ryoichi. *Population Pressure and Economic Life in Japan.* London, 1937.

Isomura, Eiichi. *Tochi shakaigaku.* [Urban Sociology]. Tokyo, 1953.

————. *Toshi* [Cities]. Tokyo, 1954.

————. *Toshi shakaigaku kenkyū* [Research in Urban Sociology]. Tokyo, 1959.

————, editor. *Gendai toshi mondai* [Modern Urban Problems]. Tokyo, 1962.

————. *Asu no toshi mondai* [Future Urban Problems]. Tokyo, 1964.

————. *Chihō toshi* [Local Cities]. Tokyo, 1964.

Ito, Oshiro. "Edo jidai shoku no toguchi chōsa" ["Study on the Population in Early Edo Period"], *Rekishi chiri* [Historical Geography], 48 (1926).

Jaffe, A. J. "Urbanization and Fertility," *American Journal of Sociology,* 48 (1942).

Japan. Bureau of Commerce, Department of Agriculture and Commerce. *General View of Commerce of Industry in the Empire of Japan.* Tokyo, 1897.

————. Ministry of Labor, Women's and Minors' Bureau. *Statistical Materials Relating to Japanese Women.* Tokyo, 1951.

————. Ports and Harbor Bureau, Ministry of Transportation. *Principal Ports in Japan: 1952.* Tokyo, 1952.

————. Kōseisho Kenkyūsho jinkō minzokubu [Public Health Institute Population Bureau]. *Jinkō tōkei sōran* [Population Statistics Summary]. Tokyo, September, 1943.

————. Naikaku tōkei kyoku. Bureau de la Statistique Générale. *Résumé Statistique de l'Empire du Japon.* Tokyo, 1887-1941.

————. Naikaku tōkei kyoku [Cabinet Bureau of Statistics]. *Taishō kunen kokusei chōsa hōkoku* [Reports of the 1920 Census]. Tokyo, 1920-1933.

————. Naikaku tōkei kyoku [Cabinet Bureau of Statistics]. *Taishō jūyonen Kokusei chōsa hōkoku* [Reports of the 1925 Census]. Tokyo, 1925-1934.

————. Naikaku tōkei kyoku [Cabinet Bureau of Statistics]. *Shōwa gonen kokusei chōsa hōkoku* [Reports of the 1930 Census]. Tokyo, 1930-1938.

————. Naikaku tōkei kyoku [Cabinet Bureau of Statistics]. *Shōwa jūnen kokusei chōsa hōkoku* [Reports of the 1935 Census]. Tokyo, 1935-1939.

————. Prime Minister's Office, Bureau of Statistics. *Summary Results, Surveys of 1944, 1945 and 1946.* Tokyo, 1949.

————. Sōrifu tōkei kyoku. Prime Minister's Office, Bureau of Statistics. *Shōwa nijūninen rinji kokusei chōsa kekka hōkoku. Reports on the Special National Census, 1947.* Tokyo, 1948-1949.

————. Sōrifu tōkei kyoku. Prime Minister's Office, Bureau of Statistics. *Shōwa nijūgonen kokusei chōsa hōkoku. Population Census of 1950.* Tokyo, 1951-1955.

————. Sōrifu tōkei kyoku. Prime Minister's Office, Bureau of Statistics. *Shōwa sanjūnen kokusei chōsa hōkoku. 1955 Population Census of Japan.* Tokyo, 1955-1959.

————. Sōrifu tōkei kyoku. Prime Minister's Office, Bureau of Statistics. *Nihon tōkei nenkan. Japan Statistical Yearbook.* Tokyo, annually from 1949.

————. Sōrifu tōkei kyoku [Prime Minister's Office, Bureau of Statistics]. *Nihon hyōjun toshi chizu bunri* [The Standard Metropolitan Areas of Japan]. Tokyo, 1954.

Kawada, Shiro. "The Income and Living Conditions of the Agrarian Population in Japan," *Journal of the Osaka University of Commerce,* 4 (1936).

Keene, Donald. *The Japanese Discovery of Europe.* New York, 1954.

Kiss, George. *Le Probleme de la Population au Japon.* Paris, 1936.

Kizaemon, Ariga. "The Family in Japan," *Marriage and Family Living,* 16 (1954).

Kneedler, Grace M. "Economic Classification of Cities," *The Municipal Yearbook,* 1950.

Knight, Melvin M. *Economic History of Europe to the End of the Middle Ages.* New York, 1926.

Kojima, Reikichi. "The Population of the Prefectures and Cities of Japan in Most Recent Times," translated by Edwin G. Beal, Jr., *Far Eastern Quarterly,* 3, 4 (1944).

Lampard, Eric E. *Urbanization and Economic Growth: The Creative Force of Cities.* New York, 1954.

Levine, Solomon. "Labor Patterns and Trends," *The Annals of the American Academy of Political and Social Sciences,* 308 (1956).

Levy, M. J., Jr. "Contrasting Factors in the Modernization of China and Japan," *Economic Development and Cultural Change,* 2 (1953).

Lloyd, T. E. "Kyushu and Honshu Islands, Focal Points of Japan's Industry," *Iron Age,* April, 1952.

Lockwood, William W. *The Economic Development of Japan: Growth and Structural Change, 1868-1938.* Princeton, N. J., 1954.

Lorimer, Frank. "Dynamic Aspects of the Relation of Population to Economic Development," in Joseph J. Spengler and Otis D. Duncan, editors, *Demographic Analysis.* Glencoe, Ill., 1956.

Masuoka, Jitsuichi. "Urbanization and the Family in Japan," *Sociology and Social Research,* 32 (1947).

Matsuda, Taijiro. "The Family Budget Enquiry in Japan, 1926-27," *Bulletin de l'Institute Internationale de Statistique,* 25 (1931).

Matsumiya, Kazuya. "Family Organization in Present-Day Japan," *American Journal of Sociology,* 53 (1947).

Matsuo, Kosaburo. *Tōkyōshi no rittaiteki kōsatsu* [Statistical Examination of Tokyo]. Tokyo, 1932.

Matsuoka, Asa. "Labor Conditions of Women and Children in Japan," *Bulletin of the United States Bureau of Labor Statistics*, Industrial Relations and Labor Series, 558 (1931).

McCune, Shannon. "Recent Growth of Japanese Cities," *Geographical Review*, XXXII (1942).

McKenzie, R. D. *The Metropolitan Community*. New York, 1933.

Mihara, Shinichi. "Internal Migration in Japan," *Proceedings of the World Population Conference, 1954*. New York, 1954.

Mitsubishi Economic Research Bureau. *Japanese Trade and Industry: Present and Future*. London, 1936.

Mitsubishi Economic Research Institute. *Mitsubishi Enterprises*. Tokyo, 1955.

Murdoch, James. *A History of Japan*. 3 vols. London, 1925-26.

Murphey, Rhoads. "The City as Center of Change: Western Europe and China," *Annals of the Association of American Geographers*, XLIV (1954).

Nakazawa, Benjiro. *Toshi nōson sōkan keisairon* [Economic Study of the Interrelation of Cities and Farm Villages]. Tokyo, 1935.

Nasu, Shiroshi. *Land Utilization in Japan*. New York, 1929.

Nef, John U. *Industry and Government in France and England, 1540-1640*. Ithaca, New York, 1957.

Nihon UNESCO kokunai iinkai [Intra-Japan UNESCO Committee]. *Jinkō mondai kankei bunjo mokuroku* [Bibliography of Materials on Population Problems]. Tokyo, 1952.

Norman, E. Herbert. *Japan's Emergence as a Modern State*. New York, 1940.

————. "Ando Shoeki and the Anatomy of Japanese Feudalism," *Transactions of the Asiatic Society of Japan*, third series, 2 (1949).

Oikawa, Jinnojo. *Nihon jinkō chiri* [Demographic Geography of Japan]. Tokyo, 1932.

Okazaki, Ayanori. *Nihon jinkō no jisshiteki kenkyū* [A Factual Study of the Population of Japan]. Tokyo, 1950.

Okazaki, Fuminori. *Nihon jinkō zusetsu* [Explanatory Diagrams of Japan's Population]. Tokyo, 1954.

Ono, Akitsugu. "Toshi no hattatsu," ["Development of Cities"], *Shikō dainihonshi*, 12 (1939).

Ono, Giichi. *War and Armament Expenditures of Japan*. New York, 1922.

Ono, Hitoshi. *Kinsei jōkamachi no kenkyū* [Study of Modern Castle Towns]. Tokyo, 1928.

Ono, Yeijiro. *The Industrial Transition in Japan*. Baltimore, Md., 1890.

Orchard, John E. *Japan's Economic Position*. New York, 1930.

Parsons, Talcott. "Population and Social Structure," in Douglas G. Haring, editor, *Japan's Prospect*. Cambridge, Mass., 1946.

————— and Robert F. Bales. *Family, Socialization and Interaction Process*. Glencoe, Ill., 1955.

Pelzel, John. "The Small Industrialist in Japan," *Explorations in Entrepreneurial History*, 7 (1954).

Penrose, E. F. *Population Theories and Their Application with Special Reference to Japan*. Stanford, Calif., 1934.

—————. "Japan, 1920-1936," in E. B. Schumpeter, editor, *The Industrialization of Japan and Manchukuo, 1930-1940: Population, Raw Materials and Industry*. New York, 1940.

Pirenne, Henri. *Economic and Social History of Medieval Europe*. London, 1949.

—————. *Medieval Cities*. Garden City, N. Y., 1956.

Ratcliff, Richard U. "Efficiency and the Location of Urban Activities," in Robert M. Fisher, editor, *The Metropolis in Modern Life*. Garden City, New York, 1955.

Redlich, Fritz. "European Aristocracy and Economic Development," *Explorations in Entrepreneurial History*, 6 (1953).

Rein, J. J. *The Industries of Japan*. London, 1889.

Reischauer, Edwin O. *The United States and Japan*. Cambridge, Mass., 1950.

—————. *Japan Past and Present*. New York, 1953.

—————. "Japanese Feudalism," in Rushton Coulborn, editor, *Feudalism in History*. Princeton, N. J., 1956.

Reiss, Albert J., Jr. "An Analysis of Urban Phenomena," in Robert M. Fisher, editor, *The Metropolis in Modern Life*. Garden City, N. Y., 1955.

Reubens, Edwin P. "Small-Scale Industry in Japan," *Quarterly Journal of Economics*, 61 (1947).

Roger, F. A. "Japanese Emigration and Japan's Population Pressure," *Pacific Affairs*, 14 (1941).

Rogoff, Natalie *et al. Demographic Indices of the World's Urban Population*. Bureau of Applied Social Research, New York, 1953. Mimeographed.

Sakanishi, Shio. "Women's Position and the Family System," *The Annals of the American Academy of Political and Social Sciences*, 308 (1956).

Sansom, George. *Japan: A Short Cultural History*. New York, 1943.

—————. *The Western World and Japan*. New York, 1951.

—————. *A History of Japan*. 3 vols. Stanford, Calif., 1958-1963.

Sawada, Goichi. "Narachō jidai no jinkō no kenkyū" ["Study of the Population of the Nara Court Period"], *Shigaku zasshi*, 37 (1926).

Schlesinger, A. M. "The City in American History," *Mississippi Valley Historical Review*, XXVII (1940).

Schnore, Leo F. "The Functions of Metropolitan Suburbs," *American Journal of Sociology*, LXI (1956).

————. "The Growth of Metropolitan Suburbs," *American Sociological Review*, 22 (1957).

————. "Metropolitan Growth and Decentralization," *American Journal of Sociology*, LXIII (1957).

———— and Gene B. Petersen. "Urban and Metropolitan Development in the United States and Canada," *The Annals of the American Academy of Political and Social Sciences*, 316 (1958).

———— and David W. Varley. "Some Concomitants of Metropolitan Size," *American Sociological Review*, 20 (1955).

Schumpeter, E. B., editor. *The Industrialization of Japan and Manchukuo, 1930-1940: Population, Raw Materials and Industry.* New York, 1940.

Seki, K. *The Cotton Industry of Japan.* Tokyo, 1956.

Sekiyama, Naotaro. *Nihon jinkōshi* [History of Japan's Population]. Tokyo, 1942.

————. *Kinsei nihon jinkō no kenkyū* [Study of the Population of Modern Japan]. Tokyo, 1948.

Sjoberg, Gideon. "Comparative Urban Sociology," in Robert K. Merton, Leonard Broom, and Leonard S. Cottrell, Jr., editors, *Sociology Today.* New York, 1959.

————. *The Preindustrial City, Past and Present.* Glencoe, Ill., 1960.

Smith, Guy-Harold and Dorothy Good. *Japan: A Geographical View.* New York, 1943.

Smith, Neil Skene. "Materials on Japanese Social and Economic History: Tokugawa Japan," *Transactions of the Asiatic Society of Japan*, second series, 14 (1937).

Smith, Thomas C. "The Introduction of Western Industry to Japan During the Last Years of the Tokugawa Period," *Harvard Journal of Asian Studies*, 11 (1948).

————. "Old Values and New Techniques in the Modernization of Japan," *Far Eastern Quarterly*, XIV (1955).

Sorokin, Pitirim A. and Carle C. Zimmerman. *Principles of Rural-Urban Sociology.* New York, 1929.

Stead, Alfred, editor. *Japan by the Japanese: A Survey by its Highest Authorities.* New York, 1904.

Taeuber, Irene B. "Family, Migration and Industrialization," *American Sociological Review*, 16 (1951).

————. *The Population of Japan.* Princeton, N. J., 1958.

————. "Demographic Research in the Pacific Area," in Philip M. Hauser and Otis D. Duncan, editors, *The Study of Population.* Chicago, 1959.

————. "Japan's Demographic Transition Re-examined," *Population Studies*, 14 (1960).

————— and Edwin G. Beal, Jr., "The Dynamics of Population in Japan," *Demographic Studies of Selected Areas of Rapid Growth.* The Milbank Memorial Fund, New York, 1944.

————— and Edwin G. Beal, Jr., "Guide to the Official Demographic Statistics of Japan. Part I: Japan Proper, 1868-1945," *Population Index,* 12 (1946).

————— and Frank W. Notestein. "The Changing Fertility of Japan," *Population Studies,* I (1947-48).

Takahashi, Bonsen. *Nihon jinkō tōkeishi* [Statistical History of the Population of Japan]. Tokyo, 1942.

—————. *Nihon jinkōshi no kenkyū* [Study of the History of Japan's Population]. Tokyo, 1941.

Takekoshi, Yosoburo. *The Economic Aspects of the History of the Civilization of Japan.* London, 1930.

Takizawa, Matsuyo. *The Penetration of Money Economy in Japan.* New York, 1927.

Thompson, John H. "Urban Agriculture in Southern Japan," *Economic Geography,* 33 (1957).

————— and Michihiro Miyazaki. "A Map of Japan's Manufacturing," *The Geographical Review,* XLIX (1959).

Thompson, Warren S. *Population and Progress in the Far East.* Chicago, 1959.

Thrupp, Sylvia. *The Merchant Class of Medieval London.* London, 1948.

Tobata, Seiichi. "Through the Eastern Window: Excess Farm Population," *Japan Quarterly,* 1 (1954).

Toyoda, Takeshi. *Nihon no hōkentoshi* [Feudal Cities of Japan]. Tokyo, 1952.

Toyoura, Asakichi. "Tōkyōshi ni okeru jinkō kōshin no ryō to shitsu," ["Quality and Quantity of Population Renewal in Tokyo"], *Shakai seisaku jihō,* April-June, 1939.

Trewartha, Glenn T. "Japanese Cities: Distribution and Morphology," *The Geographical Review,* XXIV (1934).

—————. *Japan: A Physical, Cultural and Regional Geography.* Madison, Wis., 1945.

Tsuchiya, Takao. "An Economic History of Japan," *Transactions of the Asiatic Society of Japan,* second series, 15 (1937).

Tsuru, Shigeto. "Internal Industrial and Business Trends," *The Annals of the American Academy of Political and Social Sciences,* 308 (1956).

Ueda, Teijiro, editor. *Nihon jinkō mondai kenkyū* [Study of Population Problems in Japan]. Tokyo, 1933-34.

United States Strategic Bombing Survey. *The Effects of Air Attack on Japanese Urban Economy.* Washington, 1947.

Uyeda, Teijiro and Tosuke Inokuchi. *The Cost of Living and the Real Wages in Japan, 1914-1936.* Tokyo, 1936.

————. *The Growth of Population and Occupational Changes in Japan, 1920-35*. Tokyo, 1936.

———— and associates. *The Small Industries of Japan*. New York, 1938.

Violich, Francis. *Cities of Latin America*. New York, 1944.

Wakukawa, Seiyei. "The Japanese Farm-Tenancy System" in Douglas G. Haring, editor, *Japan's Prospect*. Cambridge, Mass., 1946.

Weber, Adna F. *The Growth of Cities in the Nineteenth Century*. New York, 1899.

Wilkinson, Thomas O. "Urban Structure and Industrialization," *American Sociological Review*, 25 (1960).

————. "Agricultural Activities in the City of Tokyo," *Rural Sociology*, 26 (1961).

————. "Family Structure and Industrialization in Japan," *American Sociological Review*, 27 (1962).

————. "Agriculturalism in Japanese Urban Structure," *Rural Sociology*, 28 (1963).

————. "A Functional Classification of Japanese Cities: 1920-55," *Demography*, 1 (1964).

William-Olsson, W. *Economic Map of Europe*. Stockholm, 1953.

Yamamoto, Noburu. "Toshisei ni kansuru taido" ["Attitude Concerning Urbanity"], *Jimbun kenkyū*, 3 (1952).

Yanaga, Chitoshi. *Japan Since Perry*. New York, 1949.

————. *Japanese People and Politics*. New York, 1956.

Yanagida, Kunio. *Toshi to nōson* [City and Village]. Tokyo, 1929.

Yazaki, Takeo. *Nippon toshi no hatten katei* [The Process of Japanese Urban Development]. Tokyo, 1962.

————. *Nippon toshi no shakai riron* [The Social Theory of Japanese Cities]. Tokyo, 1963. Published in English as *The Japanese City*, Tokyo, 1963.

Yoshida, Hideo. *Nihon jinkōron no shiteki kenkyū* [Historical Study of Japanese Population Theory]. Tokyo, 1944.

Yoshii, Tojuro. "Chikiteki idō to jinkō kōsei" ["Population and its Mobility"], *Jimbun kenkyū*, 3 (1952).

Yoshikatsu, Ogasawara. *Japan, Labour Population and Urban Functions*. Chiba, 1950.

Zachert, Herbert. "Social Changes During the Tokugawa Period," *Transactions of the Asiatic Society of Japan*, second series, 17 (1938)

Index